P9-CSH-378

THE GEOPOLITICS OF LENINISM

STANLEY W. PAGE

EAST EUROPEAN MONOGRAPHS, BOULDER
DISTRIBUTED BY COLUMBIA UNIVERSITY PRESS
NEW YORK

1982

EAST EUROPEAN MONOGRAPHS, NO. XCVII

Stanley W. Page is Professor of History at the
City College of the City University of New York

Library of Congress Card Catalog Number 81-69397
ISBN 0-914710-91-5

Printed in the United States of America

Four hundred years ago, Germany was the starting point of the first upheaval of the European middle class: as things are now, is it outside the limits of possibility that Germany will be the scene, too, of the first great victory of the European proletariat?

April 20, 1882 Friedrich Engels

This book is dedicated to my beloved children,

Nicole and Bennett

TABLE OF CONTENTS

PREFACE

The start of World War One sent Lenin to Switzerland, haven for most Russian exiles. Viewed from there, Europe, including Russia, appeared in a different light. Germany, above all, became the central motif in Lenin's thinking. He believed that Marx's vision of Germany, as the center of Communism, was finally about to materialize, ushered in by the imperialist war. Lenin's ideas, beginning with the latter portion of 1914, predominantly reflect his hopes for a German proletarian revolution coinciding with a German military conquest of Europe. However, it was Russia which unexpectedly spawned the first war-born revolution, which Lenin promptly designated as merely the first stage of the all-European revolution to be led by Germany.

Lenin returned to Russia expecting events to develop as he had anticipated. But Germany, even though defeated, did not give rise to a social revolution. That left Lenin at the head of a revolutionary regime which his April Theses had cloaked in conceptions invented for Germany, although Russia's economic and social conditions were better fitted for Asia than for Western Europe. Lenin realized this fully after having, in 1919, tried to export his Soviet Communism into Europe, where it was met with brusque rejection. Thenceforth he began to predict that the world revolution would start not in the proletarian but in the agrarian and colonized portions of the world.

This much having been said, a reader might be inclined to ask: "But where is the Marxism in Marxism-Leninism?" To such a question the answer is that Lenin's conception of the world revolution's course grew largely out of the leadership role he intended to play in shaping it. That, in turn, was determined by the location from which he was operating.

Marxism postulates economics as the determining force in the shaping of history. But economic determinism could not possibly be expected to account for the factor of Lenin's location at any given moment. But, since it was Lenin who provided the theoretical framework, (integrating Marxism and Russian agrarian socialism) for the existing world revolutionary movement, the geographically determined theorizing of Lenin must be given its due in explaining this phenomenon.

*****

At this point I should like to express my deepest appreciation for the efforts of Professor Andrew Ezergailis with whom I collaborated on our article "The Lenin-Latvian Axis in the November Seizure of Power," *Canadian Slavonic Papers,* XIX, No. 1, March 1977. Without Professor Ezergailis' superb understanding of the revolution in Latvia, I would not have been able to arrive at conclusions about events in 1917 on which such vital parts of this book hinge.

I have employed the Library of Congress system of transliteration except for such well known names as Trotsky and Kerensky.

Social-democracy is hyphenated when applied to Russian empire parties or when used by members of such parties.

S. W. P.

INTRODUCTION

THE FUNCTION OF A REVOLUTION IN RUSSIA: THE DEVELOPMENT OF LENIN'S VIEWS TO 1914

A. *What Is To Be Done?*, or The Adjustment of Marxism to a Peasant Society.

Which way for the people of Russia? For the Populists, or narodist "friends of the people," the answer was to promote agriculture and peasant handicraft industry. The growth of factory industry, sponsored by the government, was, they thought, destroying the Russian people, as evinced, above all, by the great famine of 1891.[1] This answer did not satisfy the Russian Marxists of the 1890s. The famine's horrors had radicalized youth as never before, the ranks of Marxists were growing.[2] They believed that technological development was inevitable, yet from where was the market for industrial products to come, if, as the narodists claimed, the rise of capitalism was impoverishing the people? The growth of industry was destroying the internal domestic market for commodities. "The question of markets," notes Krupskaia in 1893, when Lenin made his initial appearance among the St. Petersburg Marxists, "interested all of us young Marxists very much."[3] This explains the striking success of the two early essays by Lenin. Circulated in manuscript among young men and women, most of whom had read only *Capital I,* of Marx's works, Lenin created the impression that he had actually found the answer to the problem of markets.

Lenin's first article used a paper on peasant farming in South Russia by an official of Tavride Guberniia, V. Y. Postnikov, to "prove" decisively that Russia was a capitalistic society. Lenin prides himself in taking from Postnikov's paper "far more important and wide ranging conclusions" than the author himself had been able to draw. Lenin's "conclusions" were distorted in still another sense. Postnikov's painstakingly collected statistics applied to a few provinces of South Russia. But Lenin read into them "the basic fact," applying to the entire Russian domain, that "the small producers (peasants and domestic workers) were dying out, explaining our urban and large-scale capitalism, and destroying the myth that the peasant way of life was anything but typically bourgeois, except for its greater entanglement in feudal relationships." The "so-called 'workers' were merely the top layer of that huge mass of peasants which already earns its living more from selling its labor power than from its own farming." Lenin "so greatly" valued Postnikov's material because it "factually" disproved current absurdities concerning the peasant "commune" and revealed "that our life style, basically, is exactly that of Western Europe."[4]

The second of Lenin's essays was presented before an awed circle of Marxists as criticism of Herman Krassin's paper "The Question of Markets." Lenin asked rhetorically whether it was *"possible for capitalism to develop fully in Russia when the masses of the people are poor and becoming ever poorer?* The development of capitalism requires a broad-based internal market, but the ruins of the peasantry diminishes this market, threatens quite to eliminate it, thus making impossible the organization of a capitalistic order. Indeed, it is said that the conversion of the natural economy of our direct producers into a market of manufactured goods capitalism is by that token creating a market for itself. [In *Capital I* Marx had predicted the destruction of rural domestic economy as a prerequisite for the rise of capitalism.] But is it conceivable that the pitiful remnants of the natural economy of our pauperized peasants can develop for us the kind of powerful capitalist production which exists in the West? Is it not obvious that the impoverishment of our masses alone means that our capitalism . . . is incapable of becoming the *basis* of our social economy?

These are arguments forever presented in our literature against the Russian Marxists. The notion of an absence of a market is one of the principal arguments offered, denying the applicability of Marxist theory to Russia."[5]

To refute this major argument, Lenin cited Marx's statement that *"in capitalist society,* the production of [machinery] increases *faster than the production of the means of consumption,"* (italics are Lenin's) and that "capitalist society employs more (*Nota bene*) of the annual labor at its disposal in the production of the means of production (ergo of constant capital) which can not be transformed into income either as wages or as surplus value, but can function only as capital."[6]

Marx's *Capital,* of course, drew its inferences from the economy of Great Britain, whose expanding industry supplied most of the world. But that did not at all apply to turn of the century Russia. Krupsakaia's reverent description of Lenin as that "erudite" Marxist who had just "arrived from the Volga"[7] (compare for a moment the commercial activity of South Russia with that of London around 1890) tells us much about the St. Petersburg Marxists' wishful economic thought. The inspiration of Lenin's "ideas", however, did help them to combat the influence among the peasants, then flocking to the factories, of those narodist "friends of the people," whose idealization of the peasant commune and "small deeds" was so out of accord with the restive mood of the young radicals who had close contact with a brutally exploited, if small and illiterate, working class.

The "erudite" man from the Volga was harsh and uncompromising in tone and manner. Having barely appeared on the scene, he caused excitement with his caustic ridicule of a proposal that the Marxists make contact with the workers through the "Committee for Illiteracy."[8] The readiness of the Marxists to accept his leadership, must, in turn, have fired the stranger from the provinces to ever bolder gestures, and he proceeded to stress that Marxism, even in backward Russia, was not merely a subject for study. He helped encourage Marxist militancy with his 1894 pamphlet *What the Friends of the People Are, and How They Fight the Social-Democrats* by using sarcastic irreverence to demolish the narodists not merely as intellectuals but as people. Stressing the motif that capitalism had penetrated the villages to cause their division into classes, and that "the exploitation of the working people in Russia *is everywhere capitalist in nature,*" Lenin argued that the time had come for the Marxists to transform their current preoccupation with sporadic economic struggles into conscious class war, "whereupon the RUSSIAN WORKER would place himself at the head of all democratic elements to overthrow absolutism and to lead the RUSSIAN PROLETARIAT (together with the proletarians of ALL COUNTRIES) directly into open political war for the VICTORIOUS COMMUNIST REVOLUTION."[9]

It was one thing to employ the dialectic against non-Marxists. But to use it against the Marxists themselves meant re-interpreting his own movement's theoretical base, thus threatening to disrupt an already minuscle group with a schism. However, Lenin plunged ahead, as he invariably did on later occasions when he meant to cleanse the movement of its moderate elements. By 1895 he had written *The Economic Content of Narodism and the Criticism of it in Mr. Struve's Book.* Lenin while cleverly using Struve's *Critical Remarks on the Subject of Russia's Economic Development* (1894) to further cudgel the narodists—not disdaining to use Struve's ideas when they supported his own—was also apparently out to undermine the acknowledgedly leading theoretician of Russian Social-Democracy. He attacked Struve for failing to support all of Marxism as universal truth, generally for misinterpreting Marx, for remaining partially trapped in narodist views, even on the question of markets (which Lenin had already explained) and above all for regarding capitalism in Russia "as something of the future and not of the present," causing him, therefore, to ignore the need for theoretical thinking to "cope immediately with the problem of capitalism."[10]

Lenin, as Neil Harding writes, was re-asserting "the Russian mutation of the Marxian position," as "outlined" initially by Plekhanov. (Plekhanov's attack upon the narodists was largely his proof that class division in the villages was a direct outgrowth of capitalism.) Harding astutely points out that Lenin was able to make a stronger case than Plekhanov, because he had "a great volume of reliable statistical data . . . collected by Zemstvo statisticians" at his disposal.[11]

Lenin rejected the motif in Struve's work, which posited an invisible hand inexorably leading to socialism in Russia, as an encouragement for evolutionary Marxism. Such a "comfortable" view of the course of economic history would allow Marxists to sit on the sidelines. Lenin, however, demanded a Marxism ready to fight the tsarist order and its supporters as well as liberals who called themselves socialists but were not prepared to bloody their hands. Nevertheless, in 1897, when Lenin, in prison, began work on *The Development of Capitalism in Russia,* he did not yet deny that the party of the working class—i.e., Social-Democracy as he conceived of it—was still temporarily allied to bourgeois democracy in the general struggle against tsarism. But he made every effort to distinguish tactics used jointly by moderate and extremist Marxists, in the achievement of political democracy, from accomodation with the class values and goals of the bourgeoisie. It is quite clear from

Struve's memories of his "contacts and conflicts with Lenin" that this then seemingly slight matter lay at the heart of their polemic, which constantly widened in scope until the two finally became mortal political foes.[12]

The proletariat, Lenin wrote in *The Tasks of the Russian Social-Democrats* (1897) stood alone in the economic struggle against both landed nobility and bourgeoisie. Because Social-Democrats recognized that the political revolution had to precede the social revolution, it was essential for them to "unite with all political forces fighting autocracy, (national minorities, religious groups, and the like) temporarily setting aside socialism." But such support "neither presumed nor demanded any sort of compromise with non-Social-Democratic programmes and principles," but was merely support "to an ally against a *particular* enemy. Social-Democrats expect nothing for themselves from these temporary allies, nor do they yield anything to them."[13]

In the 1897 pamphlet, Lenin attacked *narodovolets* P. L. Lavrov, who, in 1895, had written mockingly of the idea that a revolutionary party could function in an autocratic state without resorting to conspiratorial organization. At least part of Lenin's hostile reaction must have risen from the implication in Lavrov's article that peasant Russia was not capitalistic (i.e. democratic) enough to do without *narodovoltsy* tactics. But only three years later, when he was writing *What Is To Be Done?* (1900-1902) Lenin recognized that he could not have it both ways.

Insist though he might that Russia was capitalistic, he could not disown its peasant essence. Although he was forever referring to peasant-proletarians, he could just as accurately have used a term such as proletarian-peasants to describe the factory workers. Realistically, then, he had to admit, however obliquely, that the revolutionary way had to be a conspiracy, led by intellectuals, a modernized *narodovolets*-type of operation. "For this we need a staff of specialist-writers, specialist correspondents, an army of reporter social-democrats, having connections here, there and everywhere, able to penetrate into "all the secrets of government," (which the Russian official so values and which he so readily divulges) able to sneak "behind the scenes, an army of people duty-bound to be ubiquitous and omniscient."[14] Lenin's *What Is To Be Done?* diatribe against Economism represents the monumental impatience of a man who knew the toiling masses were unable, without a revolutionary elite corps, to convert their spontaneous protests into a rising.

In short, the "new" Marxism of *What Is To Be Done?* was the product of Russia's industrial backwardness, and that made it, to say the least, a peculiar Marxism. All the more was it, therefore, necessary to make noise enough to drown out rational criticism.

To give his shaky polemic a better foundation, Lenin boldly asserted that his Marxism was identical with that of Kautsky. Thus he mocked any attempt to attack his own revisionism as Bernsteinian trade unionism –in a word, Economism–declaring that any such critique was the same as opposing majority opinion in German Social-Democracy. There, he noted superciliously, some "insignificant minority" had tried to revise the "old programme and tactics" of revolutionary Social-Democrats and had so timidly proposed "innovations," that it was understandable why they were warded off with "a dry rejection."[15] What Lenin took to be a passionless rejection may, in fact, have grown out of the then already revisionist Marxism of Kautsky and the other "revolutionary" Social-Democrats of Germany, although lip service was still given to orthodoxy. (As noted below Lenin did not become aware of that state of affairs for another fourteen years.) Lenin also used "Kautsky's profoundly true and important statement" about the "projected programme of the Austrian Social-Democratic Party," to bolster a major argument of *What Is To Be Done?,* namely that socialist consciousness had to be injected into the proletariat by *"bourgeois intellectuals."* Kautsky's emphasis is noted by Lenin, who adds, "it was in the minds of individual members of this stratum that modern socialism originated, and it was they who communicated it to the more intellectually developed proletarians. . . ."[16]

This realistic estimate of the limited potential of the proletariat, whether stated by Kautsky, or with Lenin's vicarious help in *What Is To Be Done?* (the same thought is implicit in *The Communist Manifesto*)[17] made it theoretically possible for a backward country to initiate the revolution. That idea was fully in accord with the Hegelian concept of *Zeitgeist.* Marx and Engels, having based their *Manifesto* on conditions observed in England, made it plain, nevertheless, that Communists looked "chiefly to Germany" because its imminent bourgeous revolution would occur "under a more advanced civilization and with a more developed proletariat," as compared with their counterparts in 17th Century England and in 18th Century France.

But things went sour in the German revolutions of 1848-49, and Marx and Engels decided to back oppressed nationalism (an expedient contradiction to their theory of history) as the key to revolutionary incitement. In this connection, the restoration of martyred Poland, partly within Prussia, became a major rallying cry for Marx and Engels along with German democrats in general. They hoped to see a united Germany warring against barbaric Russian reactionism.[18]

By 1849, Marx, far from being happy with the failures of all the European revolutions, first found the reason for it in English control of the world markets. Until England was "overthrown in a world war" social reform in France and the rest of Europe remained hopeless. But a revolution in France, overthrowing the bourgeoisie would lead to British financing of the counterrevolution, whereupon the English Chartists would bring about an English revolution.[19]

Such fantasizing was probably an attempt to breathe a glow into the dying embers of the proletarian-oriented *Manifesto.* However, there was always the Gendarme of Europe to hate and the Russian intervention in June 1849, gave Marx something more solid to sink his teeth into. He became obsessional about Russian reactionism as the continuing cause for the failure of revolution to get off the ground in Germany. Even after Prussia in 1866 had revealed her military prowess in the Seven Weeks War against Austria, Marx could admit only grudgingly that Prussia, and not Russia, was the continent's prime military power and that Russia was "less to be feared than ever before,"[20] an admission implying that the Prussian regime would need no Russian help to suppress a German rising.

The outburst of class war in Paris in 1871, coming after two quiet decades, tended for the moment to rekindle in Marx and Engels the hope that Western Europe had come back to life. But the Communards were crushed within two months, and, except for an echo in Algeria, the first "proletarian dictatorship" sank in France without causing a ripple elsewhere. By 1877, Marx so desperately hated tsarism that he predicted the start of "the revolution in the East, formerly the impregnable citadel and reserve army of the counter revolution." In the same strokes of his pen Marx continued irrationally to insist that the tottering Russian monarchy remained the "last prop" of the Hohenzollerns, whose fall would follow that of tsarism.[21] In the same delusory vein, Engels' famous 1875 reply to Tkachev, had predicted that Russia was "undoubtedly on the eve of revolution," which, especially if it involved the peasants, would be "of the greatest importance for the whole of Europe if only because it [would] destroy at one blow the last . . . reserve of . . . European reaction."[22]

In a preface to Plekhanov's Russian translation of *The Communist Manifesto,* both Marx and Engels, in 1882, agreed upon the possibility "that Russian collective landownership [might] prove the starting point of communist development."[23] And, in 1918, Kautsky recalled, in his *Dictatorship of the Proletariat,* that "the Russian Revolution of 1905 brought the idea of a mass strike to a head [within] German Social Democracy. This was recognised by the 1905 Congress."[24]

The German prophets, despairing of a proletarian revolution in the booming centers of 19th century capitalism, were seeking help from peasant Russia. If Lenin was so ready to seize upon the "last ditch" Marxian postulation of a European revolution ignited by one in Russia, this is understandable considering how deeply he was steeped in the ideas of Herzen, Chernishevskii, Bakunin, Nechaiev and Tkachev, all of whom had asserted that socialism in Russia could bypass capitalism.[25] To build on that tradition, Lenin, the Marxist, needed only to present Russia as a capitalist society, hence the "mutated" (perhaps mutilated?) Marxism referred to above, begun by Plekhanov and blown up to grandiose proportions by Lenin. Lenin would never concede that he had changed the essence of Marxism by projecting as reality an image of Russia that lay in some Utopian distance, and this helps explain the doctrinaire rejection of any but his own reading of Marx. Almost every attempt to refute a position Lenin took was met with fierce *ad hominem* vituperation, a classically defensive reaction.

By asserting that Russia had long since entered the capitalistic stage, Lenin had already found a way of linking the Russian revolution and himself to Western revolutionary currents. His concept of revolutionary party formation continued that trend. In *What Is To Be Done?* he went Engels one better, shoving Russia to stage center not merely as the instigator of European revolution but as the world's leading Marxist nation. History had given Russia's proletariat the "*most revolutionary* of all *immediate* tasks confronting the proletariat of any other country," that being the destruction of tsarism "the most powerful bulwark, not only of European, but. . . also of Asiatic reaction." In accomplishing that task, the Russian proletariat would become "the vanguard of the international proletariat. And we can rightly assume that we shall gain the title, already earned for us by our predecessor revolutionaries of the 1870s. We need only infuse our thousand times broader and deeper movement with the earlier generation's dedication and energy."[26]

Around 1870 Marx was still hoping for the revolution to start in Germany. The Germans, he mused in 1868, had the advantages of a late start, in addition to which they "had on their shoulders heads that could generalize" being "the most theoretical people in Europe" and having "preserved a theoretical frame of mind."[27]

Lenin was delighted with the Hegelian (*Zeitgeist*) thinking of Marx and Engels and the idea that a nation's progressive philosophers could breathe life into the revolutionary hopes of a nation, however backward. Lenin drew upon Engels' introduction to his *Peasant War in Germany* to help support his claim that Russia was the leading revolutionary country. As Marx had done some years earlier, Engels explained that the German workers had "two natural advantages over the rest of Europe's workers." 1) They "belonged to the most theoretically-minded people of Europe and have maintained in themselves that sense of theory which the so-called 'educated' classes of Germany had completely lost. Without the leadership of German philosophy, especially that of Hegel, there would never have been German scientific socialism [Engels complimenting himself and Marx] the only scientific socialism ever to exist." Because other nations lacked the philosophical background which had "infiltrated" the German workers "flesh and blood" with scientific socialism (like the body and blood of Christ) they lagged behind the Germans. 2) The second advantage of the Germans was that they were "almost the last of all to have taken part in the workers' movement. Thus, German socialist theory had been able to benefit from the brilliant, if fantastically erroneous, Utopian socialism of St. Simon, Fourier and Owen" and to avoid the errors of the English and French workers' movement.[28]

Borrowing that ego and ethnocentric thought pattern, Lenin likened the Russians of the turn of the century to the German workers of a generation earlier. The Russians, last to enter the working class movement, therefore, had the experience and mistakes of their predecessors—those of the Germans, included—to guide them. And like the Germans, the Russians had the heritage of such socialist giants as Herzen, Belinskii and Chernishevskii, and the "brilliant galaxy of revolutionaries of the seventies," (who, although failing to make the slightest impact upon the peasantry, had produced a Lenin). Perhaps a bit abashed at comparing himself with Engels and wishing to divert his readers from such a thought, Lenin asks them to "ponder the worldwide significance which Russian literature had attained; to think about . . . oh, let it go, that is enough!" (To think of all those illiterate Russian peasant-proletarians reading Tolstoy and Dostoevsky is not only enough, it is too much, unless one shares Engels' belief that the body and blood of the philosopher transsubstantiates into the people's flesh.) However mystical the explanation the case was proved to Lenin's satisfaction. The conception of Russia's working class as the vanguard of world revolution remained one of Lenin's basic canons until World War I.[29]

In *What Is To Be Done?* it was crucial for Lenin to link his essential brand of Russian Marxism with European Marxist thought and even to make it relevant to Asia, the latter concept constituting an enormous broadening (and a very original one) of Marxist thinking. All of that helped to reinforce the argument that the Russian empire needed a militant, rather than a revisionist, Marxist organization. By overstating the extent of Russia's capitalistic progress, Lenin compensated for his country's tiny proletariat. In a similar process of exaggeration, a society not even ready for revolutionary Marxism—even in the West the idea of violent revolution had expired—was presented as the dynamo of a global revolution.

The "world-wide importance" of Russian Marxism, one might say, was stuffed into *What Is To Be Done?* because the notion added a dimension to Lenin's quasi-religious theorizing. As it happens, given the inherent internationalism in Marxism, this auxilliary notion has far greater validity in Lenin's pamphlet than does the central idea which it is meant to support. For the idea that "capitalistic" Russia was quite ready for a militant Marxist party is contradicted by the elitist structure envisaged for it by Lenin, since the need for such a party demonstrates Russia's economic backwardness. However, once Lenin had introduced the idea that Russia stood at the center of the world's revolution, then that motif took on a life of its own, providing Lenin with a visionary's sense (or delusion) of grandeur. That, scorning the democratic traditions of Russian Social-Democracy and the resultant trend toward revisionism, led to the creation of the new type of Communist, or the Bolshevik.

Lenin justified the need for Nechaiev-type revolutionaries largely in terms of the police-state conditions under which they had to function. But an unstated reason why Lenin wanted the twenty four hour a day activist—whether he be worker or student—was that Lenin wanted a party moulded to fit such as Chernishevskii and his strong, silent hero of *What Is To Be Done?*, Rakhmetev; in short, a party of fanatical isolates, much like Lenin himself. Such people would by nature tend to oppose, indeed hate, the fraternal spirit of intra-party democracy, which led to softness, to revisionism, that is, to the dissolution (or "liquidation") of the revolutionary spirit and hence of the revolutionary party.

That all of the party members' energies be devoted entirely to revolutionary activities was exactly Lenin's aim. Only such a party could raise the sluggish political consciousness of the Russian (semi-peasant) proletarian to the level of a revolutionary.

This new style revolutionary would not only be a conspirator *par excellence,* he would, at the same time, be an organizer of the masses, understanding how to propagandize among them and prepare them for action. He would not, as the Economists wanted, allow the party to sink to the level of the worker.

The Germans, with all their forces, Lenin wrote, understood that talented agitators "seldom rise from among the usual workers." Therefore they trained "every capable worker" to become a "professional agitator," gradually widening his sphere of activities "from a single factory to the entire industry, from one locality to the entire country. He acquires experience and cleverness in his [revolutionary] work, expanding his outlook and his knowledge" and learning to size up "the outstanding political leaders of other localities and other parties." [Lenin was drawing upon his own technique in coming to grips with rivals and opponents.] "He strives to raise himself to their level [This seems almost autobiographical] and to combine his understanding of the workers and his dedication for socialism" into the kind of professional skills "without which the proletariat *cannot* hope to win against its excellently trained enemies. This is how the Bebels and Auers rise to leadership of the working classes. But that which happens to a large degree automatically in a politically free country, we in Russia, must systematically inculcate into our organization."[30] In fact, Lenin had demonstrated that the German method was not automatic but systematic. It seems he meant to say that if even a country like Germany had to train its elite propagandists, then Russia, having to cope with far greater problems, needed even more intensively to pursue such a course of action.

In the new revolutionaries, as Lenin depicted them, an understanding of the techniques of secret organizational methods, Russian style, would become fused with the ability of Western Marxists to educate the masses to understand such abstractions as "class struggle" and "economic determinism." What Lenin had drawn up as a model for members of his envisaged party was moreover a reflection of his belief that all problems had to be approached both theoretically and practically.

In addition, since the date of tsarism's overthrow was certainly not predictable (in 1901-1902) the new style party, led by democratic-minded elitists was at the same time a common sense accomodation to the harsh fact that there would be a continuing need for a durable revolutionary underground in an economically and hence politically backward society.

Referring once more to Lenin's way of combining theory and practice, it should be noted that even as he was proclaiming Russia's leadership in the world proletarian revolution, he was not blind to the weakness of Russia's proletariat. Although he had in part retreated from his assertion of 1897 that the party of the proletariat needed help from any and all oppressed elements in the Russian empire (so long as no compromises were made with Social-Democratic programmes and principles) one thing is surely clear from his *What Is To Be Done?* prediction of revolt in Europe *and* Asia. Even if he did not yet fully articulate it, Lenin sensed that Russian and world revolution required peasant and oppressed nation risings the world over. In the Russian empire, specifically, peasants and national minorities–to a great extent those categories overlapped–had to be harnessed to the effort of overthrowing autocracy.

B. Lenin and the Peasants

The *Communist Manifesto* recognized that there was a place for the peasant in the victorious revolution of the proletariat. This was unavoidable because provision had to be made for land as part of the "means of production." So, almost as an afterthought, the *Manifesto* proposed that waste lands be brought into cultivation, that the soil be generally improved "in accordance with a common plan," and, since all were equally to be liable to labor, it suggested the "establishment of industrial armies, especially for agriculture." Reference is also made–surely without a technical understanding by Marx and Engels of what was entailed–to a "combination of agricultural with manufacturing industries." The *Manifesto* further proposes a gradual abolition of "the distinction between town and country, by a more equitable distribution of the population over the country."[31]

That same phenomenon–also occurring in the German baronial estates of Russia's Baltic Provinces–[32] was to have immense importance in later Russian history–[33] and to a lesser, if noteworthy degree, in the south Russian *gubernii* about which Lenin wrote so voluminously in *The Development of Capitalism in Russia.*

It would make little sense at this point to criticize the *Manifesto's* authors, either for their ignorance and lack of interest in agriculture, or for failing to research the subject at least to the extent of being able to offer some meaningful observations about its possible organization in the new society. Still, as practical revolutionaries in the Germany of 1848, Marx and Engels were willing enough–as Lenin was later–to utilize any force, including the peasants, who might further their cause.[34] However, the political activism of Marx and Engels in 1848 was of no great interest to Marxists a half-century later;[35] it was the theory that excited them and that theory "underestimated"[36] the peasantry as a factor in the doctrine.

Marx and Engels, along with their disciples throughout Europe, had a need to ignore the flesh and blood peasants. His existence intruded upon the neatness of their theory. In addition, there had been no rebellious peasantry of consequence since the French Revolution, so that Marxists had no recent experience, where peasants were concerned, to guide them.

A special factor, reducing the importance of the peasant in Russia, was the total collapse of the narodnik movement in the "quiet" 1880s. Plekhanov's League for the Liberation of Labor offered the peasants "a radical review of our agrarian question," but specified no action beyond a reconsideration of the terms of the Emancipation Settlement.[37] The Western Marxists, led by Marx, Engels and Kautsky, understandably clung to a doctrine born and raised in the time of a swiftly advancing technological revolution. Nevertheless, around the turn of the century, even Germany was still largely a land of peasants. Their tools of labor, it is true, were becoming increasingly mechanized, a fact which Kautsky, as indicated above[38] did not fail to note in his re-evaluation, around 1900, of the importance of the peasants in a revolution.

In the 1890s, Lenin's extensive comments about agriculture did not include a role of any kind for the peasants in the "democratic" revolution. However, in conceiving an activist Marxist movement in a predominantly peasant society, it was only natural that he would try more earnestly than Plekhanov had done to add the force of the peasantry to his revolutionary equation. In his efforts to find a place for the peasant within the parameters of Russian Marxist thinking, Lenin did so, initially, by way of a purely dialectical approach.

Lenin's anti-narodist *Friends of the People,* as we know, stressed class division among the peasantry. That same line of thought fostered the notion that it was necessary to support the class strivings, however petty bourgeois, of the peasants, for they were natural radicals in their desire to destroy what remained of medievalism, i.e., large landownership. Beyond that, Lenin insisted that Marxists demand that land taken from the peasants be returned to them, and he also proposed nationalization of the land to bring about the complete abolition of landed propietorship "that bulwark of serfdom's institutions and traditions." That such actions would mark progress toward capitalism in agriculture was, he said, less important than the fact that it would be a move toward democracy. "In general, the Russian . . . followers of Marxism [who] call themselves SOCIAL-DEMOCRATS should never in their activities, forget the tremendous importance of DEMOCRACY."[39]

The sum total of Lenin's pre-1900 views on the metamorphosis of peasants into proletarians emerged in *The Development of Capitalism in Russia,* but that book did not yet concern itself with the peasant as anything but a statistic. Lenin's general conclusions about the peasant as a victim of capitalism were certainly reinforced, when, almost simultaneously with his own *magnum opus,* there appeared Kautsky's *The Agrarian Question. Part I, The Development of Agriculture in Capitalist Society.* Lenin's enthusiasim for that work is especially understandable in that, as he noted, Kautsky's analysis of agriculture under Western capitalism had uncovered various phenomena identical to those described in *The Development of Capitalism in Russia.* These included the progressive division of labor and the employment of machinery as well as the process of polarization among the peasantry. The latter was evident from the spread of wage labor, creating a class of worker-peasants, with two results: 1) the migration of small peasants to towns and factories, and 2) the transplantation of large-scale industry to rural areas. In the preface to his own book, Lenin expressed regret that he was not able to make use of Kautsky's, which reached him too late. He cited Kautsky as "categorically" rejecting the idea that a village community might adopt large-scale modern agriculture.

He was further pleased by Kautsky's comment that West European agronomists, who were demanding the strengthening and development of communes, were "not at all socialist," but were the "agents of big landowners," who, by alloting land to agricultural workers, were seeking to create a modern form of serfdom. Thus, via Kautsky, Lenin was able to take another poke at the narodists. Kautsky, writes Lenin, also called for the most determined struggle against "all attempts to help the small peasantry by implanting handicraft industry (*Hausindustrie*)–that worst form of capitalist exploitation." Lenin thought is necessary "to stress the common opinion held by both West European and Russian Marxists, in light of the latest attempts of the representatives of *narodnichestvo* to demonstrate a marked difference between one and the other."[40]

Reviewing Kautsky's book, in *Nachalo* 4 April, 1899, Lenin called it the most important economic work since *Capital III.* Kautsky, by demonstrating agriculture to be an integral part of the capitalist economy and subject to the same basic forces, had exposed the errors of "our narodnik press in its attempts to prove that small peasant farming was viable, or even that it was superior to large-scale agriculture," thereby ruling Marxism out as applicable to peasant economics. But according to Kautsky, agriculture was caught up in the changes wrought by capitalism.

And so peasants became ever more impoverished as urbanization inexorably took the best workers from the farms and the cities appropriated an ever greater portion of rural wealth. The rural population could no longer "return to the soil what had been taken from it." Although Kautsky "fully admitted" that the middle class farmers suffered less than the poor from labor shortages, he denied that a peasant renaissance, as the narodists hoped, might rise out of that class, because like the poor this class also suffers from "usury, tax burdens, poor farming practices, soil exhaustion, etc. Therefore the children of the middle peasants flee to the cities along with the farm hands. The views of optimistically inclined petty bourgeois economists," writes Lenin, were refuted. Moreover, Kautsky had demonstrated the impact upon agriculture of the competition for world markets in agricultural products. This would lead not only to a decline in European grain production—which could also happen to Russia—but also enhance the trend toward polarization within the peasantry, hasten the development of agricultural technology, and, even replace some branches of agriculture by industrial production. "Optimistic economists, says Kautsky, who think that such changes in the appearance of European agriculture can save it from crisis are deluding themselves; the crisis is growing and can culminate only in the general crisis of capitalism."[41]

In *Zhizn'*, January 1900, Lenin tore angrily at Bulgakov's comments on Kautsky's book. Kautsky's work was a brilliant Marxist treatise, its critic a maligner of Marxism. "Even before Mr. Bulgakov takes on Kautsky, he throws a punch at Marx for his 'false representations.'. Who is mistaken here, Marx or Bulgakov?" To Lenin, anyone daring to criticize Marx was *ipso facto* in error. In conclusion, Lenin wrote: "Capitalist agriculture is now in the same unstable condition that is characteristic of capitalist industry and is forced to adapt itself to new market conditions. The agrarian crisis, like every crisis, is destroying many farmers, producing major changes in the established property relations, and in *certain places* is leading to technical retrogression, to the revival of medieval relations and forms of economy. In general, however, it is speeding up social evolution and is forcing patriarchal stagnation out of its last refuge, necessitating further specialization of agriculture (one of the main features of agricultural progress in capitalist society) further introducing agricultural machinery, etc. On the whole, as Kautsky shows. . . even in

Western Europe, we see not stagnation in agriculture in the period 1880-1890, but technical progress. We say–*even* in Western Europe–because in America, for example, this progress is still more obvious. In a word, there is no basis for viewing the phenomenon of the agrarian crisis as something that could hold back capitalism and capitalist development."[42]

Lenin, of course, was using Kautsky to whale away both at peasant-loving narodniks and at "legal Marxists," like Bulgakov, who dared to question the ubiquitous truth of the Marxist scripture. Less obviously, but perhaps more importantly, Lenin was letting it be known that, like Newton and Leibniz in 1700 (discovering calculus), both he and Kautsky, two centuries later, had simultaneously, but independently arrived at a great "scientific" discovery; namely that agriculture, just as every other industry, was subject to Marx's universal laws of economics. However, the fact that Lenin and Kautsky had landed on the same site at the same time does not necessarily mean that they had traveled the same route or that each had studied the impact of capitalism on agriculture for the same reasons.

Kautsky, it may be assumed, had become painfully aware that trade unionism was diverting the factory proletariat away from revolution. He may have been seeking in a peasantry, destroyed by industry, but lacking the trade union cushion enjoyed by the proletariat, a reserve army in which the militant spirit, defunct among the urban workers, might yet be sparked.[43] Just before that time, it should be recalled, Engels had turned his sights back to the peasant wars in Germany, as though seeking in the agrarian past what seemed so lacking in the proletarian present. Even earlier, as mentioned, both Marx and Engels had begun to seek in Russia's revolutionary peasant the spark to ignite the European revolution. Following their lead, or, at least, using their reasoning to substantiate his own, Lenin's writings since 1894 had concentrated upon the capitalist contradictions in Russian agriculture (highlighted by *The Development of Capitalism in Russia*) thus providing the theoretical basis for a militant Marxist party in an agricultural society. (*What Is To Be Done?*)

If the parallels which Lenin drew between Kautsky's findings in the West and his own in Russia were so exciting to Lenin, as his ecstatic praise of Kautsky, leader of Marxian orthodoxy, indicates, that was because it showed Lenin to be roughly Kautsky's equal as an interpreter of Marx. Beyond that, Kautsky had underlined the importance of agriculture in Marxist thinking everywhere, even in the West.[44] Lenin could therefore claim that his own ideas, although originating in a land of peasants were equally relevant to the West, if not to the entire world. So, by offering the reserve army of Russia's "peasant-proletarians" to the drive for world revolution, Lenin had provided himself, at least to his own satisfaction, with the stature of an outstanding Marxist theoretician.

If the peasant of Russia or of the West was, like the factory worker, a victim of capitalism, then he had to be harnessed to the revolution. Lenin's article, written in February 1901, but published in the summer of 1902, in connection with the elaboration of the agrarian programme of the Russian Social-Democratic Workers' Party (RSDWP), reveals the transition in Lenin's perspective. Its earlier portion reflects Lenin's ambivalence, taking note of the peasants' personal sufferings while still treating them as objects. As though attempting initially to cushion the "heresy" expressed in the latter part of the article, Lenin depicts the peasants as politically useful to Social-Democracy because their plight could be blamed upon an insensitive government. The peasants, in other words, would be useful as tools in the regime's overthrow, but only revolutionary workers and students were expected to participate actively. The peasants "political" function as the article's early portion has it, lay in the mechanical process whereby the peasantry "liberates itself from the yoke of capital . . . by linking up with the working class movement, by helping it in its struggle for socialism; for converting the land as well as other means of production (factories, machines, etc.) into social property." Any attempt "to save the peasantry by defending small scale farming and small holdings from the advance of capitalism [another slap at the narodists] would be to hold back social development to no purpose," actually deceiving the peasants into believing they had a chance to prosper "even under capitalism."

The phrase "even under capitalism" is noteworthy, because, offered casually, as though quite beyond dispute, it highlights the extent to which Lenin had internalized his distorted image of Russian conditions. In the same article, Lenin, expressing pity for the famine-ridden peasants, whose misery, ignorance and oppression placed an Asian stamp on Russia, introduced a motif, new to Russian Marxism, calling for *"carrying the class struggle into the countryside."*[45] That statement, stressed by Lenin, marked an abrupt change of focus toward the peasant, further manifested by demands having specific appeal for the peasantry, including the restitution of lands cut off from the peasant commune by the Emancipation Laws. Coming from a Marxist such a proposition was incongruous because it offered to add property to the commune. Indeed, as delegate Gorin at the RSDWP Congress in 1903 argued, such a plank in the Social-Democratic platform would, by presenting a hope for property, enhance an anti-proletarian spirit among the pauperized peasantry.[46] But, where peasants were concerned, Lenin, by 1901, had begun to mix political opportunism with dialectics. Moving even further along those lines, he proposed the setting up of peasant committees—an extraordinarily high level of peasant political awareness being presumed here—to oppose Committees of Nobles established by the Government. This proposal, paralleling workers' committees in the factories, was obviously intended as a means of blending the image of the peasant with that of the factory worker. Lenin further advocated agitation among the peasantry, based upon their most pressing everyday needs, yet not confined to those alone but to be "geared ceaselessly toward broadening the peasants' understanding and elevating their political consciousness."

The article, naturally reflecting a long process of thinking by Lenin, reveals that he had finally begun to perceive the peasants as people, and therefore, ready to be wakened to a desire for representative government and for the "overthrow of authoritarian officials," and ready for a role in the struggle against tsarism and the landlords.

Common sense dictated an accomodation between Social-Democracy and the misery-laden peasantry, and Lenin pressed for the inclusion of demands for peasant liberation in the Social-Democratic program if it wished to "stand at the head of the whole people in the struggle against autocracy." But whether controlled by Marxian conditioning or not wishing to appear too abrupt a violator of tradition, Lenin cautioned against sending urban "active revolutionary forces" into the villages. "Of doing that there can be no question. There is no doubt but that the militant elements of the party must concentrate upon the industrial proletariat, urban and factory centers" the only forces able to conduct "an irrevocable and massive campaign against the autocracy." Peasant demands were included in the program not so that "convinced Social-Democrats should be sent from the towns to the villages [narodnik-style]

. . . but to give leadership to the activities of such forces who *cannot* act in any place but a village."

Probing carefully into this virgin soil, Lenin was seeking to use the vast peasant reserve army of the revolution without seeming at the same time, to be sliding into the narodist bog. And so he wrote of "sowing seeds" about class struggle and political awareness among the "multi-millioned peasantry," about their increasing interest as they come to towns and witness the workers' struggle, so that they come to understand that the workers fight for "all the people."[47] But even Lenin's hesitant attempts to adjust this new and untried peasant dimension to the Marxian strictures were met with quizzical opposition, which, in turn, had to be countered with the subtlest of casuistical polemics.

Lenin began his comentary to the agrarian section of the Russian Social-Democratic Party's draft program[48] with the bold statement that there was "hardly any need to prove at length that an agrarian programme" was "essential to the Russian Social-Democratic Party." But, aware that he was treading on treacherous ground, Lenin proceeded at once to explain what he meant even by the phrase "agrarian programme," which he described as the "guiding principles of Social-Democratic policy on the agrarian question, i.e., policy concerning agriculture and the various classes and groupings of the rural population." In other words, the peasant was still to be viewed as an object of Social-Democratic theory rather than as a person with mind and sentiments of his own. However, this attitude was not a far cry from that expressed toward the proletariat in *What Is To Be Done?* who were to be guided every step of the way, except for the fact that being factory workers they were the legitimate and central focus of Marxism. Yet, as Lenin implied, Social-Democracy's concern for the proletarian's country cousin, was not at all abnormal. As long as the issue involved the "big landowners, the agricultural wage workers and the 'peasants' [small landowners] of any capitalistic country, Russia included," and if even in the West "the crux of the agrarian program of Social-Democracy was precisely the 'peasant question', then how much more so was this the case with Russia?"[49] Lenin was turning necessity into a virtue, but because the road was full of dialectical pitfalls which had to be circumvented, he persistently justified the Russian party's concern with the "peasant question." But reluctant to state candidly, as he would somewhat later, that for Russia's Marxists there was no chocie about taking account of the preponderant peasants, Lenin delicately explained the party's need for a peasant orientation in terms of the newness of the Russian Marxist movement and because all of "the old Russian socialism was, in the final analysis, a 'peasant' socialism."[50] Having with such sophistic comment tried to resolve the issue, Lenin, again, lest he become suspect of having strayed into narodist heresy, went on splitting hairs. To demonstrate that his purity remained unsullied, he declared, rather meaninglessly (except in the sense that he was defending himself) that in those radicals who consider themselves to be inheritors of our "Narodnik Socialists there remains almost nothing that is socialistic."[51]

In constructing a "Marxian" rationale for an agrarian programme which viewed the peasant as a person, Lenin was like an explorer about to venture into *terra incognita.* What were the natives like? Lenin's description of the peasant was a composite of what Marxist scripture made him out to be and the revision of the scripture by Lenin to fit a pre-scriptural society. Lenin was trying to present the Russian peasant as a factory worker, if still mired in village mud. But since the factory worker in accordance with the minimum programme of Social-Democracy, was as yet progressing only toward the goal of bourgeois democracy, then, too, if moving very sluggishly forward, was the rural wage worker. But the small-propertied peasant, as Lenin intimated, was ready for violent revolutionary action because history had, so to speak, brought "peasant wars" to the foreground in the struggle against the survivals of serfdom in Russia. However, the notion that the propertied peasant was more radical than the rural wage workers was so obviously unrealistic that it was soon ejected from the evolving agrarian programme of Russian Social-Democracy.

In *To the Village Poor, An Explanation for the Peasants of What the Social-Democrats Want,* (March 1903), Lenin daringly expressed his vanguardist views on the peasant's role in the revolution. As the subtitle tells us, the pamphlet was written to be read by the peasants themselves, so that it depicts in the simplest terms the ideas presented in *The Development of Capitalism in Russia,* including, of course, the exaggerations which Lenin had drawn from Postnikov's statistics.[52] What gave this work its major historical importance, however, was Lenin's creative deviation from Marxist thought in crediting peasants with a capacity to learn. Provided with Marxist gospel they would be able to grasp what their "brains" (the Social-Democrats) had in mind for them and they would understand how they themselves could help in achieving those goals. Lenin, hitherto bound to Marxist dogma regarding the peasant, had become a full fledged peasant "humanist." Such flexibility, in turn, provided him with insight into the vast revolutionary potential which lay formant among the hordes of rural destitutes. If only for the "peasant" dimension that he added to Marxism, Lenin fully deserves the title of leader of the Russian revolution.

At the same time Lenin never could admit (probably not even to himself) the extent to which he had accomodated Marxism to narodism. In the final chapters of *Capital I,* Marx, the vanguard intellectual who probed into factory conditions, had graphically exposed *laissez faire* capitalism as the principal cause of popular suffering. By the same token, Lenin's *Village Poor* was a simplified handbook with which the Marxist narodniki (the Bolsheviks) could go to the "people" to explain, in terms of their personal suffering, the horrors of Russia's capitalist agriculture which made the peasant essentially identical to the factory worker. "A horseless peasant," wrote Lenin, "is in fact propertyless. He is a proletarian. . . . He is a natural brother to the town worker." The peasant, owning a single horse, Lenin labeled semi-proletarian, i.e., one who barely eked out a living, and "they were also blood brothers to the town workers. . . . All these horseless and single-horsed peasants! All these rural proletarians and semi-proletarians! And what a huge number of such people in Rus!"[53]

But all Russian peasants, whether rich or poor, Lenin wrote, were "still serfs to a large extent; . . . a lower, 'black', tax-paying class; [subordinates] of the police and the land captains. . . . *All* of the peasants want to be liberated from this newly imposed serfdom [and] want full rights, *all* of them hate the landlords. . . . For the most part even the rich peasant is abused by the landlord. This means that the rural poor must fight together with the rich peasants [to win] their rights."[54] Thus emerged the concept of the two-stage revolution (further developed in Lenin's *Two Tactics*), the first stage uniting workers with all the peasants against landlords (and factory owners), the second, linking workers and poor peasants in the struggle against the rich peasants, who would, in the revolution's course, have seized the landlord's holdings.

Worth noting, if only because Lenin's eventual triumph put the concept into practice, was the great stress, in *The Village Poor* upon freely elected peasant committees. Here, for the first time, Lenin clearly envisages them as political and social activists. They would know how to right the wrongs of the nobles' committees, who, in drawing up the Emancipation settlement, had, by cutting off grazing areas, watering areas and the like, kept the peasants dependent upon their former masters.[55]

In February 1901, Lenin had rejected the thought that urban "revolutionary forces" be sent into the villages. But early in 1903, although not yet locating permanent "active revolutionary forces" in the villages, Lenin was urging that "class conscious Social Democrats, gathering in a town or village" collaborate with peasants "to the best advantage of the entire working class." How perfect a blending of old narodism with the "new" Marxism. But Lenin must do his best to camouflage it. He provides an example of the *modus operandi.*

The Social-Democrat might at once contact the "most sensible, intelligent and trustworthy peasants who are seeking justice and are not afraid of the first police dogs," to explain to them the various ways in which the village is being cheated, and, as though applying the technique of the factory courtyard leaflet to the fields, getting the peasants to complain in concert, "just as the urban workers make their demands to the factory owners." In time, Lenin suggests, the peasants may become organized for the "common struggle together with the Social-Democratic workers in the towns," or even occasionally manage to stage a strike against landlords or rich farmers "in the manner of urban workers."[56] The function of the peasantry in Lenin's projection of Russia's revolutionary future had obviously risen to much greater importance.

Given its shockingly heretical nature, it was to be expected that Lenin's agrarian program would encounter vigorous opposition at the 2nd Congress of RSDWP. Lieber, Egorov and Martynov argued that Lenin in his attempts to woo the peasant, was muddling the Marxian road map to socialism. "Is it a programme to suit our purposes?" asked Egorov. "Does it define our demands, or do we want to make it popular?" He added, "If all we want from the peasants is their participation–*a la* the French Revolution–and if all we offer them are the *otrezki,* [pieces of land the peasants considered their own which the landlords had taken during the Emancipation], then we shall be outbid by the SRs who offer to give them all the land."[57] Martynov found fault with the demand that the peasants were to reacquire exactly the lands they held in 1861 because Social-Democrats denied in principle that even before 1861 the landowners held legitimate title to the lands they occupied.[58] Comments of that general nature abounded at the Congress, proving mainly that the Social-Democrats, Lenin included, were not in their element where agriculture was concerned. Makhov remarked rather bluntly that "the majority of the speakers" had no idea what to make of the program or what its aims were, adding that it "was hard to perceive it as a Social-Democratic agrarian program," but seemed more like some toying with the idea of "correcting historical injustices" which had a flavor of "demagoguery and adventurism."[59]

In *One Step Forward, Two Steps Back,* (May, 1904) a bitter critique of the 2nd Party Congress, Lenin denounced his Congress opponents as "vulgar" Marxists. Proof was precisely their failure to grasp "that an underestimation of the significance of the peasant movement. . . and our insufficient strength to utilize it, constituted the weak side of our Social-Democrats when the first famous peasant risings occurred [in 1901 and 1902]."[60] To Lenin, Marxism had come to mean the achievement of revolution in Russia, using every opportunity that historical circumstances offered. The failure to seize upon and to encourage the revolutionary potential of the Russian peasant and not to offer him every possible inducement to tear down the remnants of the past, was to Lenin a distortion of the letter of Marxist thought for the purpose of perverting, or vulgarizing, its spirit.

Lenin's polemical approach to the subject of agricultural revolution was exactly that which he had employed against the Economists in *What Is To Be Done?.* Therein he had stressed that "the fundamental flaw in Russian Social-Democracy's 'new direction' was its tendency to bow before spontaneity, while failing to understand that mass spontaneity demanded great consciousness from us Social-Democrats. The greater was the spontaneous stirring among the masses, the broader the movement," so much more urgent became the need for "consciousness in the theoretical, political and organizational work of Social-Democracy." *What Is To Be Done?* had deplored the failure of the young Social-Democrats to cope with the rapid acceleration of spontaneous mass upsurges, "continuing incessantly," and spreading to ever "new localities and to new social classes," including "even the peasantry." But the revolutionaries had *"lagged behind"* this trend in their 'theories' and in their activities, and they had failed to create organizational continuity enabling them *to lead* the movement."[61]

Lenin barely mentioned the peasants in *What Is To Be Done?* but until 1902 they had barely entered his consciousness as a potential revolutionary force. By 1904, however, Lenin had come to view the peasants as "spontaneously" ready for revolution so that Social-Democrats, if they were true Marxists, had to utilize their powerful anger.

In his "Resolution on Relations to the Peasant Movement," offered at the All-Bolshevik 3rd Party Congress (London, April-May, 1905) Lenin noted "the now expanding peasant movement," however unconscious it still was politically, along with the duties of Social-Democracy to support "every revolutionary movement." Social-Democrats "must try to cleanse the revolutionary democratic content of the peasant movement of all its reactionary traits" while raising the revolutionary consciousness of the peasants and imbuing them with democratic aspirations. Most importantly "the party of the proletariat, must in every case and under all conditions unswervingly strive to create an independent organization of the rural proletariat, making clear to it the irreconcileable antagonism of its own interests to those of the peasant bourgeoisie."

Hence the Congress charged all party organizations with "a) propagating among the broadest layers of the people that it could expect energetic Social-Democratic support for peasant revolutionary measures aimed at improving their situation. This support would include demands for confiscation of landlord, crown, monastery and allotted lands," a marked advance beyond the demand for the return only of the *otrezky* (cutoffs) which Lenin had backed at the Second Congress.

"b) As a means of arousing the peasant movement to the highest pitch of political awareness, to stress the need for the immediate organization of revolutionary peasant committees guiding the entire revolutionary-democratic transformation, rescuing the peasantry from the police, the bureaucracy and the landlords.

"c) to disorganize the autocracy and to support the revolutionary attack upon it, to call the peasantry and the rural proletariat to all possible political demonstrations, [including] collective refusal to pay dues and taxes, to serve in the army or to obey decrees and orders of the government and its agents.

"d) to strive toward an independent peasant-proletarian organization which should be guided to unite with the urban proletariat, under the banner of the Social-Democratic party, members of which would enter the peasant committees." (This was clearly the mechanism through which Lenin expected to control the peasants.)[62]

In the session following Lenin's proposals, Bar'sov of the Caucasian union supported them so ardently that it is difficult not to suspect Lenin's coaching. The proposals Bar'sov proclaimed, had dealt "brilliantly" with the theoretical and practical "importance and necessity for the Russian Social-Democratic Workers' Party to provide energetic support to the peasants and he made the point–further suggesting his collaboration with Lenin–that Lenin had remained fully within the bounds of orthodoxy. Bar'sov alluded to authorities such as Plekhanov, Engels and Kautsky to back his statement. Therefore, said Bar'sov (sounding almost like Lenin) he had no reason to dwell upon the "already settled" (a phrase typical of Lenin) "purely principial theoretical order" of the question.[63]

Bar'sov's task, then, was essentially to call attention to peasant affairs in the Caucasus, based upon "our party's experiences [mainly in Georgia] where, in an important sense, it has worked to organize for leadership of the peasant movement." Bar'sov concurred fully in Lenin's view that Social-Democratic support of the peasant movement was vital as was the creation soon of Revolutionary-Peasant Committees and "in order better to instruct the party in this matter," he went on to depict the revolutionary situation in the Caucasus. He then told of the suffering rural proletariat, most of whom were Georgian "the most literate of all Caucasian peoples," and of brutal governmental measures in 1902. The peasant response of strikes and boycotts, leading to military retaliation, had given "the peasants their first direct lessons in political warfare [another Lenin phrasing], large numbers of old and young men and even women having been arrested." In the overfilled jails, the peasants responded enthusiastically to "our comrades–the 'political' Social-Democrats," some of whom they subsequently joined in exile in Archangel or Siberia.

From its very inception, in 1903, as Bar'sov reported, the Caucasian Union Committee was able successfully to disseminate its propaganda among the landless peasants. The initial Committee proclamation was distributed in May 1903, and soon thereafter came the organization of the revolutionary *kruzhki,* (circles) "and now [1905] Georgia is covered with a network of *kruzhki.*" The organization worked as follows: "We organize members of a *kruzhok,* including up to ten members. One such [group of ten] then meets with other ten-membered cells of the same village and elect the village representative–and so it goes in each village. In each of the four or five regions into which Georgia is divided there is an agent of the Committee, who, acting in conspiracy with all village representatives, links them together." Since Georgia adjoined Batum, Bar'sov explained, the Committee was able daily to send agents through Georgia, who, by means of literature and agitation had produced large meetings, some of which, since February 1905, had convened 5,000 persons.

The Union Committee, Bar'sov boasted, had carried its tactical and political slogans into the villages, "distributing among the villagers *the very same literature* [my italics] that it had spread among the urban workers." The Committee, additionally, had published some original and some translated brochures for the villagers–the latter including *To the Village Poor*–along with leaflets and proclamations. "In the past year the peasants of Georgia and part of Imperatia and Mingrelia had organized May Day demonstrations," which, in Georgia, had led to violent clashes with the police.[64]

It seems evident that Bar'sov's experiences influenced Lenin's congress resolution as well as his *Two Tactics,* written in June-July 1905, directly after the congress.

Lenin was not in Russia until late 1905. He then discovered that the Russian peasants who, from afar, seemed so admirable–thanks in part to Bar'sov's reports, had, in fact, manifested nothing better than primitive anarchistic behavior. However, his growing pro-peasant or peasant-dependent orientation was given fresh stimulation because of peasant militancy in the Western Provinces of the empire, particularly in Latvia.[65] Lenin, eager to seize upon whatever suited his formative theories did not pause to analyze the highly special Latvian conditions that created the organized peasant violence of 1904-1905, and this resulted in a further distortion of his agrarian views, as recorded in 1906-1907.

In general, *Two Tactics* postulates a rising revolutionary consciousness among the peasantry, expressing the sentiment that both "semi-proletarian" and "petty bourgeois," peasant were "capable of becoming wholehearted and *extremely radical* fighters for the democratic revolution."[66] [My italics] Ignoring the fact that the very peasants who had stimulated his ideas were themselves oppressed by Russians, adding xenophobia to class hatred, he prophesied that the "bourgeois democratic" revolution in Russia would "attain its greatest strength only when the vacillating bourgeoisie turn their backs on it and when the masses of the peasantry emerge alongside the proletariat as active revolutionaries."[67] (Looking back twelve years later, Lenin blamed the failure of 1905 to complete its mission on the lack of organization and aggressiveness of the Russian peasants!)

Two Tactics extented the motifs of *What Is To Be Done?* to the peasantry and was intended to serve as a manual for the elitest revolutionary cadres.

"We have now [mid-1905] undoubtedly entered upon a new epoch," wrote Lenin, "a period of political disturbances and revolutions has begun."[68] This, of course, was true. Quite unexpectedly the young Social-Democratic party found itself amid a powerful revolutionary movement and facing the possibility, given the disastrous war with Japan, that the Romanov dynasty would be overthrown. What then?

The question of what manner of party for Russian Social-Democracy, so ardently debated since 1903, had now expanded to include the matter of what role, if any, the party should play in a provisional government following the tsar's downfall. In the Menshevik view a government formed by the property owning classes was now due. Social-Democrats could not cooperate in such a government; that would constitute Millerandism and betray the proletariat.[69] But Lenin, not satisfied with such a self-defeating response, decided it was properly Marxist to utilize a provisional government, not to entrench the bourgeoisie but to further the ends of the revolution. Once the tsar was overthrown, he meant at once to initiate the by-passing of the bourgeois order and to move towards socialism.

But how could this be done in a country with so scanty an industrial base? Lenin's answer was: Use the spontaneous peasant revolution, which, harnessed to that of the proletariat, could establish a dictatorship of proletariat and peasantry. Such a regime would introduce all the democratic reforms called for by the Bolshevik minimum program. Thereupon it would be a matter of waiting for the European revolution, unleashed by the great events in Russia, to carry Russia, along with Europe as a whole, into the socialist phase of the revolution. Lenin called for Social-Democracy to lead the revolution rather than to be led by it. "We must propagate the idea of action from above," he wrote, "we must prepare for the most energetic offensive activities, and must study the conditions and forms of such action."[70]

Lenin's thought remained consistent with the ideas expressed in *What Is To Be Done?* A party of professional revolutionaries would continue to direct the proletariat even after the revolution overthrowing tsarism, but, as we have seen, he had extended the concept of elitist leadership to the peasantry as well. Starting from this ideological base, the notion of using the ongoing revolution as a steppingstone to power was to him as natural in 1905 as it would be latter in 1917. As envisaged in *Two Tactics,* the peasantry, having seized the landlords' property, would combine with the urban workers in stage two of the revolution, to assail the property holders of city and country. The petty bourgeois instincts of the peasants would need to be kept in tight rein, but that, Lenin, was sure, could be done after the revolutionary dictatorship of proletarians and peasants had been established. (In this thought lie all the components of what would much later be called a People's Republic.)

In summary, Lenin conceived of the revolution as taking a course in which the peasant committees (which Lenin had referred to at the 1905 Congress) would, like red ants, overrun the ancient and more recently established property holdings, whereupon the Social-Democratic organizers of the peasant revolution would bring the peasants into unity with their urban brethren. In this way the peasants would come under control of their "elected delegates" to the new revolutionary governent–i.e., Lenin's agents–who, using terminology which the peasants would not understand, would soon deprive them of their newly-acquired landed possessions. These ideas are implicit in Lenin's statements at the 1905 congress and in *Two Tactics.* (In 1918 Lenin tried unsuccessfully to put them into practice, his later actions being mentioned here because they clearly had their roots in his schemes of 1905 when he was prepared to lead the revolutionary masses in ways not previously forseen by Russian Marxism.)

The spectacular events of October 1905, although momentarily eclipsing Lenin, and probably even prodding him into precipitous action, served, in the long run, to suggest that he, rather than Trotsky, who flashed briefly like a meteor, had been on the right course. The sudden and utterly incredible appearance of the Petrograd Soviet, Trotsky its president, shaking its fist under the tsar's nose, made something like a proletarian dictatorship in Russia seem a real possibility (at least for several weeks) giving further encouragement to Trotsky to move beyond his co-theorist Parvus-Helphand. Having with the older man in 1904, formulated the notion of "permanent revolution," meaning that political upheaval in Russia might start a chain reaction of events leading to a world revolution, Trotsky, in 1905-1906, daringly proposed that a Russian dictatorship of the proletariat was a possibility and that it would trigger the socialist revolution in Europe and thence the world.[71]

Lenin, in *What Is To Be Done?* had previously predicted that the Russian proletariat would become "the vanguard of the international proletarian revolution," but he could not agree that the provisional government would be a proletarian dictatorship, as hoped for by Trotsky, but a revolutionary dictatorship of proletarians combined with peasants, as described above. Such a regime could inspire but not instigate European socialist dictatorships. Russia's revolution would stop short of proletarian dictatorship, until Europe had made its revolution and exported it, along with its advanced technology into Russia, enabling Russian socialism to blend with that of Western Europe.[72]

Trotsky, did not believe, as did Lenin, that a proletarian party could live in a coalition with peasants, or that it could survive the counterrevolution. The workers, therefore, had "to link the fate of their political rule, and, hence, the fate of the entire Russian revolution, with the fate of the socialist revolution in Europe."[73]

The conflicting precepts of Lenin and Trotsky regarding the post-tsarist government of Russia, each a product of the revolutionary ferment of the period 1904 to 1906, remained alive at least until 1914. Polemicizing against Martov in an article of April 1909, Lenin contended that Trotsky's "basic error," in predicting a proletarian dictatorship and permanent revolution was that he ignored "the bourgeois character of the revolution" and that he had "no clear conception regarding the transition from bourgeois to socialist revolution." Lenin also attacked what he regarded as Trotsky's assumption that in a coalition of proletarians and peasants, the latter would "either fall under the sway of an existing bourgeois party, or would form a powerful independent party," for this implied that the proletariat would be unable to maintain its supremacy over the peasantry.[74]

Lenin's conception of a Russian revolutionary government awaiting the importation of socialism from Europe seems timid compared with Trotsky's view that the Russian revolution would supply the shock troops of world revolution. However, Lenin believed that a proletarian party structured according to the blueprint offered in *What Is To Be Done?* and operating according to the prescriptions set forth in *Two Tactics of Social-Democracy,* would give the workers, led by intellectuals, the discipline and the flexibility required for controlling a revolutionary coalition, even having a minority of delegates, and that they could hold power for a least a certain period of time. However, Lenin conceded that such a government would eventually collapse if a European revolution did not come to its support. But being content, at first, with a revolutionary government in Russia would not, Lenin thought, compel the proletariat to act out of fear of being instantly crushed by counter-revolution, giving them no alternative but to bank entirely upon an immediate European revolution.

Whatever the theoretical differences between Trotsky and Lenin, the latter portion of 1905 provided both men with opportunities for political action. By November, when Lenin, returned to Russia, Trotsky had become the president of the Petrograd Soviet. Lenin naturally was jealous, although he praised Trotsky for his "tireless and striking work."[75] Trotsky's autobiography tells us that Lenin was in full accord with all the Soviet did under Trotsky's guidance. In fact, Lenin urged that the Soviet move beyond its trade unionist and economist orientation and strive to become the provisional government in Russia, more or less along the lines of his proletarian-peasant coalition.[76] If understandably careful about diminishing the Soviet, a remarkable proletarian achievement, Lenin remained critical of it and of its leader. And, as though needing to demonstrate that he was still the helmsman of Social-Democracy, he instigated the December rising of the Moscow Soviet, resulting in an armed clash with government troops. This needless butchery of thousands of Moscow's workers gave Lenin the opportunity to make an invidious comparison between the failure of the St. Petersburg Soviet, which had not ventured beyond the strike tactic, and Moscow's "heroic proletariat," which had proved that "active" (i.e. armed) struggle was possible. Lenin later claimed the December Moscow rising to have been the most important event of 1905 (Lenin referred to November and December, when he was in Russia, as the two great months of the revolution) and, indeed, hailed the rising as the legitimate successor of the Paris Commune.[77] Thus, having allowed expendable proletarians to pull his chestnuts out of the fire, Lenin, despite his late arrival upon the scene, was able to emerge with his leadership credentials intact. And even though Trotsky remained a heroic figure, aided by his cause celèbre trial soon after his arrest in December 1906, the idea of a permanent revolution, led by a Russian proletarian dictatorship, seemed like mere rhetoric compared with Lenin's much solider notion of a proletarian-peasant coalition making up a provisional government.

At the so-called Unity Congress, which met in Stockholm, during April 10/23 to April 25/May 8, 1906, Lenin spoke out with the assurance of one whom events had proven correct.[78] On the subject of the agrarian program, the first item on the agenda, Lenin's call for the nationalization of all the land was opposed mainly by Mensheviks who argued for municipalization of all the confiscated land and the administration of it by "liberal zemstva" but not by the peasants. This was an expression of Menshevik refusal to move beyond the limits of a bourgeois revolution. In the debate Comrade John termed Lenin's nationalization program an invitation to counterrevolution "not only on the fringes but in the center of Russia." Were Lenin's scheme to materialize, John predicted "not merely a Vendee but a general peasant rising against the attempted governmental interference in the disposal of the peasants' own alloted land." John cited from *To the Village Poor,* wherein Lenin had written that the bourgeoisie lied about the Social-Democratic position. Lenin had charged them with saying that the Social-Democrats intended to take away the properties of the poor and middle peasantry, when, in fact, it was only the properties of the large landowners–those who lived off the laborers –which would be confiscated. Lenin had written that the Social-Democrats would "never take away the lands of the small and middle farmers! Now Comrade Lenin wants to introduce this [bourgeois] 'lie' into the programme. . . . Lenin proclaims that in the program for municipalizing the land there is no mention of a democratic republic as a necessary precondition." But it was not decrees that made a democratic structure, it was "the organization of democratic social forces," such as municipalization, which would create "the material conditions for the organization and consolidation of democracy."[79]

Plekhanov described Lenin's plan as "closely tied to the Utopian seizure of power by revolutionaries," in other words, a narodovoltsy-type of scheme, and further argued for municipalization on the grounds that placing the land under control of "the organs of Social Self Government of the owners of the land" was a bulwark against reaction that would preclude the return of the land to their former owners in the event of "a restoration."[80]

"The only guarantee against restoration," replied Lenin, "is a socialist revolution in the West." Otherwise, restoration is "absolutely inevitable, regardless of what solution to the land reform question is decided upon. The Russian revolution can win with its own forces but it cannot hold and consolidate power. . . unless there is a socialist overturn in the West."[81] Lenin, of course, was striving for the proletarian-peasant dictatorship which, economically, would have to be founded on nationalized land. Plekhanov's charge of Utopian scheming by Lenin was quite off target if only because Lenin's programme was unequivocally realistic in its design to deceive the peasants. Lenin's draft programme, presented to the 1906 Congress, bluntly called for elitist manipulation of the politically naive peasantry. In addition to calling, as usual, for violent peasant committees to root out landlords, police, and the like, and, of course, for the election by the peasants themselves of government officials—what could be more democratic?—Lenin cynically asked support for peasants who wanted "only and exclusively to enlarge their small farms and nothing more." Their "bourgeois" desire, Lenin explained, was, at the moment, a revolutionary stimulus that should be backed.[82]

Lenin described a peasant deputy to the Duma who had requested that all land be transferred to the state, as a man voicing "a reactionary prejudice, for in constitutional Russia" the state was and would remain "a police and military despotism." (Shades of ideas Lenin would later expand upon in *State and Revolution.*) But instead of rejecting the peasant's demand as harmful prejudice, Lenin proposed that the party "hook onto it," thereby revealing to the peasants the "actual" state of affairs, to wit; their demand, although meaningless at the moment, would become "very useful" to the peasants at such a time when the state had become "a fully democratic republic," (again the seeds of *State and Revolution!*) with all its officials elected by the people, the standing army having been abolished.[83] As though the peasants could have understood what he really meant, Lenin was telling them to look joyfully ahead to the time when the land had become "nationalized" (he never used the word "socialized") as a result of their revolution.

Nothing in the term "nationalization" indicated that Lenin meant anything but that which each peasant longed for–land–to be gained in the most just and democratic manner. But in reality Lenin was giving the peasant a shovel for digging his grave, and allowing him to elect a government that would turn him into a landless proletarian.

In the Menshevik-controlled Congress of 1906 the project for municipalization carried the day. But soon thereafter the Social-Democrats had to debate the agrarian question on the floor of the Duma along with representatives of the peasants themselves. For the Bolshevik delegates Lenin chose a line supporting the peasant deputies demanding nationalization. This was the so-called "project of the 104," representing a majority among the peasant deputies in the First and Second Duma calling for a division of land taken from the rich, the state and the church.

The "project of the 104" had connotations useful for agitation and was in any case better than the Stolypin program which threatened to create a group of conservative peasants who would identify their interests with those of the landlords. Lenin was greatly impressed by the mood of the landless peasants in the first two Dumas, especially by the class hatred reflected in their speeches.

Lenin hailed the speeches of the "revolutionary peasants" as "far more revolutionary" in spirit than those of the "revolutionary workers," lauding the peasants' passion for destroying the regime of landlords and "immediately" creating a new system. The peasant "burns with desire to strangle the enemy at once," whereas the workers seemed to be "aiming at a more distant goal." Lenin perceived the peasant as "making *his* bourgeois revolution now, at this moment, and does not see its internal contradictions, nor is he aware of the contradictions. The Social-Democratic worker does see them and since his goal is world socialism, he *cannot* link the fate of the working class movement to the outcome of a bourgeois revolution. That does not mean that the worker must support the liberals in the bourgeois revolution [i.e., go the way of Menshevism]. The conclusion to be drawn is that while merging *with no other* class, the worker *must with all his energy* help the peasant to carry through this bourgeois revolution *to the end.*" (I have stressed the words "to the end" because of the extremely important significance that often repeated phrase had for Lenin. Of course, it stood for the proletarian-peasant dictatorship, and if such a regime had actually materialized is there any reason to doubt that Lenin would have become the chief of state?)

The above-cited material is drawn from *The Agrarian Programme of Social-Democracy In the First Russian Revolution, 1905-1907,* which Lenin completed in December 1907. Written to defend his nationalization programme, that pamphlet also reflects his conviction, by that date, that the Russian peasant was the true locomotive both of the revolution in Russia and of a socialist revolution in Europe. In effect, he had accorded the agrarian "bourgeois" revolution carried "to the end" the number one priority in the achievement of what he then considered to be his aims. That being the case, the reforms introduced by Stolypin became to him a matter of greatest anxiety, since they threatened to defuse the time bomb of peasant revolution upon which all else hinged. Lenin's expressions of hatred for Stolypinism are more intense than the usual anti-reactionary phraseology of a revolutionist. But in them lay a reflection of Lenin's deadly fear that the agrarian reforms were undermining the scenario for revolution upon which Lenin had labored long and hard.

Early in 1908, Lenin attributed "enormous historical importance" to the support being given the Stolypin agrarian policy by "the government of the tsar, the landlords and the big bourgeoisie." He prophesied that the fate of the bourgeois revolution in Russia, "not only the present revolution, but possible future democratic revolution as well, depends *most of all* upon the success or failure of this policy."

C. Lenin and the National Minorities

With respect to national minorities, Lenin's views were based upon the *Communist Manifesto's* references to fatherlandless proletarians who were seeking predominance within the state that ruled them, whether that state was national or multinational. In any case the function of the revolution was to destroy all states and to unite all nations. The *Manifesto* was aimed primarily at a Germany on the eve of a bourgeois national revolution that would convert the German Confederation into a unified nation. But the new state was to exist only until the proletarian revolution should have brought Germans into brotherly coalescence with the workers of the world. The Marxian concept of self determination, then, had meaning only as a transitional stage on the historically-determined road to internationalism. Lenin frequently pointed out that Marx, Engels and Kautsky never viewed the liberationist struggle of an oppressed nation as an end in itself but related each such case to the eventuality of internationalism.[86]

The programme of the Second Congress of the Russian Social-Democratic Workers Party accepted the transitional nature of national self-determination in a statement which contradicts itself. It calls for the replacement of tsarist autocracy by a democratic republic, the constitution of which would guarantee "the right to self determination for all nations entering into [the new democratic constitutional] state."[87]

Marxism, in the long run, was expected to wipe out nationalism everywhere. However, just as the Marx-Engels views on Germany exposed their deep attachment to their native land, it was Great Russian nationalism that influenced both factions in the Russian Social-Democratic Workers' Party to support the famous paragraph 9 of the party programme, if for different reasons. Both sides were united to the extent of wishing to rule out the Jewish and Polish Marxists' preference for "reactionary" federalism and cultural autonomy in the programme,[88] federalism because it decentralized the state and delayed economic unification, cultural autonomy because it enhanced national bourgeois separatism.[89]

The Mensheviks feared the Jewish Bund for its claim on Jews within Menshevik ranks.[90] Beyond that, without, like Lenin, thinking about the issue as likely to inhibit party centralization, they were automatic adherents of the idea that self determination was an undeniable democratic right. Mainly for these reasons they went along with Lenin in 1903, insensitive, at the time, to the sacrifice they were demanding of non-Marxists. Lenin, for his part, had made his own position clear well in advance of the Congress.

In an *Iskra* article of February 1903, Lenin had attacked the Armenian League of Social-Democrats for refusing, unlike their Georgian and other Caucasian neighbors, to accept the Russian-made formula, for preaching "federalism and national autonomy" rather than "the establishment of an autonomous class." The proletariat, he wrote, should attempt to bring the greatest number of workers of every nationality into closer unity "for struggle *in the broadest possible arena* for a democratic republic and for socialism." The proletarian party recognized every nation's right to self determination. But this command was to be understood in the sense of a negative imperative to "*oppose any attempt* to influence national *self determination* from the outside *by force and injustice.* The essential proletarian desire was not to struggle for self determination of peoples and nations but for the proletariat in each nationality."[91]

The same month another *Iskra* diatribe attacked the organ of the Foreign Committee of the General Jewish Workers' Union of Lithuania, Poland and Russia, for proclaiming that "The Jewish proletariat had organized itself (sic!) into an independent (sic!) political party, the Bund." Reprehensibly, the Jewish proletariat had acted on its own. ("sic!") Lenin writes sarcastically that he had almost slipped into terming the Bund's Foreign Committee "the new party's Central Committee." For the Jewish distrust of Russian proletarians who took part in pogroms, Lenin had only scorn. It was a "Zionist fable" that "anti-Semitism was eternal." Lenin was particularly outraged by the Bund's use of the words "our comrades of the Christian workers' organization." Lenin denied knowledge of any "Christian" working class organizations because "organizations belonging to the Russian Social-Democratic Workers' Party have never discriminated because of religion, have never asked about religion and will *never do so* even then when the Bund shall *in actual fact*" have become an independent political party.[92]

The "Autonomy in the Rules," adopted at the Minsk Congress of 1898, Lenin wrote, had given the "Jewish working class movement" all it needed. It had the right to agitate in Yiddish, to have its "own literature and congresses, the right to propose its special demands in the drawing up of a single general Social-Democratic programme and the right to satisfy local needs and problems relating to the special qualities of the Jewish ways." In all other respects Lenin demanded their "*closest* fusion with the entire Russian proletariat" in the interests of common struggle.[93]

Somewhat later Lenin vented his fury upon the Polish Socialist Party, whose journal *Przedswit* had labeled his notion of self determination "astonishing, confused, doctrinaire and anarchistic." The Poles, he wrote mockingly, had the idea that Lenin believed the worker had no business to be concerned "with anything but the complete destruction of capitalism," since he (Lenin) believed that "language, nationality, culture and the like" were characteristically "applicable only to the bourgeoisie."[94]

To Lenin the rejection of an all-embracing and purely temporary state form by socialists was contemptible, and his feelings toward them paralleled those he had expressed toward working groups, i.e., intelligenty, who had rejected his concept of an elitist-dominated party. In matters of organization Lenin's principal concern lay in centralizing authority. His "draft resolution on the place of the Bund in the party," written in June-July, on the eve of the Second Congress, stressed the idea that the rapid attainment of the party's goals, given the "conditions of the existing society [this was the police state argument advanced in *What Is To Be Done?*] made absolutely essential . . . the closest unity of the militant proletariat."[95]

The Bund's response to Lenin at the Second Congress was best summarized by Bundist Goldblatt, who correctly predicted that the disputed questions–Lenin had intentionally moved the question of the Bund's place in the party to the head of the agenda–"would lead to a disagreement between the defenders and the opponents of centralization. We, in the Bund, fully adhere to the policy of centralism. All of us are convinced partisans of it, yet I, unhesitantly, declare Lenin's project to be monstrous. The centralist principle proposes the control and observations over the lower organs of the party by the highest ones, but cannot and must not in any case lead to the destruction of the lower organs. Control can be [limited if] some competency is given to the subordinate organizations. The control of the central organs means keeping an eye on the lower organs to prevent them from wrecking proposed congresses or from acting to oppose the party program and basic principles. Certain temporary or local conditions might at times permit the power of the center to be broadened somewhat but the basic principles should remain intact, and such basic principles are althogether incompatible with the bases of Lenin's project. He is obsessed with the desire to provide the center with unlimited power, including its right of unlimited interference in the affairs of each separate organization. Lenin places no limits on such interference and would destroy all authority for separate subordinate organizations thereby eliminating their possibility of existence. An organization cannot exist, if it is not provided with a single right." Goldblatt concluded his blunt statement by expressing astonishment "that not a single delegate from the committee objects to such a monstrous project."[96]

Warszawski and Hanecki, the delegates of the Social-Democratic Party of Poland and Lithuania (SDKPiL), arrived late to the Second Congress where they were welcomed enthusiastically. However, Warszawski, besides conveying the best fraternal wishes from the Polish comrades, dampened the general ardor by stating that SDKPiL would require autonomous status if a union of his party with RSDWP was to be effected.[97] Although Warszawski claimed at the time not to be certain of his party's exact position, because it had not yet had the opportunity to discuss the matter, he was soon thereafter given his marching orders by Luxemburg and Jogiches. The two leaders of the Polish party in Berlin, in the meantime, received Lenin's article on self determination in the July issue of *Iskra.* The article was so much more arbitrary in tone than any previous *Iskra* article on the subject that it had completely turned them away from the possibility of fusion. Not even troubling to consult their party, Luxemburg and Jogiches instructed Warszawski and Hanecki to tell the Russians that Lenin's article had destroyed SDKPiL's sole motive for uniting with the Russians; that having been the hope of constructing a weapon against the nationalistic PPS (Polish Socialist Party). But the Russian insistence that the right of self determination be in the programme would have forced the Polish working class to adopt the nationalistic slogans of its mortal foe, the PPS.[98]

The reasons why Luxemburg and Lenin were mutally opposed on the national question is lucidly explained by Paul Frölich as the result of circumstances which "had placed the two great working class leaders in different positions." Luxemburg, a defender of an oppressed people, had, he writes, "to guard against the proletarian class struggle being misrepresented and swamped by nationalist tendencies," which was why she considered "a fighting alliance of the Polish and Russian working class to be of such great importance. By contrast, Lenin, member of an oppressor nation, needed to combine the revolutionary dynamism of the oppressed against absolutism, and that meant "unequivocally" granting them their historical right of complete political separation from Russia," i.e., self determination. But this "right," notes Frölich, Luxemburg cogently proved "to be inapplicable to the given situation, though it was to become an important psychological factor indeed for Russian Social-Democracy."[99]

Luxemburg's "Organizational Questions of Russian Social-Democracy," published in 1904 as a response both to *What Is To Be Done?* and *One Step Forward, Two Steps Back,* reveals a still broader dimension to Luxemburg's anti-Lenin polemic, and the passage below, while inadequately conveying Luxemburg's complete argument, does clarify her objections to the entire spectrum of the Leninist programme.

"Lenin's thesis," she writes, "is that the party Central Committee should have the privilege of naming all the local committees of the party. It should have the right to appoint the effective organs of all local bodies from Geneva to Liege, from Tomsk to Irkutsk. It should also have the right to impose on all of them its own ready-made rules of party conduct. It should have the right to rule without appeal on such questions as the dissolution and reconstitution of party organs. This way, the Central Committee could determine to suit itself, the composition of the highest party organs as well as of the party congresses. The Central Committee would be the only thinking element in the party. All other groupings would be its executive limbs. . . . Lenin . . . presents the opinion [in *One Step Forward*] that the revolutionary social democrat is nothing more than a Jacobin indissolubly joined to the organization of the proletariat, which has become conscious of its class interests. For Lenin the difference between Social-Democracy and Blanquism is reduced to the observation that in place of a handful of conspirators we have a class conscious proletariat. He forgets that this difference implies a complete revision of our ideas on organization and, therefore, an entirely different conception of centralism and the relations existing between the party and the struggle itself."[101]

In answer specifically to the Polish arguments, Lenin pointed out that "no Marxian slogan must ever be doctrinaire and out of context of historical relativity." The Russian Party was under political obligation "not to tie its own hands, but to reckon with all possible circumstances. The most important task for the Polish proletariat was to raise the slogan of a free and independent Polish Republic–leaving the removal of such a slogan a possibility–so that even under such an interpretation of the right of nations to self determination, the party of the proletariat would not deprave the proletarian consciousness, would not delude the working class with bourgeois democratic phrases, would not destroy the unity of the contemporary struggle of the proletariat."[103]

By such "metaphysics," as Luxemburg later termed them, did Lenin attempt to brush aside the problems of Polish Social-Democracy. However, he did not explain how the proletariat could be made to follow such subtle reasoning, how it could ever be explained to the working class that though the programme of the Social-Democratic Party on the national question sounded identical to that of the petty bourgeoisie, it was really different in that it could be changed at a moment's notice, depending on the dictates of history and the position of the international proletariat. Lenin, in 1903, would not admit that his real aim was party unity and that his insistence upon the right of self determination was merely propaganda of an intra-party nature and was not intended for much use among the masses of the border provinces; that the existence of independent nations had no real meaning anyway in a socialist world –which was essentially Luxemburg's position–and that he was, in a sense, trying to squelch parochial dilemmas, considering them to be of little consequence as compared to the all-decisive solutions that would be wrought by the Russian and world revolutions.

Although Polish and Bund delegates abandoned the Congress of 1903, one minority sector of the Social-Democratic movement as previously noted, did agree to accept the Russian point of view at that time. In the Transcaucasus, a complex of multi-nationality, the Social-Democrats prior to 1903 had found organizational progress possible only through genuine internationalism. Hence they agreed with the Russians that the recognition of national sections within the party was wrong. Though they required a certain amount of autonomy in local affairs because of the multiplicity of languages and so forth, they were content to accept the final jurisdiction of the Russian Party.[104] This type of local or "regional" autonomy had been offered to the Bund, which had rejected it. The acceptance of it by the Transcaucasian delegation provided support for the idea of party centralism which Lenin so desired.

Between 1903 and 1912 the national question was left pretty much out of the polemics of the various factions of Russian Social-Democracy. The growing split in the Party as a whole, as Lenin clung to party centralism and illegality, while the Mensheviks tended ever more toward revisionism, overshadowed the problem of whether one or another national group was to go the way of the Russian Party. Apart from the national issue, the national groups during this period took no special sides in the Bolshevik-Menshevik argument. The Latvians split within themselves into Bolshevik and Menshevik factions. Among the others, some agreed with the Mensheviks on one issue, with the Bolsheviks on another. On the whole one can say that the national groups, in elections to the Central Committee, jockeyed their strength about in such a way as to maintain Party parity so that neither Bolshevik nor Menshevik ideas could predominate. In 1912, however, the national question once again came to the forefront of attention as Lenin began to write article after article reiterating his 1903 stand on self-determination, and denouncing those who disagreed with him in no uncertain terms.

Various Bolshevik writers, among them Stalin, attribute the revival of Lenin's interest in the national question at this time to causes such as the intensification of Great Russian nationalism, accompanied by persecutions, pogroms, and the like, the impetus to nationalism given by national representations in the Duma, and the imminent European war which would change from academic to real problem the question of Polish liberation.[105]

Of whatever importance these factors may have been, the main cause for the revival by Lenin of the national question was the drift of the national groups away from their neutral positions in the Party toward unity with the Mensheviks.[106] The reason for this development is clear. The Unification Congress of 1906 (Stockholm), while bringing the national groups into the Russian Party, had left unresolved the question of how self-determination was ultimately to be interpreted.[107] Therefore, the autonomous status within the Party which Poles, Bund and Latvians desired and continued to practice, while sending delegates to Party congresses, helping to elect Central Committees and so forth, also remained hanging in the air.

However, as time went by, partly as a consequence of the inherent revisionist tendency of Menshevism, but partly as a result of the police measures of the Government, which had effectively severed the links between the Social-Democratic leadership and the Russian proletariat, there was developing in the Menshevik movement, in the hopes thereby of re-establishing contact with the working class, an ever-growing trend toward legal and open existence. By definition, this implied "liquidation" of the illegal Party center which, put into effective practice, would have destroyed Lenin's hope for the centralized party. But a legal party, not being unitary, could have no special complaint against federalism. Thus the Mensheviks, at first perhaps inadvertently, were opening the gates to unity with the national parties who, though willing enough in some instances to follow Lenin on organizational and other Bolshevik principles, could not sufficiently lose their national identities to become part of a monolithic Russian-dominated party. Already, by 1910, the Bund, the Latvian SD's and some elements of the Polish Party had joined forces with the Mensheviks. The bulk of the Polish Party remained neutral, supporting the Bolshevik formula on organization but continuing to insist upon autonomy within the Party.

The climax to this process of fusion came about in 1912. By this time, after years of exile and underground for most revolutionary leaders, it once again became possible for them to engage in open organizational activity. The Mensheviks, hoping for mass response to their newly conceived but thus far untried legal programme, found instead that Bolshevism, emphasizing conspiracy and violence, was far more attractive to the proletariat. Lenin's appeal to what Menshevik Dan calls the "mass instinct of vengeance" was cutting the ground of working-class support from under the feet of the Mensheviks. Adding insult to injury, as it were, Lenin secretly called for an "All-Russian Party Conference" to meet at Prague in January 1912. Inviting only Bolsheviks to attend, Lenin had this conference designate itself the "Sixth Congress of the Russian Social-Democratic Workers' Party." This bold stroke immediately placed all those in opposition to Lenin on the defensive and forced them to action designed to convince the Russian proletariat that they were still in the Party. Reconciling their differences, then, the various non-Bolshevik social-democratic factions decided to unite for self-preservation against Lenin and his tactics. This unity was theoretically achieved at a conference held in Vienna in August 1912 and the groups participating became known as the August Bloc—"the August Bloc of liquidators"—

as Lenin and his Bolshevik followers, in general, were ever after to term them.

Lenin did not fail to note the non-Russian delegates in the August Bloc. And though, for the moment, he held the upper hand, this still meant that the exponents of organizational decentralization[108] had combined with elements favoring national decentralization to constitute a serious threat to the "centralized party." And the menace to Lenin's *leitmotif* became even further marked when, unkindest cut of all, within Transcaucasian Social-Democracy, since 1903 the "national" model of Bolshevik perfection, a rift began to develop as the Menshevik faction, led by the Georgian Jordania, rejected "regional autonomy" and demanded cultural autonomy for each Transcaucasian nationality in the best traditions of the Bund, Poles and others.

Lenin's revival of the national question in 1912-1913 was his counterattack to the double-barrelled offensive of liquidationism and federationism upon party centralism. Sizing up the enemy coalition, Lenin decided to strike at its weakest link—the newly wavering Caucasian "liquidators." It was at this point that Lenin suddenly discovered that "amazing Georgian,"[109] Stalin, who was put to work by Lenin to write an article on the national question. Lenin might have written the article himself instead of, as it seems, dictating its ideas for Stalin to write down,[110] except that this Georgian, or any other Transcaucasian of Bolshevik persuasions[111] who might have come to Lenin's attention at this time, was regarded as useful for proving that the Caucasus was still in the centralist camp where the national question was concerned. Also, this representative of exemplary Transcaucasian Social-Democracy might serve to show the path of salvation to Jewish, Latvian, Polish and other recalcitrants. Stalin's article, as most of Lenin's on the national question, during 1912-1913, attacked the virus which had infected Jews, Georgians and Latvians and had prompted them to take the nationalist road to liquidationism (or vice versa) via the Austrian scheme of cultural autonomy. Cultural autonomy was berated as inevitably leading the working class to nationalism. It was bringing about national antagonisms even within the socialist movement. Thus, in Austria, as Lenin pointed out, the Czech Social Democrats had broken with the Austrians, and in Russia the Bund battled the Polish, Latvian and Russian Social-Democrats. In the elections to the Fourth Duma, the Bund had voted against the Polish SD's, etc. In the Caucasus, Stalin wrote, cultural autonomy was an especial evil—as it had to be wherever culture was an upper-class monopoly. Instead of the backward Caucasian peoples being drawn into the "common stream of a higher culture" (proletarian culture), the concept of cultural autonomy would "shut up the nations within their own shells" and allow the "separate national groups to be exploited by their few literates" (religious and bourgeois).

On the other hand, self-determination was the only honest socialist programme. This slogan, in accord with the economic plan of history, would break up the composities of Russia, Austria and Turkey, enabling the working class in each country, no longer confused by national strivings in common with their bourgeoisie, to recognize its real enemy—its own bourgeoisie—and overthrow it. Then, acting upon the principles of working class democracy, such a proletariat could fuse with other nations into a united world proletariat.[112]

It is clear that Lenin's notion of self-determination was something that would lead to unity and not to separation. But to expect independent nations, once arrived at or being restored to freedom, to unite again with their former oppressor—this seemed to be trusting entirely to a mystical Marxian dynamic—from oppressed minority to bourgeois nation, to proletarian revolution within the bourgeois nation and thence to internationalism; just as it was writ in the *Communist Manifesto.* To the Polish Social-Democrats the idea of a liberated Poland reuniting with Russia seemed fantastic. But, Utopian as Lenin's scheme may have seemed, his critics overlooked or ignored the fact that his overriding concern was that of revolutionary unity. In several of his articles of 1913 and 1914 on the national question, Lenin directed polemical broadsides against Luxemburg's "The National Question and Autonomy," written in 1908-1909. Among these was his lengthy "The Right of Nations to Self Determination," (early 1914) which began with the declaration that various "opportunists" on a "campaign" against paragraph 9 of the Russian Marxists' programme (Lenin specifically mentioned a Russian "liquidator," a Bundist and a "national-socialist" Ukrainian) had lately, in their "nationalist vacillations," merely repeated the arguments of Rosa Luxemburg.[113] In this article Lenin was striking at Luxemburg for isolating him within the International. In December 1913, she had criticized him for his splitting tactics, as evinced by the convening of the Prague Congress of 1912 and his separating, in 1913, of the Bolsheviks in the Duma from the Menshevik delegates.[114] Lenin hoped, with his attack upon Luxemburg to cause a split between the Berlin-based (Luxemburg-Jogiches-Marchlewski-Warszawski) faction of SDKPiL and its Krakow-based opposition, or Rosamowcy. Both factions, however, the latter including Felix Dzerzhinskii, favored the unification of Poland.[115]

Because the situation in Poland was classically conducive to an anti-self determination stance and because Luxemburg was so powerful a defender of this ideological position, Lenin's polemic even against her writings of 1908-1909 was of great importance to him. If it succeeded, it would, he believed, help to establish his centralistic vision of All-Russian Marxism among the national minorities. To demonstrate Luxemburg's "reformism," Lenin points out, firstly, that one of her "trump cards" was to state that "recognition of the right to self determination was the same as supporting the bourgeois nationalism of oppressed nations. On the other hand, says Luxemburg, if we understand this right only as the struggle against all violence of one nation toward another, then a special clause in the programme is not needed since Social-Democrats are, in general, opposed to all national oppression and inequality."

In her fears of the nationalism of the bourgeoisie of oppressed nations, wrote Lenin, "Luxemburg was *in fact* playing into the hands of the Great Russian Black Hundreds nationalism!" In fact, Luxemburg feared alienating the nationalism of the Polish proletariat. "Her second argument," Lenin went on, "is actually a timid evasion of the question: Does recognition of national equality include recognition of the right to secede? If so, then Luxemburg also admits in principle the correctness of article 9 of our programme. If not, it means that she does not recognize national equality. Evasions and dodges will not help matters here!"[116]

Luxemburg's stance was the only one that made sense in terms of Polish reality, and Lenin's arguments were those of a man who did not have to face the consequences of the position he advised.

CHAPTER I

LENIN AND THE ORPHANED GERMAN PROLETARIAT DURING THE FIRST YEAR OF WORLD WAR ONE

The news of an imminent European war, in which Russia was bound to be involved, reached Lenin in Poronin, Galicia along with rumors of the erection of barricades in St. Petersburg. Having since 1902 been predicting that a revolution in Russia would light the torch for a European revolution, he naturally became very excited. He wrote to V. M. Kasparov, late in July 1914, pleading to be kept posted on *"the progress of the revolutionary days in Russia.* Here we sit without newspapers. I beg you." He asked for "Berlin" papers–those carrying "*the most extensive* news from Russia"–and, his imagination running wishfully ahead of the pace of Russian developments, he requested telegrams telling of "exceptionally important events, if they occurred, . . . such as revolts in the army, etc."[1] Another letter sought information "on Petersburg workers movement, manifestoes, etc." to be used in the Central Organ, and he wanted "clippings from bourgeois papers about the currently stormy events in St. Petersburg. Hurry!"[2] By July 25 his frenzy for news was such, that compelled by "the latest revolutionary events in Russia," and even apologizing for his "audacity" he turned for help to two German Social Democrats then living in Stockholm, whom he had never met but whose addresses he had come upon in *Vorwärts.* He wanted one or more secret addresses in Stockholm through which he might receive mail from St. Petersburg.[3]

Had the time now come for the Russian proletariat and its leader, Lenin, to play their "due" role in European affairs? Lenin certainly hoped so. Between July 28 and July 31, after Austria had declared war on Serbia, but just before Germany and Austria were to declare war on Russia, Lenin drafted an article, provisionally entitled "Revolution and

War," revealing the manner in which he linked the revolutionary developments in Russia with the war in Europe. Under Roman numeral I of the draft's first section, item 1 states: "July days in 1914 vs. January, 1905." Thus (as is clear from what followed) Lenin distinguished the militant Petersburg workers of 1914 from the sheeplike throng that had marched to slaughter on Bloody Sunday. Item 2—"banners—barricades," was Lenin's shorthand, contrasting the ikon-bearing crowd of January 1905, with the determined revolutionaries of 1914. Item 3—"Gapon—Social-Democratic illegal organizations," flashed the message that a disciplined Bolshevik party rather than a priest, as in 1905, had taken command in 1914, and item 4—"naive attitude—stubborn struggle," tells us that a regularly functioning and dependable political apparatus had, in Lenin's view, replaced the futile demonstrations of a decade earlier. The phrases under Roman numeral IV of the draft's first section are self-explanatory.

IV. Militarism, imperialism.
Guns go off by themselves.
Struggle against war
resolution of Jaurès vs. Guesde
experience of Russian workers.
Best, war against war: revolution.

The second section of the draft contains eight items. The first few, running parallel, as it were, to their counterparts in section One, concern themselves with Russia. But the later-listed items of section Two are not in the same trajectory with the later-listed items in section One, but sweep far more boldly into the international arena. It appears that Lenin, having used section One of the draft as a springboard for testing the resilience of his ideas, had decided in section Two to let them fly off to Europe. Item 4 of Section Two—"Liquidationism rejected and little groups abroad," expressed Lenin's intention to instruct the Bolsheviks in exile throughout Europe to propagate the view that all reformist Marxism be shunned. This policy had proved its value in 1914 Petersburg,[4] and what had been learned in Russia—namely, that only revolutionary action, combining conspiracy and legal activity, could bring an end to wars and other outgrowths of capitalism—needed to be taught to European

Marxists by Lenin and his disciples. The problem then posed by item 6—"imperialism and militarism," (capitalism being the presumed dynamo of imperialist war) could be solved only by item 7—"War against war," or revolution. Concluding item 8—"The world situation and tasks of the Russian proletariat,"—asks, in effect, what Russia's Bolshevism and its leader should do at this critical juncture in European affairs?[5]

G. L. Shklovskii later wrote, providing very sound reasons for his belief, "that the fundamental slogans of Lenin's tactic in the imperialist war had been worked out by him in [Galicia] during the first days of the war, for he brought them to Bern completely formed. More than that I have every reason for stating that this tactic had ripened in Lenin's mind. . . on the very first day of the war" and "that Lenin had not a moment of doubt or vacillation" and "was already thinking of a war against war, i.e., of converting the imperialist war into a civil war."[6] But granting that Lenin's basic tactic regarding the war was formulated on "the very first day of the war," (July 18) it should, nevertheless, be stressed that his decision to become a prime mover of a revolution in Europe came about a week later, that is, after the August 4 vote of war credits by the German Social Democrats. This and identical events in France, Belgium, Austria-Hungary and Great Britain exposed the hypocrisy of Europe's "internationalist" leaders, which, as the Bolsheviks believed, had caused the proletarian ferment in Russia to be drowned in waves of chauvinism and *Slavianstvo.* Lenin, the leader of the sole Russian party to gird itself for revolution in the summer of 1914, had perhaps a personal reason to consider himself betrayed. At the same time, thanks to the chauvinist "heresy," he had overnight won the sacred right to provide the European masses with the kind of direction which, on the eve of the war, had led to the Petersburg barricades.

From the very outset of his career as a Russian Marxist leader, Lenin had never failed in his "duty" to declare as "vulgarizers" of Marx, such men as Struve, Martov, Plekhanov and Trotsky; at the same time, asserting his own reading of Marx to be the correct one. When, in 1914, therefore, Kautsky, Guesde, Vandervelde, et al., proved, like their Russian counterparts, to be nothing better than reformists, Lenin's course of action was clearly charted. But the old familiar pattern of supplanting each successive leader with himself, would this time carry him far beyond his Russian habitat. For a Russian revolutionary leader to become leader of a revolution in Europe required a period of time, during which, gradually, a major change in Lenin's perspective would occur.

Arriving upon the European (Swiss) scene, Lenin delivered his so-called "Theses on the War"[7] to a Bolshevik handful in Bern, and his frame of reference was still clearly Russia. The Theses demanded that Russian Social-Democracy call for socialist revolutions in all countries, i.e., for a struggle against chauvinism and patriotism of the Second International, "one of the most urgent slogans" being propaganda for a republican United States of Europe. Russian Social-Democracy was to opt for a revolution in Russia despite the war, because Russians regarded the downfall of the tsar and his armies "as the least evil." Defy patriotism, convert the imperialist war into civil war, and strive for defeat of one's own country. Such were the guidelines offered by Lenin.

The high priority given the slogan for a republican United States of Europe reflected an updating of that which Lenin had been propounding persistently since 1898. Russia, he maintained, had already entered upon its capitalist phase of development. She was therefore in the same general economic category not only with Austria-Hungary but with Germany as well. Russia was marching shoulder to shoulder with those and other monarchies toward bourgeois republicanism. (Somewhat later when Lenin started thinking like a European, he ceased to stress the idea that the European states were all advancing at about the same rate, or that Russia was in a class with Germany.)

Also rooted in Russia was Lenin's call for the defeat of one's own country.[8] Lenin apparently assumed that, like the population of the Romanov empire, each of the peoples hated its government and stood more or less ready to rise in revolution. In explaining his views–and partly to defend against criticism that he was pro-German,[9] if not, in fact, a traitor–[10] Lenin argued that defeatism in every warring nation was intimately linked to the drive for revolution. "Lenin," writes Isaac Deutscher, "did not ask his followers to engage, or to encourage others to engage in sabotage, desertion, or other strictly defensist activities. He merely argued that although revolutionary agitation would weaken Russia's military strength, Russian socialists were bound in duty and honor to take this risk in the hope that the German revolutionaries would do the same so that in the end all the imperialist governments would be vanquished by the joint efforts of the internationalists. The defeat of any one country would thus prove only an incident in the revolution's advance from country to country."[11] While providing a good reading of Lenin's polemical line of thought, Deutscher's apologetic ignores its Utopian dimension. It was totally unrealistic for Lenin to expect the belligerents all at the same moment to divest themselves of the Jingoism which had so enthusiastically sent their sons into the slaughter.

Lenin further justified his "defeat of one's own country" slogan by postulating that the destruction of oppressor states would pave the way to self-determination for subject nations.[12] This would mean progress toward internationalism. Bukharin, among other Bolshevik exiles, bitterly charged that Lenin was wrong to welcome the appearance of new nation-states (and cradles of national chauvinism) precisely at the time when the spirit of internationalism had attained its historic crest and ought to be supported.[13]

In the course of October 1914, Lenin began to test his ideas in public, lecturing in Swiss cities such as Bern, Lausanne, Geneva, Clarens and Zurich to politically "safe" groups of Russian emigrés, the only audiences available to him because of Swiss police surveillance. Along with applause, he encountered scathing criticism, most notably in connection with his "defeat of one's own country" theme.[14]

In *Sotsial-Demokrat* of December 12 he lashed out against the pride of the "Great-Russians" in their imperialist past, which he distinguished from ethnic pride. "Precisely because of our national pride," he wrote, "we *particularly* hate *our* slavish past (when the landed nobility led the peasants into war in order to extinguish the freedom of Hungary, Poland, Persia and China) and our slavish present when the very same landlords, aided by capitalists, are leading us to war for the purpose of strangling Poland and the Ukraine . . . . Nobody can be blamed for being born a slave; but a slave who not only shies away from an effort to free himself, but takes pride in his slavery (as, for instance, when he describes the smothering of Poland, the Ukraine, etc., as a 'defense of the fatherland' of the Great Russians)–such a slave is a loathsome eunuch."[15] At about this time too, Lenin gave public, if cautious, sanction for the prospective German seizure of Kiev, Helsinki, Riga and Tiflis and he called for Ukrainian independence.[16]

The expression of such views, along with a manifesto by the Bolshevik Central Committee, broadening the early September "Theses on the War" to include all of Europe's Social-Democrats,[17] illustrates Lenin's ability to blend in, like a chameleon, with the political environment in which he was functioning. When his base was Russia he had been the torch bearer for a revolution that would signal the oppressed of Europe to rise. But operating from Europe he would be the leader of a revolution that would sweep into Russia, Germany being its logical place of origin.[18] One aspect of this change of stance, as we shall see, was Lenin's attempt to rid himself gracefully of the tenet that Russia's revolutionary potential was at least equal to, if not greater than that of the other European countries. This–the heart of his republican United States of Europe slogan–now had to be replaced with a prophecy of imminent German revolution. And, since he sought to become the leader of European internationalism, a position previously held by Germany's Social Democratic high priest, he needed as soon as possible to acquire an international identity as Kautsky's heir apparent.

The Bolsheviks, he wrote to Shliapnikov in late October 1914, should with all their strength "support the just hatred" toward the German Social Democrats, and they should use this hatred as a device for combating "opportunism or any conniving with it." Admitting that this was an "international" task, Lenin emphasized his belief that the Russians–Lenin and his group–"more than any others" must take this burden upon themselves. "On the other hand," he wrote, "for presentation in the international arena, it is necessary that such an action be based upon some kind of collective decision in the customary manner,"[19] i.e., by way of an international conference. For his European "debut," however, Lenin needed an internationalists' conference with status enough to provide an expression of his views with a stamp of respectability. A conference to suit his purpose was not readily available. Lenin cautioned Shliapnikov not to attend the conference at Copenhagen, scheduled for January 17-18, 1915, because he suspected German-Scandinavian intrigue.[20] On the other hand, a conference of Entente nation Socialists, which met in London on February 14, invited Mensheviks but not Bolsheviks. Lenin sent Litvinov anyway, if only to object to the character of the conference and the manner in which it had been convened. (The Mensheviks in London refused to attend the conference on the ground that they did not represent their party's official opinion.)[21] At the same time, Trotsky failed in his attempts to bring together the two branches of Russian Social-Democracy in exile.[22]

Thus, desiring a dependable forum of "internationalists" which might offer a kind of official sanction of what he wanted to proclaim,[23] Lenin called together the Bolsheviks in exile. This handful convened in Bern, February 27 to March 24, in a meeting, later "officially" designated "Conference of the R.S.D.W.P. Groups Abroad." The eight resolutions[24] to emerge from the conference were drafted by a Lenin whose ideas were changing to accord with his new base of operations.

Henceforth, it was no longer Russia that was to set off the European powderkeg of revolution. The imperialist war, outgrowth of capitalism's latest stage (cartellization, internationalization of economic life, complete partition of the world, and the like) had become the key. "World capitalism's productive forces" had "outgrown . . . the national framework" so that "the objective conditions" for the achievement of socialism had "matured fully" as the result of "the extreme war-caused misery of the masses."

Lenin's tactical ideas, while shifting to Europe, had retained their Russian roots. For Europe, as for pre-war Russia, Lenin insisted upon a complete break with a policy of "class truce," while proposing, in line with his pre-war anti-liquidator views, that the revolutionary party utilize both legal and illegal means of struggle. His call for fraternization among troops at the front was likewise an outgrowth of his 1912-1914 polemics on self-determination with the Menshevik liquidators.[25] Europe, he said, should be organized by a new (Bolshevik) international, with Germany expected to serve as its nucleus. "A defense of the socialist viewpoint" in that country, he declared, "had been made possible only" because of "a decisive break with the wishes of the majority of the Social-Democratic party's top leaders." (Lenin's all-Bolshevik Prague congress of 1912 had similarly declared its independence from the Menshevik-liquidator majority of the Russian Social-Democratic Workers' Party.) "It would be a damaging illusion," Lenin added, in effect offering his person as leader of a German-led European revolution, "to hope for the restoration of a truly socialist International without a total organizational breach with the opportunists."

His December 1914, article "Dead Chauvinism and Living Socialism, (How Can The International Be Revived?)"[26] was a thrust in the same direction. Contrasting the Second International's "most authoritative writer" of the year 1909 with "the very same Kautsky" in October 1914, Lenin noted that Kautsky's pamphlet *Der Weg Zur Macht* had predicted an early seizure of state power by West Europe's proletariat and had based that prediction on the rapid growth of the German working class in the years 1895 to 1907 (as compared to the minuscule increase of the capitalists) and the sharpening of the class struggle resulting from a war. "A world war," Kautsky had written, "means also revolution." Declaring as vulgar the theory that socialism might be won through peaceful tactics, Kautsky called for an "unwavering, consistent and irreconcileable Social Democracy."

"Thus wrote Kautsky in ancient times, fully five years ago," Lenin wryly noted. "This is what German Social Democracy was, or rather, what it promised to be." But, "Look how the same Kautsky is writing in his article 'Social-Democracy in Wartime,' (*Die Neue Zeit,* No. 1, October 2, 1914) . . . 'The practical question now is: victory or defeat of one's own country'. . . . 'Social-Democrats of all countries have the same right or obligation to participate in the defense of their fatherland'." Lenin pointed out that he had deliberately gone to the original source for his citations, having found it hard to believe that Kautsky had actually written such things. The Kautsky of 1909, Lenin was saying, had proved that the time for a German revolution had come. What had held it up? Nothing less, Lenin implied, then the heresy of its prophet leader. By the very process of authoring so caustic a critique, Lenin was letting it be known that he—forever true to the faith—stood ready to replace the turncoat.

Lenin still needed to explain how the revolution in a single country might assume a socialist form—a contingency for which the Kautsky of 1909 had provided no theoretical basis—and he needed further to expound upon the manner in which that single country, having achieved a socialist order, might proceed to export it to other countries. Lenin's thinking, to judge by his conclusions, took the following approximate course. The war had destroyed communications among the peoples of the belligerent states.[27] Necessarily then, if socialism was to rise at all, it would first have to make its appearance in some single country. Most logically the place of origin would be Germany, where, as Kautsky had written, the proletarian dictatorship in Western Europe was portended by the rapid pace of proletarization in the years 1895-1907.

The aforementioned Bern Conference became, among other things, a platform from which Lenin's diminishing interest in a "Russian-oriented" republican United States of Europe was broadcast. After first firmly urging the slogan upon the conferees, Lenin performed an overnight *volte-face,* proposing instead to the Conference–in reality dictating to it–that discussion on the slogan be deferred. Six months later, acting on his own initiative, Lenin, in a *Sotsial-Demokrat* article of August 1915, smoothly removed from his repertoire of slogans the "United States of Europe" which had become an impediment to his grand design. Its replacement, in the same article, was a completely new "theory": socialism in a single country. Lenin explained that a United States of Europe was impossible under capitalism, because capitalism and hence imperialism developed unequally. It was therefore inconceivable that the capitalist nations of Europe would be willing to share equally their imperialist booty. But the very inequality of economic and political development which made impossible a republican United States of Europe, also provided the basis for "the possible victory of socialism at first in several or even in one capitalist country alone."[29] By jettisoning his formerly precious axiom that Europe's revolution had to begin in Russia, Lenin also rid himself of the burden of always having to prove the unrealistic proposition that his peasant homeland possessed a Marxian mission of global importance.

Thus he no longer needed to insist that Russia was, somehow or other, in a category with countries far more advanced, and to claim, as he had–in *What Is To Be Done?*–that it was precisely Russia's backwardness which had made her the most progressive of countries.

Lenin's celebrated "theory" on the inequality of capitalist development was at best a common sense observation. But to Lenin's mind, so rigid where his self-made Marxist dogma was concerned, the dawning of the obvious seemed like a major breakthrough derived through the science of Marxism. There was, of course, nothing scientific about the perceptual process whereby Lenin exchanged one "outmoded" doctrine for another more suited to the "current situation." The same driving force which had produced the earlier "theory" (or tactic) was always available to provide the creative energy for the "theory" that was to replace it. In the progression of ideas leading to the inequality "theory," Lenin's catalyst was the reading or rereading, in 1915, of Kautsky's 1909 observations on a coming German revolution, coupled with the contemporary triumphs of the German army. That Lenin had decided to stake his hopes on a victorious Germany is clear from his further thoughts on "the victory of socialism in one country." That country's proletariat, he predicted, "having expropriated the capitalists and organized socialist production [the dictatorship of the proletariat] would stand up against the capitalist rest of the world, attracting to its cause the oppressed classes of other countries. It would stir up among them revolt against their capitalists, and if necessary, even advance with military might against the exploiting classes and their states." Only Germany, among the warring powers of late 1915, could have been thought sufficiently powerful to perform such a task. In addition to her triumphs in the West, the Germans, particularly on the Ukrainian front (Galicia) had enormously damaged the Russian forces. The awesome German offensive, toppling Lvov and Przemysl,[30] had made of Kiev a front-line city, "full of wounded."[31]

Lenin was quick to utilize these events for propaganda intended to attract Ukrainian nationalism. Shortly after the catastrophic Russian defeats he wrote an article placing the Kadets and all the Russian socialist factions (except, of course the Bolsheviks) in the camp that was seeking to "grab Galicia, to take part of Poland from Austria and Germany, and to take Constantinople, the Straits and Armenia from Turkey."[32] (By the Fall of 1915 the Germans held all of Poland, Lithuania and Courland.)

On the initiative of Lenin, the International Women's Conference convened in Bern, March 26-28, dovetailing with the Bolshevik Conference which had just concluded. Chairwoman Klara Zetkin, was initially sympathetic to Lenin on the position the Women's Conference should take. Through her Inessa Armand, well in advance of the event, had labored to convert the conference into a secretly Lenin-controlled conclave of exclusively leftist delegates.[33] The largest and best organized contingent at the conference was made up of mainly Liebknecht-Luxemburg-oriented German women.[34] Lenin could not participate in person, but working through Krupskaia, Armand and Zinoviev's wife, Lenin tried stubbornly, but in vain, to induce the Conference to express itself in favor of the formation of a new international. However, he was frustrated by pacifist sentiment, that of Zetkin included.[35]

Lenin pursued the same goal a few weeks later, when a conference of Socialist youth,[36] also having strong German representation, met in Bern. Its organizer was Willi Münzenberg, a young migrant from Germany to Switzerland, later to become Lenin's disciple. Lenin again failed to have his program adopted, but a study of his approach to the successive conferences clearly foreshadows the line he would later take in jousting with the German left centrists at the September Zimmerwald Conference. The Bern conferences, Balabanova would later write, had first made her aware of Lenin's tendency to consider "every individual and every social event from the viewpoint of the revolutionary strategist. His whole life was a matter of strategy and every word he uttered in public had a polemic interest."[37] Balabanova sensed correctly that some sort of "master plan of revolutionary strategy" occupied Lenin's mind.[38] But she did not suspect the extent to which it focused on Germany, a country with whose socialist movement or working class he had no direct contact. Hence his feverish efforts to use such marginal opportunities as the Women's and Youth Conferences to make himself and his views known in Germany. At the time, he could not have anticipated Zimmerwald.

Lenin, ironically, was offered a role of consequence in German affairs well before that crucial September meeting, but it was one he found it necessary to disdain. Late in May 1915, Alexander Helphand tried to persuade Lenin to join him as an agent of the German Foreign Office. Helphand's bait was German financial aid in promoting a revolution in Russia, thereby abetting victory for the country having the most advanced proletarian movement. "The armies of the Central Powers and the revolutionary movement" would, in Helphand's words "shatter" the Romanov empire "and conquer the stronghold of political reaction in Europe." Helphand suddenly surfaced in Zurich with his scheme combining aspects of the Helphand-Trotsky theory of permanent revolution and Lenin's erstwhile *leitmotif* (borrowed from Marx and Engels) that the tsar was the "gendarme of Europe." Helphand dwelt "on the social-revolutionary consequences of the war," asserting "that as long as the war lasted, *no revolution could occur in Germany*" (Emphasis mine) adding that, as matters stood, *"a revolution was possible in Russia only"* if brought about by the successes of German arms. But Lenin, according to Helphand's scornful words, dreamt "of the publication of a socialist journal, with which he believed, he could immediately drive the European proletariat from the trenches into a revolution."

Another version of this discordant exchange comes to us from Siefeldt, a Bolshevik, to whom Lenin, soon after the discussion, allegedly denounced Helphand as an agent of German socialist chauvinists, like Scheidemann, with whom he wished no further contact. Katkov doubts the accuracy of Siefeldt's account on the ground that an "open breach" between Lenin and Helphand would have precluded their subsequent relations, Katkov, in particular, stressing Helphand's allegedly vital role in enabling Lenin to return to Russia in 1917.[39] In fact, Lenin rejected all further attempts by Helphand to communicate with him, and Helphand, contrary to Katkov's belief, had nothing to do with Lenin's return to Russia.[40] However, there is little reason to doubt but that Helphand's 1915 proposals greatly disturbed Lenin. Helphand's scheme posed a serious threat to Lenin's aim of taking charge of the German revolution, which had prompted him to cease concentrating upon the question of revolution in Russia. In 1905, moreover, it had been the very same Helphand whose proposed structure for a provisional revolutionary government in Russia had competed with Lenin's own design.

Another cause for annoyance with Helphand was that Lenin's aim, the success of which depended upon a German victory *following upon* a revolution within Germany, might too easily become confused with Helphand's support for the victory of the Kaiser's Germany, and Lenin, not even having connections with the German Government, was already suspected of being a traitor. Moreover, Helphand's scheme for a victorious Germany offered nothing whatsoever to the non-Russian nations of Eastern Europe and made no mention of the right of nations to self-determination. All told, one is inclined to surmise that Lenin abruptly rejected Helphand's proposition basically because it threatened to interfere with Lenin's own carefully nurtured plans. It can be assumed that Lenin was hopeful that Italian and Swiss mid-May proposals for an international anti-war conference of socialist parties would help bring those plans to broad public attention.

Such a conference was perfect grist for Lenin's mill. The project, directed by the Swiss Socialist Grimm, whom Lenin suspected of wanting deliberately to exclude the Bolsheviks,[41] moved rapidly toward realization after a July 11 preliminary conference in Bern. Lenin's hopes for a conference exclusively of Lefts, which had been inspired by the initial proposal of the Italians, were dashed by the preliminary conference, which over Zinoviev's protest, voted to include Centrists. But half a loaf was better than none, and during July and August Lenin did his utmost to prepare the impending Zimmerwald meeting to be the launching site for a German-centered but Lenin-led new international.

Krupskaia recalls a "worried" Lenin sending "letters in all directions –to Zinoviev, Radek, Berzins, Kollantai and the Lausanne Comrades– to make sure that places were secured for genuine lefts at the forthcoming conference and to insure the greatest possible unity among them."[42] Should any of those contacted be unable to attend, Lenin wanted their proxies assigned to him.[43] Meticulous in every detail, Lenin, in conjunction with Wynkoop, Radek, Armand and others, had managed to draw up a manifesto, draft resolution and a draft declaration "which were forwarded to comrades of the extreme left for consideration."[44]

Lenin, in a letter to Radek, strongly suggested that his group's preparations (including materials being readied) for Zimmerwald were Marx's 1847 activities brought up to date. But having added the *What Is To Be Done?* motifs to Marxism, Lenin's letter also asked, rhetorically, whether the German leaders were being properly Marxist in waiting for the masses to make the first move, and whether it was not the task of a handful of revolutionaries to stir up the German revolution? "What was the 1847 'Communist Manifesto' and [Marx's] group? Was it a stirring of the masses? Or was it a small band of revolutionaries? Was it the *one* or was it the other?"[45]

A highly significant passage in the draft resolution interpreted the slogan of defending the fatherland as "the defense of the 'right' of 'one's own' national bourgeoisie to oppress foreign nations; it is national-liberal working class politics, it is an alliance of a tiny part of the privileged workers with 'their' national bourgeoisie against the masses of the proletarians and the exploited. Socialists, conducting such a policy are in fact chauvinists, social chauvinists. The policy of voting war credits, of entering ministries, of *Burgfriede,* etc., is a betrayal of socialism."[46]

Lenin's reference to social chauvinism in this resolution was directed not only at types like Scheidemann but also at German socialists not nearly so far to the right.

Two days before the general conference Lenin's clique met in Bern to receive final instructions for the strategy, the essential purpose of which was to inform the German proletariat about Lenin and his ideas about Marxist internationalism. Lenin's behavior at the Conference, most notably his "duel" (Zinoviev's expression) with the German delegation's leader, Lebedour, was a reflection of this purpose. Another device was the pamphlet "Socialism and War (The Attitude of the R.S.D.W.P. Toward the War)" distributed among the delegates in the Russian and German languages. This attacked the fatherland-defending, war credit voting, "Kautsky-type" betrayers of socialism. Kautsky, the Second International's "outstanding authority" (a status Lenin hoped to occupy in a Third International) was singled out as exemplifying perfectly the way in which "lip service to Marxism became converted in practice to 'Struvism,' or to 'Brentanoism.' We see the identical phenomenon in the case of Plekhanov."[47] The two Russians, among the three mentioned, had each in turn been exposed by Lenin as a "petty-bourgeois reformist." The pamphlet stressed the failure of Kautsky in Germany and of his Menshevik counterparts in Russia to utter any protest against "social chauvinism," whereas the Russian Duma Bolsheviks had "expressed the political line of our party," (obeying Lenin) and, suffering arrest and lifelong Siberian exile, "went with their protest against the war to the very guts of the working class, carrying their preaching against imperialism to the broad masses of Russia's proletarians." The pamphlet proudly cited official Russian publications, alluding to "certain members of Social-Democratic societies" whose "antiwar agitation, underground appeals, and vocal propaganda was intended to undermine the military might of Russia." The pamphlet went on to boast that "*only* our party, in the person of its central committee [a tribute to Leninist discipline] had given a negative reply to Vandervelde's well-known appeal for a 'temporary' halt in the struggle against tsarism."[48]

Although, in his pamphlet, he indicted the German Social Democratic Party, "which had been the most powerful and leading force in the Second International," for having dealt proletarian internationalism a fierce blow, Lenin explained that it was the top leadership of the party and not the entire membership that he had in mind. Indeed, he lauded the German, among the major European socialist parties, because within it, comrades who had "remained true to the banner of socialism" (referring to Liebknecht and his group) were the first to "raise a loud voice of protest." It was with joy that Lenin had "read the journals *Lichtstrahlen* and *Die Internationale,*" and "with even greater joy to learn that illegal revolutionary appeals were being spread all over Germany, including, for example, the slogan [Lenin's pride] 'the major foe is in our own country,'" proving to Lenin "that the spirit of socialism was still alive among the German workers, and that there were still people in Germany capable of defending revolutionary Marxism."[49]

Generous, if general, praise having been given, Lenin felt free to make specific criticisms concerning the clear lack of purpose and other basic weaknesses still present within the dissidents of the Social-Democratic party. There was uncertainty and regrouping among them, "some elements being more, others less resolute," as *Die Internationale* had admitted. Lenin's proffer of such criticism was implictly a suggestion that he who was criticizing was also sufficiently resolute to become the leader. And, in a roundabout way (he could not come out directly saying "Here I am.") Lenin proceeded to implant this idea. Beginning modestly, Lenin denied that "we Russian internationalists pretend in the slightest degree to have the right to mix into the internal affairs of our comrades, the German Lefts." Thus, obliquely, Lenin introduced the notion that such intervention was in fact called for, (a few years earlier, the Germans had asked the International Socialist Bureau to referee the conflict within Russian Social-Democracy) and, while continuing to maintain that "we understand that only the Germans themselves were fully competent to decide upon their means of fighting the opportunists and to figure out the proper time and place to do it," Lenin, hedging, went on to say that the Bolsheviks (implying that they would be acting as proper internationalists) considered it only to be our right and our duty to express our frank opinion on the state of affairs," i.e., to intervene. Summing up, Lenin proposed that the "independent Marxist parties in the *various* countries," Germany's "oldest and strongest" working class movement being of "decisive significance," should enter into "the formation of a new and Marxist international." He added that the Russian Bolsheviks would "joyfully enter such a Third International, cleansed of opportunism and chauvinism."[50] That such a newly-founded body would require a new leader did not have to be spelled out.

Lenin hardly expected his polemical pamphlet (the *Communist Manifesto* brought up to date) to result in an immediate mass conversion in Germany, and he allowed for that. If the opposition socialist parties were still not ready by the time of the Zimmerwald Conference to follow his proposal, then this, he wrote "would indicate that a more or less lengthy evolution would be needed for the accomplishment of such a purging." In this case, Lenin's Bolsheviks, in the meantime, would "become the extreme opposition [the Zimmerwald Left] within the former International."[51] By asserting that even if in the minority, his group would be pursuing the correct course, Lenin was true to his past form in suggesting that no compromise was possible. "Who is not with us, is against us." It is precisely such rigidity which marked Lenin's confrontation with Lebedour and his associates at Zimmerwald.

Those who arranged the invitations to Zimmerwald (the actual conference was attended by thirty-eight delegates from eleven countries) had ignored all of the Centrist opposition leaders of German Social Democracy. Neither Kautsky nor Bernstein learned about Zimmerwald until the Conference was over.[52] That was why Left-Centrist Lebedour acted as unofficial head of the five or six man majority faction of the German delegation, which Zinoviev contemptuously labeled as elements vacillating between Liebknecht and Kautsky. "Lebedour and his adherents," Zinoviev later wrote "do not vote in the Reichstag against war credits—they abstain from voting; the reason they gave to the Conference was as follows: voting against war credits by a whole group of deputies would have signified a split in the parliamentary group, and such a split would have signified a split in the party; whereas only patience was necessary in order for the Lefts to obtain a majority in the party. K. Liebknecht through his voting against credits and through his open breach of discipline, so they say, had helped the Rights. He, Lebedour, could not accept the obligation to vote against the credits. This is a question which only the Germans can solve. Such was the position of the majority delegation."[53]

Since Lebedour's views were generally shared by all but the Zimmerwald Left,[54] Lenin's polemic with the majority emerged as a vicious attack. Lenin picked that fight even before the Conference had started, using, as his arena, the resolutions' committee in Bern which met on the eve of Zimmerwald. Lenin proposed that the Conference call upon the workers and soldiers of all countries to undertake a general strike against the war. Dismissing Lenin's suggestion as purposeless, Lebedour added that delegates accepting such a resolution would, in effect, be committing suicide, because they would be court-martialed and executed upon returning home, "their death having achieved nothing." Merrheim, another German, describes Lenin as displaying no interest at all in opposition arguments, beyond becoming more and more acerbic. Tension mounted to such a degree that but for the intervention of Rakovsky, representing Rumania, the Zimmerwald Conference would not have met at all, since the French, like the Germans, refused to accept Lenin's "brainless plan." The committee finally accepted a compromise resolution, at which Lenin immediately started sniping in the resolutions' committee, continuing at Zimmerwald. Amid the bitter exchange, and replying at one point to Lenin's sarcasm, Lebedour shouted out that he was not asking Lenin to return to Russia to offer his resolution and be killed, but that Lenin, safely harbored in Switzerland, was asking Lebedour to give up his life.[55]

Lenin was following the script called for in his pamphlet, whose purpose, above all, had been to depict the German Left as "vacillating" and Lenin as the true revolutionary leader. Still, it was expedient for Lenin, in responding to this personal attack, to veil, for the time being his individual importance, saying "it was unavoidable that differences should have risen between Lebedour and our group." Thus it was "the group," not Lenin alone, that had come into conflict with the majority. Yet Lenin had plotted in advance for Zimmerwald, the "group" having been part of his plan, and the Zimmerwald Left Bloc, who were simply Lenin's spearbearers, could never have come into existence without his scheming. And, as though further to shift attention away from the puppet master, probably to suggest he was not engaged in fighting a personal battle, Lenin made it a point to protest "against the manner in which Lebedour had [earlier] attacked Radek." So he became the defender of Radek's honor and that of others in his group as well, terming it "outrageous to maintain that [the Left Manifesto] had been signed only by people who happened to be safe from harm," since Winter and Borchardt, two of the signers, were not in that category.

But then moving from trivial matters to the role of revolutionary statesman, Lenin labeled his opponents "shabby" for saying "one had no right to call upon the masses for revolutionary action, if one was not directly involved in it." Lenin further argued against the proposition that one should not mention the means of struggle (general strike, etc.) something which had been done in all revolutionary periods. Only by presenting the means of struggle to the people could they be explained and discussed. "In Russia we have always acted on that principle," and that, said Lenin, thereby advertising the methods of propaganda with which he had become identified in Russia, was the very point he had debated with Plekhanov. Marx and Engels, too, in 1847, while in London, appealed "for violence in Germany," when, as Lenin put it, the German movement stood at the crossroads. The implication, of course, was that Germany once again was at the crossroads, and that Lenin, as his letter to Radek tell us, was to the Germany of 1915 what Marx and Engels had been to the Germany of 1847.

"If there is really a revolution in the making in which the revolutionary masses will go over to revolutionary struggles, then," declared Lenin, "we must be ready to provide them with guidance. Of course, this is without purpose if we accept the revisionist conceptions of David, etc., because they don't believe we face a revolutionary epoch. We who do believe this, must act otherwise. Once cannot wish to make a revolution without explaining the revolutionary tactic. This was precisely one of the worst qualities of the Second International that it always avoided calling for revolution, which is why the Dutch Marxists quite rightly called the German Center 'passive revolutionaries'."

Then passing to the question of persecution, Lenin pointed out that if the revolutionaries in Germany really wanted action, they should stop resorting to legal methods only, but should combine legal with illegal activities. (This was, of course, another of the "made in Russia" tactics identified with Lenin.) The usual German methods no longer sufficed in the existing situation. "The Germans themselves say: We are approaching an era of great class struggles. Then they should also want to use the necessary means to win. It is not necessary to sign a manifesto; it can appear anonymously. . . . The matter stands as follows: either a real revolutionary struggle or simply idle chatter, which helps only cowards, as Liebknecht has pointed out. . . . To be for peace, has in itself no meaning. Even David writes: We are not for the war, but only against defeat. Everybody wants peace. Accordingly we must create new original means of struggle in this situation, which will resemble neither the old German nor the Russian methods."[56]

Lenin, without trying to seem boastful, was making the point that he, Lenin, had worked out the currently essential means of struggle. They therefore required his leadership. Lenin regarded Zimmerwald as a great success because it had enabled him to highlight the split between the "revolutionary Marxists" and the "vacillating, quasi-Kautskyites, making up the right flank of the Conference."[57] At Zimmerwald French Centrist Bourderon had remarked: "Lenin, you want to give us *the formula for the Third International.* We did not come here for this purpose."[58] But that, precisely, had been Lenin's reason for coming.[59]

CHAPTER II

SWITZERLAND
POSSIBLE SPARK OF THE GERMAN REVOLUTION

Although he let pass few opportunities to revile the German Marxist leaders, Lenin was not unhappy over the fact that by abandoning their responsibilities, they had vacated the "room at the top." The process of Lenin's thinking in the Zimmerwald period becomes apparent in a manuscript of September, 1915. His comment on the dissolution of the Duma captures him in the act of emerging from a Russian cocoon as a German butterfly.

The Russian crisis, he wrote, reflected the government's retaliation against the forming of an opposition bloc "of liberals, Octobrists and nationalists." The imperialist war was the dynamism of both the Russian bourgeois-democratic revolution and the proletarian socialist revolution in the West, linking the two so directly "that no separate resolution of revolutionary tasks was possible in one or another country." Thus Lenin prefaced his turning away from a now obsolete theory that the European revolution had to begin in Russia, thereby implying that its vanguard would be the "proletarian socialist revolution" of Germany. "The Russian bourgeois-democratic revolution [this very designation is intended to indicate a lower level of revolutionary development as compared with that of proletarian Germany] was no longer a mere prologue to the revolution in the West, [Lenin's erstwhile teaching] but had become an indivisible and integral part thereof." If "in 1905 it had been the task of the proletariat to fight to the end for the bourgeois revolution in Russia, so as to set off the proletarian revolution in the West, in 1915 [Note the careful way in which Lenin words his transition to a new position] the second part of this task [i.e., the Western revolution] has become of such great importance that it was not equal in urgency to what had formerly been its number one task." Lenin did not mention that his own geographic base of political activity had, in the meantime, shifted to Western Europe. It was "the lessons of the war," i.e., historical forces, (not Lenin) which had dictated the change of course, compelling even Lenin's opponents, including various Russian bourgeois elements to accept Lenin's original view that the defeat of the tsar was the least of all evils. They had begun to speak of "a rising in the rear" of the German army, which was the same as saying "civil war in *all* countries." Lenin's analysis of events in Russia, therefore, fortuitously coincided with his wish to head an imminent German revolution.[1]

The ideas contained in the above outlined manuscript appeared somewhat altered in *Sotsial-Demokrat* of October 13. For public viewing Lenin was not ready to demonstrate so complete a break with his former position. The article, therefore, still defines the Russian proletarian task as that "of promoting to the end the bourgeois democratic revolution, *thereby* to ignite the socialist revolution in Europe." But Lenin's stress on "thereby" is important in that it calls attention to the secondary importance of Russian revolution. Another subtle change in emphasis, matching the thoughts in his unpublished manuscript, diminishes the importance of the Russian proletariat as the fuse for the European revolution; to wit, "This second task [ignition of the revolution in Europe] had now come extremely close [in importance] to the first task [revolution in Russia] but still remained in second position [within the framework of Russian society] because we are talking about the *various classes* who are collaborating with the Russian proletariat; so that in task number one, we must keep in mind the petty-bourgeois Russian peasantry [and their narrow outlook] but task number two [involves] the proletariat of other countries." Reluctant to make himself too clear, Lenin was moving crabwise in suggesting that Germany's proletariat would accomplish the task for Russia's proletarians before the Russian peasants had gotten around to achieving the necessary first stage of the Russian revolution, viz., the peasant rising against the landlords.[2]

After Zimmerwald, Lenin and Zinoviev sniffed about hungrily for any scrap of information that might finally signal the great German eruption. In an unpublished item of late 1915, Lenin mentions a *Berner Tagewacht* story about several hundred (*einige hundert*) militant working women in Berlin who had protested the lack of revolutionary will in the

Social-Democratic party's leadership.[3] "On November 26," the "counter-revolutionary" Kautsky had referred "to street demonstrations as *'adventurism'*, exactly the way that Struve, before 1905, had said there was not a revolutionary people in Russia. But, on November 30, 1915, 10,000 women workers demonstrated in Berlin."[4] At about the same time, a Zinoviev letter sent to various Bolsheviks mentioned a German worker who had "painted a picture of important activities (a half million illegal leaflets, a number of demonstrations) carried through by the Berlin opposition."[5]

In January, 1916, a Lenin article, referred to *hunger and political demonstrations in Germany* of 1915, asking "What else can this be but the beginning of revolutionary mass struggles?"

"This question," wrote the French Socialist Grumbach acidly in April 1916, "reveals the whole Lenin, together with the spectacles through which he looks at everything. The hunger demonstrations in Germany are supposed to be the beginning of . . . mass struggles! He actually dared to write this! . . . Does Lenin expect to aid the cause of international socialism . . . by spreading these illusions?"[6] Lenin's language was indeed inflated, perhaps to compensate for the war-caused limitations upon his international political activity and partly, no doubt, in the hopes of orchestrating "from afar" the music of a German revolution and securing himself a coveted place on the conductor's platform.

For distributing the Kienthal Manifesto "in the trenches," writes Krupskaia, "three [German] officers and thirty-two soldiers were shot . . . in May." Then, parroting Lenin, she added: "The German Government feared nothing so much as the revolutionization of the masses."[7] In a June 1916 article, Zinoviev observed that the attitude of the masses had changed despite "the deadening influence of Kautskyism, still pressing strongly on some members of the opposition." Almost every large city was having demonstrations "against the high cost of living. The masses are becoming 'radicalized.' Should war continue until the autumn, great events are inevitable."[8]

Given Lenin's exaggerated rejoicing over every trifling news of unrest in Germany, it was understandable that the anonymous appearance of Rosa Luxemburg's *Junius pamphlet* in April 1916 (actually written a year earlier in prison) should have evoked his enthusiasm. Its scathing indictment of the German Government, the banks and the Reichstag

Social Democrats, as all bearing responsibility for the war, prompted Lenin, in July, to hail "finally" the appearance in Germany of an illegal and uncensored "Social-democratic pamphlet dealing with the questions of the war! . . . Junius's pamphlet has undoubtedly played and will continue to play an important role in the struggle against the ex-Social-Democratic deserters" to the bourgeoisie and the junkers, and we extend our hearty greetings to the author." (For reasons explained below, the bulk of Lenin's article on Luxemburg's tract was carpingly critical.)

Other than such propaganda balloons, Lenin made what use he could of young Swiss radicals, Nobs, Platten and Münzenberg, whom he had met in Bern, at Zimmerwald and Kienthal, in efforts to push the Swiss socialist movement further toward the left. The Kienthal Conference had urged young socialists to pressure their parliamentary deputies to vote "against all war credits,"[9] a tactic which caused a split within Swiss socialism on the issue of national defense. In the ensuing polemic, one side favored total disarmament, since Swiss military strength, in the event of an attack, was sure to prove futile. Swiss pacifism conveyed the same anti-militaristic spirit as Lenin's "defeat of the fatherland" idea, but it was damaging to his tactical design of the moment. He therefore exhorted the Swiss Lefts to reject a policy of disarmament. In a September 1916 article, Lenin ridiculed it as "ultra-nationalistic" and a "specifically nationalistic programme of small states [Swiss, Dutch and Scandinavian] but having nothing at all in common with the international programme of international revolutionary social democracy." Lenin argued that socialists are not opposed to all wars but favor revolutionary and civil wars, adding that "the victory of socialism in one country far from expecting an immediate end to wars in general, most definitely anticipates their continuation." He noted that it would be a "theoretical mistake to forget that every war is only a continuation of politics by other means."[10]

"Socialism in one country," had by this time become Lenin's code phrase for a revolution in Germany, which he thought long overdue. Chafing impatiently, Lenin struck upon the fantastic notion that possibilities existed for a revolution in Switzerland, which in turn might spark one in Germany. The idea was clearly one of wish fulfillment since if a country going through the tortures of the damned, like Germany, was maintaining civil order, why should a prosperous country at peace make a revolution? Nevertheless, Lenin set about to make his hope a reality.

His above-mentioned article of September 1916, had called attention to the inherently internationalistic nature of Switzerland, thanking God [sic] that the Swiss did not have a language of their own, but used "three world languages" which were spoken "in the adjoining warring countries."[11] Still agitating against the Disarmament slogan, Lenin, in an October piece, repeated his three language refrain. Again he gave thanks to God, this time because "the real Swiss Social Democrats [Lenin's friends of the Swiss Left]" were "attempting to utilize Switzerland's relatively free atmosphere, her 'international' position . . . to broaden, to consolidate and to strengthen the *revolutionary* alliance of the revolutionary elements of the proletariat of all of Europe," and he declared it the political objective of the Swiss Lefts to rouse "the revolutionary elements of the French, German and Italian proletariat," to join forces in "overthrowing the bourgeoisie." The above phraseology is Lenin's, and it was he, not necessarily the Swiss Lefts, who were thinking along these lines.[12]

By December, however, when, as Krupskaia tells us, Lenin, was positively certain that the revolution was impending, he dispensed with most of the generalizing that included France and Italy, focusing on the motif that Switzerland was the fuse that would set off the German powderkeg. Therefore, he wrote:

> it is absolutely true when we say, that the Swiss people will *either* suffer from hunger worsening each week and will with every passing day be faced with the danger of being drawn into the imperialist war [and] of being killed in the capitalists' interests, *or* they will follow the advice of the best part of their proletariat [Lenin's Swiss friends], and dedicate all their energies to the accomplishment of a socialist revolution.
>
> Socialist revolution [in Switzerland]? Is that a Utopia! . . . No, this is not a Utopia . . . . The Swiss people, thank God, [Again!] have no 'separate' or 'independent' language, but speak the three world languages spoken by their warring neighbors and the Swiss people know well what is happening in those states. In

> Germany things have reached a stage at which the economic life of *66 million people* is directed *from one centre. . . .* and tremendous sacrifices are imposed on the predominant majority of the people so that the 'upper 30,000' can pocket thousands of millions in war profits, and that millions die for the benefit of the 'finest and noblest' representatives of the nation. Having such facts and such experiences to observe, is it 'Utopian' to assume that a small people, having neither monarchy nor Junkers, having a very high level of capitalism [like Germany's] and being perhaps better organized in various unions than in any other country, that such a people, *to save itself from hunger and the danger of war,* will subject itself to *the very same experience* that has already been practically tested in Germany?

Or, as Lenin was asking, would the Swiss sit idly by and be taken in by "defense of fatherland" propaganda? The result of this, in Germany, had been "millions killed and maimed to enrich a few, to gain Baghdad, to conquer the Balkans;" all the while, in Switzerland, the revolution—an easy task, involving the "expropriating" of a maximum of "30,000 bourgeoisie" would ward off hunger and war danger, and would, in addition, "call forth a class movement of solidarity in neighboring countries."[13] i.e., spread to Germany.

Grasping at every straw that might possibly be used to ignite a Swiss-German-European chain of explosion, Lenin, at the beginning of November 1916, abruptly patched up a year of bitter wrangling with Radek. At the moment Radek's influence among the Bremen Left-Radicals was on the rise thanks to his weekly articles in *Arbeiter-Politik.*[14] In mid-January 1917, Lenin began to use Radek, inviting him to become an ally against Swiss socialist leader Robert Grimm,[15] the object being to persuade Grimm's party to reject its "defense of fatherland" position. At a special conference on Swiss affairs shortly thereafter, Radek and Lenin jointly challenged Grimm's right to call himself a socialist.[16] Their purpose was to focus Swiss proletarian hatred upon Grimm as a target.

Lenin's rationale for splitting the Swiss party emerges from his draft of a manuscript (not published in his lifetime) in which he pointed out that the Swiss bourgeoisie, by exporting over 3,000 billion francs a year, was guilty of "imperialistic exploitation of backward nations." In addition

"Swiss banking capital was tied together most closely with the banking capital of the great powers." The Swiss bourgeoisie was therefore involved in the imperialist war and was engaged in the "*sale* of its own people to one or another coalition of imperialist powers." The Swiss socialists, therefore, instead of hewing to neutrality, to civil peace, to "defense of fatherland" slogans, had, according to Lenin, every reason "to open the eyes of the people to the reality of Swiss bourgeois politics and the danger of being *sold out* by 'their own' bourgeoisie."[17]

Naturally enough the Swiss did not rise to swallow this absurd bait. Lenin's *entre nous* letters to Armand at this time reflect Lenin's frustration at the fact that neither his youthful Swiss adherents nor various Russians seemed willing to take seriously his bizarre idea that Swiss workers were ready to man barricades for no other reason than the purely financial involvement of their bourgeoisie in the imperialist war. It seems that since no one else was listening, Lenin conducted his hysterical polemic with Inessa Armand, one person whose sympathy he could always count on.[18]

It is worth recalling the striking resemblance between Lenin's writings of 1902 and his propaganda of early 1917. The only difference between the two lay in Lenin's changed perspective regarding which country was to serve as the base from which he could set in motion a secondary revolution whose sparks would light the European powderkeg. If in 1902 he had perforce to think of the fuse being kindled in Russia, in 1917 that same thought pattern was transplanted to Lenin's current base of operations in Switzerland, leading to the fantasy that a Swiss revolution might sprout from his pathetic propaganda linking Swiss and great power banking interests.[19] The same pattern, again transplanted, would soon thereafter appear in Lenin's first "Letter from Afar." That piece of agitprop charged the Russian Provisional Government of "banker-imperialists" with being tied "hand and foot to Anglo-French imperialist capital."

CHAPTER III

LENIN'S THEORY FOR REVOLUTION IN GERMANY

A. Imperialism, the Newest Stage of Capitalism

Virtually nothing in Lenin's *Imperialism* (completed in the summer of 1916) is original. The motifs it contains had been expressed by numerous German socialists, including Marx and Engels, and by such English critics of imperialism as Liberal Party M.P.s, Walton and Wallace, and most notably by Hobson in his impressive 1902 opus.[1] Hilferding's *Finanzkapital* (1912) provided Lenin's pamphlet with its subtitle *The Newest Stage of Capitalism.* Lenin had written a preface to Bukharin's 1915 book *Imperialism and World Economy,* which had demonstrated that modern capitalism was dominated by banks, whose purpose, above all, was to expedite the exporting of their funds. Bukharin had called this trend an emerging global force, inextricably binding each nation's military production to its industrial economy, a new form of mercantilism, bound to breed war among capital-exporting rivals. Bukharin used mainly German sources to prove that the United States and Germany were the countries whose policies were most influenced by monopoly capital. (Hobson had stressed the financial greed of English firms.) In his book, Bukharin had also launched an extensive attack upon Kautsky's theory of "ultra-imperialim,"[2] labeling it a reformist deviation from Marxism. Opposing Kautsky's views, he argued that "a series of wars was unavoidable."[3]

Except for some minor differences of emphasis, Lenin's book merely expanded upon that of Bukharin. Indeed, since Lenin's book is so plainly a rehash of previous writings, its monumental historical importance derives not so much from its ideas as from Lenin's attempt to use them as a weapon for starting an international revolution in Germany.

Lenin's concept of war against (imperialist) war, or civil war, had, as shown, led through the "theory" of unequal development of capitalism, to socialism in one country: Germany. In turn this presaged a permanent revolution fanning out from that center; Lenin's anti-disarmament and anti-pacifist postulations being branches from the same tree of ideas. Lenin wanted no laying down of arms by German worker-soldiers, but a victory of the German revolutionary workers' army first over its own generals and government, and then over other governments which, by Marxist definition, also oppressed their workers. This would explain Lenin's stubborn insistence that nations be given the democratic right to self-determination, whether this expressed itself in fraternization among troops at the front, or as revolutionary protests against annexations old or new (or imperialism, past or present). The nations in question (i.e., the workers of those nations) were to be "liberated," not conquered.

A link between Lenin's anti-imperialism and the prospective conquest of Europe by a revolutionary Germany, may be found in the fact that Germany possessed little colonial territory as compared with most of Europe's states. Lenin's *Imperialism,* even more than Bukharin's polemic, drew upon German sources of information, and like Bukharin's work seems largely intended to expose Kautsky's "ultra-imperialism" as a sellout to the bankers.[4] In essence, then, Kautsky was charged with justifying the conquest of Europe—and subsequently the world—by a densely populated and technically advanced "young and growing" Germany. One-third of Germany's population was under fifteen, and, therefore, according to Fritz Fischer, "there was in the German consciousness a dynamic of population pressure which additionally strengthened the cry for *Lebensraum,* for markets and for industrial growth."[5] As Hitler would later put it *"Heute Europa, morgen de ganze Welt."*[6]

"To give the reader the best possible basis for understanding imperialism," writes Lenin, "I intentionally tried to bring in the largest possible number of excerpts from the writings of *bourgeois* economists, who are compelled to admit the particularly indisputable facts about the latest form of the economics of capitalism."[7] The German "bourgeois" economists, to whom Lenin refers, were naturally interested in advocating a redivision of the world's resources in Germany's favor, although they expressed themselves far less bluntly than did Hitler some twenty years later.[8] Lenin, one might say, stood the German economists on their heads; using their apologetics for German aggrandizement as ideological weapons with which to propagate an expanded, but revolutionary empire. Thinking in dialectical terms he emerged with roughly the following formula: Germany's impulsion for a fresh division of the world's wealth had sparked the imperialist war, creating as its anti-thesis the revolutionary temper of Germany and Europe as a whole. The synthesis would be the conquest of Europe by a German-led European revolution.

Having completed the basis for this "theory" in *Imperialism,* Lenin discovered that his thunder had been stolen by the Junius Pamphlet (written in April 1915). "Junius," like Lenin, denounced imperialism as the mortal enemy of the working class, betrayed, in the name of Marx by German Social Democracy. It therefore, called for a new Third International. However, Lenin fortuitously found several "weaknesses" in Junius, among them that he (actually she–Lenin did not yet know that Luxemburg was Junius) foresaw no early revolution because the German proletariat apathetically accepted the war. Although Luxemburg, like Lenin, opposed the Fatherland's war (and this implied her acceptance of a German defeat) her logical extension of that motif attacked the notion of national self-determination. Lenin, as we know, had persistently defended the rights of each nation to self-determination, even though that position demolished the rationale for his rejection of defense of the fatherland. In order better to understand Lenin, it is useful at this point to repeat Lenin's casuistical argument against Luxemburg's cogent reasoning.

Lenin asserted that the Marxian dialectic viewed all boundary lines, "whether in nature or in society," as "conditional and subject to change," and that there was *"not a single"* phenomenon which, under certain conditions, might not be converted into its opposite. "A national war *can* be transformed into an imperialist war and *vice versa.* For example: the wars of the great French revolution began as national wars. . . . These were revolutionary wars–the defense of a great revolution against a coalition of counterrevolutionary monarchies. But when Napoleon created the French Empire by enslaving a whole series of large, well established and viable national states of Europe, then the national French wars became imperialist wars, which *in their turn* gave rise to national liberationist wars *against* the imperialism of Napoleon."[9]

The above statement proves nothing so much as the infinite elasticity of Lenin's Marxism. His ideas were subject to conversion into their exact opposite if it suited the political purposes of the "theoretician."[10]

B. Self Determination to the Point of Secession. Why?

To restate Lenin: An imperialist war, since it inspires wars of national liberation, becomes a revolutionary war. His long mid-1916 article, "A Summing Up of the Discussion on Self-Determination,"[11] explored in theory every wrinkle of the subject in order to demonstrate that every nation had the right of self-determination to the point of secession. In the period leading up to the 1905 revolution, and, for reasons described below, in 1912-1914, Lenin vigorously supported self-determination. In the course of the war, however, that idea became a key weapon in Lenin's campaign to become the leader of Europe's revolution. The reason for this was that only the right of national self determination *to the point of secession* could assure a "democratic" expansion of his "instrument," the German army in revolutionary conquest.

One advantage in propounding this message lay in the embarrassment it caused the German Social Democratic leadership. If they refuted Lenin's call they denied democracy to subject nations. If they agreed with Lenin they would have to oppose their government, but their *Burgfriede* forbade that.[12] On the other hand, the mere propagation of the slogan allowed Lenin, indirectly, to proclaim himself the leader of the coming revolution. At that time most of the European countries were captive nations and sought independence. And, after Zimmerwald, when Lenin became increasingly hopeful about his chances for captaining the German revolution, he became more than ever eager to promote the idea of self determination as a way of ingratiating himself with the subject nations about to be "liberated."

Just before the war, Lenin had antagonized many Marxists of the Russian empire, particularly among those of the national minority Social Democratic parties, by repeatedly stressing the literal validity of point 9 in the 1903 R.S.D.W.P. platform, which guaranteed "the right of all nations in the state to self determination." Lenin's opponents generally regarded his stance as an anti-Marxist incitement to nationalist passions, but Lenin saw it as a device for centering aournd himself those elements in the Russian empire which were torn between Marxism and nationalism. In his prewar anti-Luxemburg polemics, and on other occasions, as previously noted, Lenin used the idea of self determination as a means for obstructing the national minority Marxists, most of whom had joined the 1912 August Bloc, from taking the "nationalist road to liquidation,"[13] i.e., to become legal and therefore anti-Bolshevik groups.

Once the war was in progress, however, Lenin's demands for self determination became incomprehensible to Bukharin, Piatakov and other Bolsheviks. Lenin's anti-nationalism, distinctly articulated in urging his own country's defeat, contradicted any interpretation of self determination that could effect a subject nation's secession and, thereby, the creation of a new state. Only Lenin, of course, was privy to the egocentric motivation for this ideological contradiction. His arguments favoring national self determination, therefore, caused his party comrades endless irritation. Lenin defended his frequently reiterated cry for self determination in numerous ways. But he could never offer the only logical explanation for his position; namely his desire to assume leadership of the German Army when it became a revolutionary liberating force. Lenin's call for tsarism's defeat as the "lesser evil" was a logical part of a scheme wherein Lenin conceived of himself as the person who would be formulating the treaties deciding the exact status of all hitherto subject nations. The key to the puzzle, in short, was Lenin's Napoleonic conception of his role in the redrawing of the map of post-bellum Europe.

Richard Pipes, noting the "significant shift of emphasis" in Lenin's comments on self determination during the war, ascribes it to Lenin's growing awareness, as he delved deeper into the subject of imperialism, that the national question was a global phenomenon.[14] There can be no doubt that Lenin's perspectives broadened as he moved from his peripheral Russian position into the European inner circle and that viewing matters from a central vantage point enabled him to understand relationships previously beyond his perception. But I believe his reason for stressing the motif of self determination in precisely the way he did, was, as always, tied to his subjectively designed tactic which he called "theory." Granted that Lenin's horizons had expanded. Indeed, his increasing knowledge added factual and statistical weight to his arguments, and in his polemic with Piatakov he introduced non-European peoples into the self-determination equation. After all, why should he not have flung onto the scales the "more than 700 million"[15] of China, India, and others, certainly an impressive portion of humanity. Still his argument remained unconvincing because he could at no point admit that his line on self determination was based upon the dream of becoming the generalissimo of Europe's revolution.

Attacking Lenin's stream of apparent doubletalk, Piatakov, Evgeniia Bosh and Bukharin wrote their November 1915 "Theses on the Right of Self Determination." The slogan of self determination, they asserted quite logically, (as Luxemburg had done) was simply another way of saying "defend the fatherland," for "unless an appeal [was] also made for material defense of the corresponding [newly created] state boundaries," the slogan had no actual meaning, it was "an empty phrase." They argued against the inherent contradiction in Lenin's opposing "the chauvinism of the working masses of a Great Power," while at the same time recognizing the national right of self determination. This, they said, was as absurd as fighting chauvinism while acknowledging that the "oppressed 'fatherland' had a right to defend itself."[16]

C. The Polemic on the "State"

The dispute between Lenin and his opponents inevitably centered about the meaning of the word "state." Bukharin's article "The Imperialist Pirate State," appeared December 1 in *Jugend-Internationale,* but had been written in the first half of 1916, when its content had become known to Lenin.[17] The article, in effect, accused Lenin with obtuseness in confusing "state" with "nation." Like a professor lecturing to a student, Bukharin explained that "the word [country] contained a deception, for it concerned not really the country as such, its *inhabitants,* but the *state organization;* the *state* . . . ."[18] Bukharin seemed to be trying to convince Lenin that his misconception would disappear once he understood that expert Marxist theoreticians (like Bukharin) were not opposing the rights of the people who happened to be living in a particular territory. They were fighting the modern state organization which had so powerfully superimposed itself upon those people that, as the "present war" had shown, "the roots of statehood" had penetrated into the souls of the workers." Bukharin's article provided a brilliant examination of what he called "the present day monster, the modern Leviathan."

The individual enterprise, Bukharin wrote:

> . . . . the capitalist who "works" by himself and confronts only his workers, the capitalist to whom the state assures only general conditions of his "right of exploitation"—these are typical of former [economic conditions]. It is different now. The individual capitalist has become an associated capitalist. The rapid vanishing of the middle class, the victorious progress of large capital have called forth some new forms of economic life, which, naturally have originated as special forms of class life. The formation of unions, of owners of enterprises, of trusts and syndicates, and so forth, and their mutual connections through combined enterprises and the large banks have changed entirely the old forms. And if, for the pre-imperialistic epoch, individual capital ownership was characteristic, then, for present-day finance capitalist economy, a *collective* ownership by capitalists, united with one another by some organization, is characteristic. This same process however, affects not only [economic relationships]. It spreads over the entire realm of class life, and if the working class for its own sake establishes trade unions, political organizations, co-operatives, educational clubs, etc., the bourgeoisie does it on a larger scale. In this manner various bourgeois class organizations are formed . . . . But this does not conclude the process of organization. *All these organizations have a tendency to fuse with one another and to become transformed into a single organization of rulers.* This is the newest stage of development, and one which has become *especially* apparent during the *war* . . . . *So there comes into being a single, all-embracing organization . . . an omnipotent organization of bourgeois dominance with innumerable functions,* with gigantic power, with spiritual (various methods of obscurantisms: the church, the press, the school, etc.) as well as material methods (police, soldiery). . . . *The state, which at first was the only organization of the ruling class, transforms itself into a group of organizations, one beside the other, and this group by drawing in all other organizations again becomes a single organization.*"[19]

Bukharin had x-rayed the "newest stage" of capitalism and detected its "fascist" skeletal structure. Lenin's portrayal of the dictatorship of the proletariat was worked out in its final form soon after he had read Bukharin's article. *State and Revolution* provides a portrayal of the "bourgeois" totalitarian state, revealing a "democracy" armed with exactly the weapons of Bukharin's capitalist Leviathan. But the "peoples" police, "peoples" militia, and "peoples" bureaucracy (as if such institutions could ever be "people"-controlled) would overthrow the Leviathan, and, by building a new dictatorship upon the ruins prevent the old regime from re-emerging.

Bukharin's analysis was brilliant, and although Lenin subsequently tried to prove that the same ideas had been lurking, ignored and forgotten, in the Marx-Engels scripture (and although Lenin's writings of 1905-1907 reach out in the same direction) it seems clear that he plagiarized Bukharin's work completing his *Marxist Teaching on the State in the Revolution,* which "explained" the dictatorship of the proletariat.[20] In expounding his ideas for the purpose of instructing Lenin, Bukharin could not, of course, have divined the subjective reasons for Lenin's "inability" to comprehend the dialectic where it concerned the State. Citing Marx and Engels to demolish Lenin, Bukharin pointed out that to support any state was tantamount to aiding the exploiters against the oppressed. "The conception of the state," he wrote, "presupposes the conception of class rule." Expanding upon this elementary lesson in Marxism, Bukharin wrote superciliously:

> *K. Marx* has expressed this in the following words: 'Even the radical and revolutionary politicians are seeking the cause of evil not in the nature of the state but in a definite form of state which they wish to replace by a different form of state.' Entirely different are the aims of the socialists, who [Bukharin noted, citing Engels] agree that the state, and with it political authority, will vanish owing to the future revolution, [as public functions lose their political dimension to become merely administrative institutions] for the protection of social interests. . . . The state dies off. . . .[21] The society which organizes production anew on the basis of free and equal association of producers transfers the entire state mechanism . . . to museums of antiquities, along with the spinning wheel and the bronze axe.[22]

In a footnote to the above comments from his article, Bukharin, apparently proud of his ability to think problems through to their roots, took the "opportunity" to remark that it was "incorrect" to believe "that the difference between socialists and anarchists is that the former are in favor of a state and the others are against a state. The difference . . . lies in the fact that revolutionary SocialDemocracy wishes to establish a new centralized social production—i.e., which would be technically progressive—while the decentralized anarchist production would mean merely a step backward to old technique and form of enterprise."[23] In thus downgrading the importance of the revolutionary state en route to oblivion as the central issue in the Marxist versus anarchist conflict, Bukharin was not only pressing brazenly into realms hitherto untouched by Marxian theory, he was also stepping directly upon Lenin's toes. Bukharin could easily make light of the revolutionary state and of the proletarian dictatorship which it would govern, because unlike Lenin he had no aspirations for becoming its leader.

Piatakov's article of August 1916, charged that Lenin's arguments for self determination were traitorous to socialist ideals and led directly to social patriotism. "We absolutely refuse to understand how one can *simultaneously* be against defense of the fatherland and in favor of self determination—to be against as well as for the fatherland."[24] In his reply, completed in October, Lenin questioned Piatakov's failure to understand why Lenin expected "when we shall be in power" to "bring about the freedom of nations to *secede,* since the entire course of [historical] development is toward the fusing of nations?" As Lenin explained, the apparent contradiction was entirely on the level of semantics. "We advocate and, when in power, shall establish the dictatorship of the proletariat, though the whole course of events is moving toward the destruction of forcible rule by one part of society over another. Dictatorship is mastery of part of society over the whole and it therefore bases itself directly on the use of force."[25]

The puzzle is solved, once it is recognized that Lenin viewed the right of a nation to secede (the essence of bourgeois democratic freedom) and then to become a dictatorship based on coercion, as part of the first phase of proletarian control. Whoever denied the need for such a dictatorship, or recognized it "only in words," Lenin wrote, could not "be a member of the Social-Democratic party." Lenin was simply transposing the elitist schema expressed in *What Is To Be Done?* and in *Two Tactics*—i.e. Marxist theory guided by Jacobin practice—from its original Russian framework (in which the party had to cope with secret police and a backward proletariat in an agrarian society) to Europe as a whole and by extension (as he ultimately made clear) to the entire world. Lenin hoped that the same doctrine designed to achieve power for his party in prewar Russia would serve during the war period to make him the boss of a German revolution.

CHAPTER IV

FROM THEORY TO PRACTICE LENIN'S PREPARATION FOR LEADING THE REVOLUTION IN GERMANY

"By 1915-1916," Krupskaia's *Reminiscences* notes, "Vladimir Ilyich had gone deep into the question of democracy, which he examined in the light of socialist construction."[1] What does this mean?

In September 1916, a letter from Lenin, referring to Piatakov and Bukharin, instructed Shliapnikov to place on the order of the day the task of cleansing the party's theoretical line "of the accumulating nonsense and confusion, of the denial of democracy (hence the talk of disarmament, of denial of self determination, the theoretical denial 'in general' of the defense of fatherland, uncertainty concerning the question of the role and significance of the state in general, etc.)"[2] What does this mean?

In the latter part of 1916, as Krupskaia tells us, Lenin reread and took notes on *"all that Marx and Engels had written on the state,"* observing that it was the *"dictatorship of the proletariat, ensuring the proletariat's leading role in the reconstruction of the whole social fabric"* which interested Lenin *"most of all in the later half of 1916* . . . . Ilyich argued with Bukharin, who *underestimated the role of the state, the role of the dictatorship of the proletariat,* etc. He was angry with [Piatakov] for failing to understand *the leading role of the proletariat* . . . . This [rereading] *equipped* [Lenin] *with a deeper understanding of the nature of the coming revolution, and thoroughly prepared him for an understanding of the concrete aims of that revolution."*[3]

My emphases in the above lines are meant to highlight major keys to Lenin's thought process. These become comprehensible only when related to his hope of becoming the leader of Germany's revolution. In order to head that revolution, he thought it necessary to invent a theory for which he could claim authorization by Marx and Engels; hence his quest for a "deeper understanding of the nature of the coming revolution." The "concrete tasks of that revolution," he believed, centered about winning the German working class away from its faith in the existing German socialist leadership. This explains Lenin's stress upon "the leading role of the proletariat," by which, Lenin could only have meant a conspiracy of activists under his direction attempting to seize state power in the name of the revolutionary people. Since Lenin was thinking in the *Narodnaia Volia* pattern expressed in *What Is To Be Done?,* it was essential for him to *define precisely* the so-called "dictatorship of the proletariat" as a form of state, something which neither Marx, nor any other Marxist to that date had found reason to do. But Lenin needed such a definition as a theoretical foundation upon which to construct his prospective elitist revolutionary coup.

From relatively random statements on the subject of the state made over many years by Marx and (principally) Engels, Lenin derived "orthodox" notions of which he made use in the period 1916-1918, particularly in his "Letters from Afar," *State and Revolution,* and *Renegade Kautsky.* But any attempt to trace the ideas in these works back to their "Marxist" roots would be futile. The reason for this can be stated in one word—distortion. The notes Lenin made in "re-studying" Marxist comment on the state reveal quite clearly that Lenin quoted the scripture as though each item in it had full validity beyond its chronological context. In this way he was able to apply material dealing with the Paris Commune to demonstrate that the German proletariat, betrayed by Kautsky & Co., stood ready, given new leadership, to spearhead a European revolution.

In an 1871 letter to Kugelmann, Marx had referred to the disappointment his *18th Brumaire* had expressed over the Commune's failure in not taking over the "military-bureaucratic machine."[4] According to Marx this state apparatus had passed down intact from the monarch to the bourgeoisie. The latter had strengthened it for purposes of mass repression (counter-revolutionary struggle) and had further centralized its authority.[5] Having made this point, Lenin carried it chronologically out of context, and "brought it up to date" by repeating the exact motif as it appeared in Engel's preface to the third German edition of *18th Brumaire,* written in 1885.[6] By such sleight of hand, Lenin sought to create the impression that events of 1917 in Germany were linked, and, in a sense, therefore, prophesied, by what the Founding Fathers had written decades earlier with France in mind.

"'The state machine' is precisely the bureaucratic-military machine of the majority of capitalistic governments (now in 1917, one may say that this is *universally* the case). It was in France that the *universal* capitalistic process became formed with 'special' 'classical' clarity. We see on the one side the creation of this machine which got its start in the middle ages, passing through absolute monarchy to the constitutional monarchy, i.e., the parliamentary monarchy or republic. On the other side, (as is the case everywhere in 1917) it has been most nakedly exposed for what it is" thereby being "brought most closely to the struggle for its 'destruction'." It was precisely the issue of the destruction of the state machine, about which, Lenin thought, *"a conspiracy of silence"* had been "constructed by the opportunists and Kautskyites."[7] To further strengthen the connections between 1871 and 1917, via 1885, Lenin threw in comment from Engels' 1891 critique of the Erfurt program, referring to opportunism in the German Social Democratic party and to a dictatorship of the proletariat based upon a republican form of government,[8] adding an Engels letter of 1894, exhorting the French socialist party to revolt and suggesting that it make use of the popularly-based army, newly-structured since 1870. Engels' letter admirably served Lenin's purpose, concluding with the words, "The French give the signal, open fire, and the Germans decide the issue."[9]

So, using evidence from the grave, Lenin pieced together the notion that since the time of the Paris Commune, Marx and Engels had incessantly been urging the Germans to take the lead in a violent European revolution. If the Germans had not answered the call that was because of the lack of revolutionary spirit in the German Socialist Party. To prove this, Lenin cited from Engels' irritated comment (as in his critique of the Erfurt Program)[10] concerning the growing German tendency toward moderation, and he drew upon the polemics between militant Dutch Marxist Pannekoek and Kautsky, which, as late as 1910-1912, revealed Kautsky as refuting Pannekoek's talk of destroying the powers of the state through proletarian revolution. Kautsky insisted that the socialist goal remained that of winning a parliamentary majority and then raising parliament to a dominant position in Germany.[11] But since then the war had broken out and Lenin was obviously preparing to utilize the hallowed images of Marx and Engels to present wartime Germany with this question: "Why should a huge armed proletariat, provoked to the hilt by the war's butchery, and ready, by all past Marx-Engels' indices for a proletarian rising, continue in its docile ways?" His own answer was that the German opportunist leaders had convinced the workers that the German state—contrary to basic Marxian teaching—belonged to them as well as to the bourgeoisie.

Revision was an old story in Germany by 1916. What makes it worth mention here was that Lenin's eyes were opened not only to its existence but even more to its deeply rooted national pervasiveness. The "re-reading" of Marxist writings (much was really read for the first time) enabled Lenin to comprehend the true nature of German socialism. He came to understand that German Social-Democracy for at least a quarter century before the war was geared entirely to what Lenin would have termed "economism." This came to Lenin as something of a surprise, perhaps as a shock. On second thought, however, he was probably pleased since it added ammunition to his arsenal of propaganda. That Lenin had arrived at what for him was a new perception is easily appreciated. We recall that a mere two years before he had begun his voyage into the past of German Marxism, Lenin had upheld the Kautsky of 1909 as a true revolutionary, who had only later abandoned his principles. But, it had now become obvious that the man whom Lenin, in 1914, denounced as a "renegade" had been a reform-minded Marxist much earlier.

Kautsky, referring in his 1892 book on the Erfurt Program to the question of "confiscation of property" had commented sarcastically on the opponents of Marxism "who know better than we ourselves what we seek to achieve." He mocked them as able with greater certainty than we to describe the "state of the future," and ridiculed their discovery that Social Democracy could attain power "in no other way than in the expropriation of the craftsmen and the peasants, from whom all will be taken (without compensation)—not merely house and land, but also their non-essential properties and their bank accounts. Besides the allegedly forcible destruction of all family ties," Kautsky went on, "this tale of confiscation is one of the major trump cards played out against us. In reply to which it can be stated that the essence of a socialist society *in no way calls for such confiscation.* [My italics] About confiscation the Social Democratic program says nothing; not out of fear of seeming to frighten off, but simply because nothing certain can be said about it. With certainty one can only assert that the tendency of economic development makes it necessary that the large industries pass over into social property and be run for the benefit of society. But what the manner of such a transfer will be, whether the inevitable expropriation will be a confiscation or a redemption, whether it will happen peaceably or through violence, these are questions that no man can answer . . . . It goes without saying that the Social Democrats wish that the expropriation of the large enterprises, having become inevitable, should take place *as painlessly as possible, peaceably and amid universal agreement.* But the historical development will be determined *as little by our wishes* as by those of our opponents."[12]

As the *Communist Manifesto* had done, Kautsky, in 1892 stressed the deterministic nature of historical development and had thereby absolved Marxists from the need of participating directly in the making of a revolutionary upheaval. Lenin, in the course of his "re-study" of Marxism, also re-read, or perhaps read for the first time, back issues of *Die Neue Zeit* and easily recognized how wrong he had been, around 1900, to place Kautsky in the category of those untainted by revisionism; indeed had regarded him as a revolutionary militant like himself and as being at opposite poles from such men as Bernstein. Lenin's research of 1916-1917 thus was further proof that this one-time giant of Marxism had feet of clay. Among other works of Kautsky, Lenin also read *The Social Revolution,* written in 1900. In this book, made up of two essays written for an Amsterdam Socialist reading circle,[13] Kautsky had asked rhetorically:

"What will be the precise form under which the decisive battles between the ruling class and the proletariat will be fought out? When may we expect them to occur? What weapons will be at the service of the proletariat? To these questions it is hard to give definite answers. We can to a certain degree suggest the *direction* of the development but not its form nor its velocity." In effect, Kautsky, at great length, makes the point that absolutely nothing is definitely predictable about revolution and that even Marx and Engels who over "many decades" made magnificently accurate predictions on the course of economic development, erred "strikingly when" attempting to predict "the velocity and the form of the development of the month ahead." The only thing that could be said with "certainty . . . about the approaching revolution" was that it would be entirely "different from its predecessors." Kautsky disparaged revolutionaries who expected revolutions of the future to be modeled upon those of the past, claiming there was "nothing easier than to prove that such revolutions are no longer possible. The conclusion is then at hand that the idea of a social revolution is an entirely outgrown one."

Kautsky had given up on the idea of a social revolution because the revolutionary struggle, fought out by way of democratic forms created upon the foundation of democratic freedom–i.e., the Social Democratic movement within bourgeois democracy–"faced resources such as the world has not yet seen," by which Kautsky meant powerful organizations of employers "before which even monarchs bow." Democratic methods of struggle were, in short, useless against the capitalist oligarchy. Kautsky added the seemingly paradoxical (but astute) observation, that democracy strengthened the opponents of the proletariat even more than it did the proletariat, because "the exploiting class can more freely develop their organization . . . . They use their forces recklessly and more harshly than the government itself, which no longer stands above them, but rather beneath them."

According to Kautsky, then, the very nature of bourgeois democracy had made revolution practically obsolete, further obstacles rising out of the pluralism of industrial modern society and the inability of the proletariat to unite with farmers and with intellectuals–so that civil war was more likely to reflect a struggle of one class against another, rather than people against a government. He mentioned Russia as an exception. Describing the Social Revolution, Kautsky foresaw "much less of a sudden rising against the authorities than a long drawn out *civil war,* if one does not necessarily join to these last words the idea of actual slaughter and battles. We have no [reason] to think that barricade battles and similar warlike accompaniments will play a decisive role today." Militarism, Kautksy explained, could be "overthrown only by rendering the military faithless to the rulers not through its being conquered by popular uprisings."[14]

Kautsky saw equally little hope that a worthwhile revolution might grow out of financial crisis, a general strike, an alliance with liberals, or even out of a war. He expected war and conceded that it might lead to proletarian risings, but he dreaded the terrible destruction it would cause. "Any [war-spawned] revolution," he wrote, "is heavily laden with tasks that are not essential to it but which momentarily absorb all its means and energy. Consequently a revolution which rises from war is a sign of weakness of the revolutionary class, and often the cause of further weakness, just because of the sacrifice that it brings with it, as well as by the moral and intellectual degredation to which war gives rise. It also increases enormously the tasks of the revolutionary regime and simultaneously weakens its powers. Accordingly a revolution springing from a war is easier wrecked or sooner loses its motive force."[15]

Lenin's "Marxist" critique of *The Social Revolution* made note of its pessimism regarding the chance for a transfer of power to the working class, vented annoyance toward Kautsky's defeatist attitude on agitation in the army, (a view expressed again by Kautsky in *Die Neue Zeit* of 1904) and took particular issue with Kautsky's failure to mention the smashing of the bourgeois state machinery and its takeover by the dictatorship, a notion largely Lenin's, stitched together out of random comment by Marx and Engels. If Kautsky did not see it Lenin's way he could not realistically be blamed for it. But all that aside, the reformist (and, from Lenin's point of view, defeatist) tone of Kautsky's turn of the century tract was self-evident, further enhancing Lenin's convictions of 1916-1917 that German socialism was helpless, without his intervention, to take advantage of the then ripe revolutionary situation. Referring, in *State and Revolution,* to the *Social Revolution,* Lenin wrote:

> Kautsky has completely misunderstood the differences between bourgeois parliamentarism, combining democracy (*not for the people*) with bureaucracy (*against the people*), and proletarian democracy, which will at once proceed to root out bureaucracy, and which will have the ability to carry out the. . .complete destruction of bureaucracy, and fully establish democracy for the people. Here Kautsky again reveals the same old 'superstitious reverence' for the state, the same 'superstitious faith' in bureaucracy.[16]

By contrast, *State and Revolution* describes Kautsky's *The Road to Power* (1909) "as a great step forward, to the extent that in it nothing is said of a revolutionary program in general, as in the pamphlet of 1899 against Bernstein, nor does it speak about the tasks of a social revolution unrelated to the time of its occurrence, as in the pamphlet *The Social Revolution* of 1902. But it does tell us of the concrete conditions which force us to acknowledge that the 'era of revolution' is advancing. The author specifically refers to the sharpening of class antagonisms in general [which pleased Lenin] and to imperialism, as having a particularly great significance for this development."[17] While Lenin's book found Kautsky's brochure praiseworthy, if only in that it served as a yardstick for measuring the great "promise" of German Social Democracy before the war as compared to "how low it (and Kautsky) had fallen after the war's eruption,"[18] his notes (for the book) attacked *Road to Power* for avoiding "all discussion of concrete measures for replacing the parasitic state by that of the workers." In that way, Lenin berated Kautsky for failing in 1909, to interpret Marx as Lenin was doing in 1916-1917. And in *State and Revolution,* Lenin calls attention to Kautsky's warning of 1909 that German Social Democracy "could easily be assumed to be more moderate than it actually is," enabling Lenin to make the mocking assertion that "the German. . .Party was *incomparably* more moderate and opportunistic than it had seemed to be." [My emphasis] Summarizing his findings, Lenin wrote in *State and Revolution:* "German Social Democracy, in the person of Kautsky, seems to have declared: I retain my revolutionary opinions (1899). [This referred to Kautsky's pamphlet attacking Bernstein], I accept, in particular, the inevitability of the social revolution of the proletariat (1902). I acknowledge the coming of a new era of revolution (1909). But all the same, I oppose that which Marx said as early as 1852, once the question has risen concerning the tasks of a proletarian revolution in relation to the state (1912)."[19] On the whole Lenin condemned Kautsky for giving mere lip service to radicalism, and it was, of course, true that the *Burgfriede* and, indeed, the German Social Democratic *Weltanschauung* in general, was foreshadowed as far back as 1890.[20] To the Lenin of 1916-1917, the message conveyed by this discovery was simple: Germany's proletarian mentality was hopelessly wedded to the idea of living with capitalism. Such defeatism, Lenin felt, would need to be overcome before a revolution could be expected, and in his preface to *State and Revolution* he points out that without "a struggle against the opportunist superstitions concerning the 'state' the fight for the liberation of the toiling masses from the influence of the bourgeoisie in general and the imperialistic bourgeoisie in particular was impossible."[21] The motif of *State and Revolution* is thus clearly concerned with the German proletariat which Lenin intended to lead in the proper direction.

But how did Lenin intend to go about the task of re-conditioning a nation's working class, to present it with a new self-image? How did he expect to convince the workers that their only loyalty was to their class, that their identity as German nationals meant nothing, and that by placing their national feelings ahead of their class aspirations, they were obstructing the locomotive of history? "And ever more often," he says in *State and Revolution,* "do we see how German bourgeois scholars, yesterday's specialists in the destruction of Marxism, are speaking about the 'national-German' Marx, who, as it were, has so superbly educated the labor unions to organize for conducting this robbers' war."[22] Lenin also had to cope with the problem of undermining the German trait of viewing the state as something holy. That position "bolstered by bourgeois, and particularly by petty-bourgeois, ideologists, whom indisputable historical facts have forced to admit that the state exists only where there is class contradiction and the class struggle, 'correct' Marx in such a way as to make the state appear as an organ of class reconciliation." And then, as though making direct reply to such of Kautsky's writings as *The Social Revolution,* Lenin declared that such camouflage "obscured" the fact that "if the state is the product of irreconcileable class antagonisms and if it was strong, standing above society while 'ever more estranging itself from society,' then clearly the liberation of the oppressed class is impossible without violent revolution, which will destroy the apparatus of state power which the ruling class created and in which this 'estrangement' is embodied."[23]

That the state represented the ruling class was generally accepted as an integral part of Marxist doctrine. Kautsky had reasserted the principle in *The Social Revolution* and Bukharin had exposed the state as nothing less than the dictatorship of the bourgeoisie.[24] Lenin's special contribution to this theme–and in time it acquired monumental significance as revolutionary propaganda–was his interpretation of the bourgeois democratic oligarchy, stood on its head, as exactly that which Marx had intended to convey when he used the phrase "dictatorship of the proletariat." That interpretation, as previously noted, was of great tactical importance to Lenin's goals. That, in itself, could easily have persuaded Lenin, as he mulled over the idea, that –come to think of it–this was the very core of the Marxian revolutionary heritage. Indeed, Lenin had no choice but to allow his tactical goal to dominate the process of his "reasoning," if, as a revolutionary activist, he wished at the same time to view himself, and be viewed, as a true, and indeed, the truest Marxist. In contemplating the course of Lenin's thinking there seems no other way he could have gone. For in re-reading Marx, Engels, Kautsky, et al., Lenin, had he not had to blot out or repress the notion, should have perceived that the seeds of Marxian thought, when planted in bourgeois democratic soil, invariably blossomed into an evolutionary, trade unionist and anti-militant doctrine.

But it was not in Lenin's interest to expose, as a toothless hoax, the radical faith of Europe's proletarians. Although, by 1917, Lenin had become far more knowledgeable about the history of Marxism in practice than he had been two decades earlier, his mission as a European, as far as he was concerned, was an exact parallel to the mission he had set for himself as a Russian in writing *What Is To Be Done?* His function remained that of saving Marxism from its reform-minded vulgarizers and to keep burning within it the flame of individual activism, or vanguardism, as something sharply separated from the politically debilitating and fatalistic acceptance of economic determinism. Although vital to the movement's *raison d'étre,* the concept of socialism's inevitability was a dead weight which encouraged a passive (or reformist) approach to the millenium.

In Chapter II, Section 3 of *State and Revolution,* Lenin revised Marxism leftward, stating that the class struggle was not "the major point in the teaching of Marx." This kind of bold distortion, or Big Lie, goes far in explaining Lenin's success as a propagandist. Having, by his very audacity, shocked his reader into a judgment-suspending state, Lenin, without allowing him time to come to his senses, plunges spectacularly onward. He makes the startling charge that this untruth (that class struggle is the "major point" of Marxism) very often is turned into an opportunistic distortion of Marxism deliberately created for the benefit of the bourgeoisie. Lenin's "evidence" for that astounding contention was that "the teaching about the class struggle was not by Marx *but* by the bourgeoisie *before* Marx, who had created the theory to suit their own purposes."[25] Thus Lenin further confused the issue. For even if the general notion of class struggle existed prior to Marx (although never stated in the same terms), it was not the idea in and of itself, but rather the original manner in which Marx employed the concept, that made it the riverbed of so much of modern socio-economic thought. But by establishing a false premise, Lenin had opened the way for an interpretation of Marxism which is best called Leninism.

"A Marxist is one who *extends* the acceptance of class struggle to the point at which the *dictatorship of the proletariat* is attained. Herein lies the profoundest distinction of a Marxist from a common petty (or even a big) bourgeois. This is the yardstick with which one measures a *real* understanding and acceptance of Marxism."

By defining a true Marxist in terms of his ability to view Marx's central motif as bound inseparably to a phrase used only seldom by Marx—and never further explained—Lenin had laid down such new guidelines that to follow Lenin was tantamount to abandoning Marx. Yet Lenin insisted that only his way was truly Marxist and whoever rejected his interpretation was an opportunist and a reformist, or someone like Kautsky, vacillating "between reformism and Marxism."[26]

Having thus "proven" that the revolution, only if joined unseverably to its product, the dictatorship of the proletariat, was the correct, if hitherto not understood, way of explaining the Marxian prophecy, Lenin could proceed to show why the Marxist movement had drifted from its course. The reason was the Western fetish for bourgeois democratic procedure, something which Kautsky himself had admitted in *The Social Revolution.*[27] "Confidence in the judgment of the masses," as Carl E. Schorske writes, "marked the German revolutionary theorists," who "paid little or no attention to the questions of organizing a revolution." Schorske correctly states that Lenin would never have "supported Kautsky's idea, entirely consistent with the latter's concept of the purpose of organization, that the party should support the mass strike, only then and there, *where the masses can no longer be held back;* [or] that the function of the party should be to curb the masses' will to action until it was impossible to do so any longer." Schorske attributes the absence in the German

Left of Lenin type mass-manipulative elite cadres partly to a "higher degree of civil liberties" in Germany, a factor tending to obviate conspiratorial methods. But the main reason for the absence of vanguardism, according to Schorske, was that German party organization, "while more highly perfected than elsewhere," was oriented "to thwart the development of revolutionary radicalism."[28]

In the period 1915-1917, it was precisely this quality of German Social Democracy which Lenin needed to alter if he was to lead the German proletariat in becoming the heart and soul of an all-European proletarian dictatorship. That gave him reasons, other than those already mentioned, for attacking Junius (Luxemburg) who had not "completely freed himself of the German influence, even of the left Social Democrats, who are afraid of a split, fearing to follow to the end their own revolutionary slogans."[29] Lenin further found fault with Junius for not using the terms social chauvinism or social patriotism in describing the Social Democratic accommodation to its government's policies. In addition, Junius had not attacked Kautsky's Centrism as a device intended to confuse the proletariat, nor had Junius made the specific demand that the Social Democrats issue a call to civil war.

From Lenin's comments one would scarcely suspect that Luxemburg's pamphlet had lashed out mercilessly against the traitors to internationalism as the following bitter citations, selected randomly among many dozens, quite amply reveal:

> If the Maoris of New Zealand were eager to risk their skulls for the English King, they showed only as much understanding of their own interests as the German Social Democratic group that traded the existence, the freedom and the civilization of the German people . . . for the vaults of the *Deutsche Bank*. There is one difference between the two. A generation ago, Maori negroes were still cannibals and not students of Marxist philosophy.[30]
>
> The passive submission of Social Democracy to the present stage of siege and its vote for war credits without attaching the slightest condition thereto, its acceptance of a civil peace, has demoralized the masses . . . .[31]
>
> By assuring militarism of peace and quiet at home, Social Democracy has given its military rulers permission to follow their

> own course without even considering the interests of the masses. . . .[32]
>
> By voting in favor of war credits and entering upon a civil peace, Social Democracy has striven, [in every way] to prevent an awakening of the masses by the war.[33]
>
> The position of Social Democracy in this war cleared away all doubts, has torn down the dams that held back the flood of militarism. In fact it has created a power for which neither Bernhardi nor any other capitalist statesman dared hope in his wildest dreams. From the camp of the Social Democrats came the cry *Durchhalten,* i.e. a continuation of this . . . slaughter. And so the thousands of victims . . . on the battlefields lie upon our conscience.[34]

If Luxemburg did not happen to use Lenin's exact terminology, designed to befoul and to belittle German Social Democracy—no great sin—her invective against the *Burgfriede* was at least as vitriolic as Lenin's. In any case it revealed a far greater intimacy with German affairs. Such "inside" knowledge probably aroused Lenin's envy and may help to account for his nitpicking criticism of the *Junius Pamphlet* for failing to identify Centrism (which Junius never even mentions) as a ploy deliberately intended to pull the wool even further over the eyes of the already blinded German masses. It was both absurd of Lenin, and revealing of his feelings, to rail at such a "flaw" in a piece written in April 1915, because the idea of separating the leader from his followers could have occurred only to once specifically seeking to replace Kautsky as the chief interpreter of Marx. It was for his own reasons that Lenin had created archvillain Kautsky. Only a second Lenin—and there was none—could have recreated that monster. It was further unrealistic of Lenin to blame Luxemburg (Junius) for not directly demanding that Social Democracy issue a call for civil war, because German Socialists knew, as Schorske notes, that an elitist-Jacobin approach on the style of *What Is To Be Done?* could not succeed in starting a revolution. Lenin, however, was convinced that an elite could stir up a revolution in Germany, for how else could he hope to emerge as its leader? It was in exactly the same vein—after he had taken power in Russia—that Lenin continued his propaganda diatribe, attacking Kautsky as the sorry symbol of German Social Democracy's reformist nature.

But, "'we' the revolutionary Marxists," Lenin writes, recalling the position of his Russian faction around 1902-1903, "have never made ourselves an idol out of 'pure' (bourgeois) democracy." Lenin recalled a declaration made by Plekhanov at the R.S.D.W.P Second Congress (before, as Lenin explains, Plekhanov had turned from a revolutionary Marxist to a "Russian Scheidemann,") in which Plekhanov had said that "the proletarian in a revolution would, if necessary, take away the voting rights of the capitalists and *disperse any parliament whatsoever* if it turned out to be counterrevolutionary." This, Lenin asserted, was clearly in accord with "all the basic ideas of Marxism."

> 'We,' the revolutionary Marxists never made speeches to the people of the kind that Kautskyites of all nations love to make, behaving as lackeys of the bourgeoisie, ingratiating themselves to bourgeois parliamentarism, saying nothing about the *bourgeois* character of contemporary democracy and asking only *that it be* extended, that *it* be led to its logical conclusion [in which the majority would rule].
>
> 'We' said to the bourgeoisie: you, exploiters and hypocrites, talk about democracy, even as at every step you set up thousands of obstacles, forbidding the *oppressed* masses a part in politics. We seize you at your word and demand, in the interests of those masses, the broadening of *your* bourgeois democracy *in order to prepare the masses for revolution* for overthrowing you, the exploiters. And if you, the exploiters, try to offer resistance to our proletarian revolution we shall mercilessly suppress you; we shall take away your rights; and more, we shall give you no bread, for in our proletarian republic the exploiters will have no rights, they will be deprived of fire and water, for we are serious socialists and not Scheidemann or Kautsky types.
>
> That is what 'we,' the revolutionary Marxists, said, and will continue to say–and that is why the oppressed masses will be for us and with us, and the Scheidemanns and the Kautskys will end up in the renegades' cesspool.[35]

Specifically what features should revolutionary tactics assume at the time when a revolutionary wave in Europe was about to crest? According to Lenin, Kautsky had feared to pose that question, which, for a Marxist was "obligatory." "Kautsky argues like a typical petty bourgeois, a Philistine, or like an ignorant peasant: has a 'general European revolution' begun or not? If it has, then *he too* is prepared to become a revolutionary! But then, mark you, every scoundrel would proclaim himself a revolutionary!

"If it has not, then Kautsky will turn his back on revolution! Kautsky does not display a shade of understanding of the truth that a revolutionary Marxist differs from the Philistine and petty bourgeois by his ability to *preach* to the uneducated masses that the revolution is necessary, to *prove* that, to *explain* its benefits to the people, and to *prepare* the proletariat and all the working and exploited people for it."

In essence, Lenin said, when the class struggle had become intensified to a certain point, violent conflict was not at all incompatible with the notion of democracy. But persistent bourgeois propaganda has succeeded in convincing the masses that violence had no place in democracy, whereas, in truth, the entire function of the bourgeois structure was designed to perpetuate a violent dictatorship against the majority. At the same time it was necessary to correct the misconception that a dictatorship was *ipso facto* a bad thing. To reshape the conditioned proletarian thinking, which automatically regarded democracy and dictatorship as mutually contradictory concepts and as being respectively equivalent to "good" and "bad," Lenin posed the question: "Whose democracy, whose dictatorship?"

Lenin's basic message was that the quality of a given democracy (dictatorship) depended on the class that controlled the state. Violence, therefore, was necessary and desirable in overcoming and suppressing a bourgeois dictatorship, usually labelled democracy. Violence would continue to prevail in the regime of the proletarian dictatorship but since it would act on behalf of the majority it would constitute a more advanced form of democracy than that of the bourgeois regime it had replaced. Like its bourgeois predecessor, the revolutionary dictatorship would take the form of an oligarchy, and, to overcome deeply-rooted bourgeois attitudes, would be obliged to retain its dictatorial form for a very long time, probably for centuries. Lenin, in short, conceived of the dictatorship of the proletariat as a repressive and long-enduring oligarchy.[36]

The above ideas, clearly stated in *State and Revolution, Renegade Kautsky,* and other Lenin writings of 1917 and 1918, comprise a sharp turning away from the ideological road hitherto traveled by Marxists or even by Marxist-Leninists, i.e., Bolsheviks. The new Marxism-Leninism may be said to have originated in 1916-1917 and was a product of the ways in which Lenin distorted the statements of Marx and Engels on the state to suit his purposes. This process is reflected perfectly in the notes Lenin made in conjunction with the restudy, especially, because of his tendency to draw boxes around ideas he considered of great importance and to write eye-catching stress marks and other attention-drawing devices in his marginalia. Along with Lenin's actual comment, his boxes, stress and exclamation marks and other marginal comment are faithfully reproduced in their printed Soviet version. Thus it becomes a simple matter to follow the ideological footprints of Lenin as he ventured upon his voyage of discovery or, more correctly, invention.

In connection with an Engels letter to Bebel (March 1875)–according to Lenin containing the most significant and most definitively expressed Marx-Engels comment on the state–Lenin noted with a double-lined box that "freedom" and "democracy" are usually considered to have the same meaning, for which reason they are often used interchangeably. "Vulgar Marxists of the Kautsky-Plekhanov stripe often follow precisely this line of reasoning. But in fact, democracy excludes freedom."[37] Somewhat later in Lenin's notebook this reasoning is justified in terms of the previously mentioned Marxist concept of power as passing from absolute monarchy through bourgeois democracy to proletarian dictatorship on its way to the eventual disappearance of all government. Democracy, thus viewed, is a stage in the evolution of the class struggle, a system of government based on class oppression.[38]

And this explains why the "state" (democracy excluding freedom) continues in Communist society, for (referring to Marx's critique of the Gotha Program) Lenin presents the state in three stages. In the first, capitalist society, "the state exists in the proper sense of the word." In the margin Lenin wrote, "The bourgeoisie needs the state." Lenin termed the second stage "the transition (dictatorship of the proletariat) a state of the transitional type–not really a state in the proper sense of the word," and in the margin wrote: "The proletariat needs the state."

The third stage was "Communistic society–*the dying off* of the state." To Lenin this progression was "completely clear and logical."[39]

Or "in other words," writes Lenin, "democracy in stage one exists only as an exception; nowhere fully–democracy being only for the rich and a small stream of proletarians, [but not for the poor!] " (The brackets are Lenin's.) "In stage two democracy is almost completely limited only by the suppression of bourgeois democracy. Democracy exists for 9/10ths of the people who forcibly suppress the opposition of the rich. In stage three democracy is actually complete, having become the way of life and therefore being in the process of dying off. . . . Full democracy equals no democracy. This is not a paradox, it is the truth, deriving from the principle 'from each according to his capacities, to each, according to his needs.'"[40]

Lenin foresaw long "labor pains" accompanying the adjustments requred in the "first phase of Communist society" (the dictatorship of the proletariat) before it could finally evolve into the "highest phase of communist society."[41] And this conception, developed more fully in *State and Revolution*,[42] was of greatest importance to Lenin. It refuted his opponents on the left–those Marxists who agreed with the anarchists that the state would disappear at once with the coming of the revolution–and those on the right, like Kautsky, who had long since ceased to think of functioning outside the bourgeois state structure. The concept of "long labor pains" coincides with the notion of a "withering away of the state," an inaccurate translation into English of Lenin's Russian rendition of Engels' *"der Staat stirbt ab"* (the state dies off), but, nevertheless, accurately reflecting his anticipation of the long struggle which confronted the German proletariat pitted against a powerfully entrenched German bourgeoisie. The concept of the state taking a long time in dying out was, moreover, of special significance to Lenin, because it provided support, at least in theory, to his vision of nations "liberated by an invading red German army, obtaining (an unspecified amount of) time to enjoy their bourgeois democratic state form, even as they would gradually be accommodating themselves to the subordination of their national identity to the international Communist superstate. (Shades of Poland, Rumania and other post-1946 Soviet satellites evolving into People's Republics after a brief period of Russian-supervised independence).

In *Renegade Kautsky,* Lenin frankly predicts a long and bitter struggle of the conquered bourgeoisie against the proletarian dictatorship, a conception that must have grown out of his anticipation of a German revolution.

> For a long time after the revolution the exploiters inevitably retain a number of huge practical advantages: they retain their money (to abolish money all at once is impossible), they have some moveable property–often a significant amount–they retain their connections, their experience in organization and management, their knowledge of all the "tricks" of management; they have their more advanced education, they are close to technologically knowledgeable personnel, who live and think like the bourgeoisie, they retain an immeasurably great knowledge of military matters and so on and so forth.
>
> If the exploiters are defeated in one country only–and this, of course, is the typical case, since a simultaneous revolution in a series of countries would be a rare exception–they *still* remain *stronger* than the exploited, for the international connections of the exploiters are enormous. . . .
>
> In view of all this, to assume that in any kind of profound and serious revolution the issue is decided simply in terms of the relation of the majority to the minority is the very greatest stupidity, the silliest prejudice of a common liberal. It is a *deception of the masses,* the concealment from them of a well-known historical truth, namely that in every profound revolution there is *prolonged, stubborn and desperate* resistance of the exploiters, and that for a number of years they hold on to major practical advantages over the exploited. Never–except in the sugary fantasies of the foolish Kautsky–will the exploiters submit to the decision of the exploited majority without trying to establish their supremacy in a final desperate battle, or in a series of battles.
>
> The transition from capitalism to communism requires an entire epoch. Until this is over, the exploiters inevitably retain the hope of restoration, and this *hope* turns into *attempts* at restoration. And after their first serious defeat, the overthrown

> exploiters, who had not expected to be overthrown, had never allowed the idea to occur to them, hurl themselves with a furious passion into the battle to regain their lost 'paradise.' They do it for their families, who had been leading such sweet lives and whom now the 'common herd' is condemning to ruin or destitution (or to 'common' labor). Behind the capitalist exploiters follow the large numbers of petty bourgeoisie [who, as the revolution approaches run panic stricken from one opposing camp to the other].
>
> In such circumstances, in a period of desperately acute war, when history places on the order of the day the question of whether age-old and thousand-year-old privileges are to be or not to be—to talk, at such at time, about majority and minority, about pure democracy, about dictatorship being unnecessary and about equality of exploiter and exploited!! What infinite stupidity, what an abyss of Philistinism is needed for this!
>
> But, during the decades of comparatively 'peaceful' capitalism, the years 1871 to 1914, the Augean stables of Philistinism, stupidity, and apostasy accumulated in the socialist parties which were accommodating themselves to opportunism.[48]

The above passage makes a special point of referring to socialism in a single country. Lenin wrote this pamphlet in 1918, but judging from his comments on managerial classes, technological know-how, international connections, and large numbers of petty bourgeois elements, it was clearly not Soviet Russia, his power base at that time, to which he had reference. He was writing as the leader-to-be of a German-centered European revolution, which had begun in Russia and was by late 1918 spreading to Germany, even though the German proletariat had, at Brest-Litovsk, betrayed "the Russian (and the world) revolution when it strangled Finland, Ukraine, Latvia and Estonia."[44] Lenin naturally made it clear that for this he was not actually blaming the "masses, who are always downtrodden," but "those *leaders,* who like the Scheidemanns and the Kautsky's *did not fulfill* their duty to conduct revolutionary agitation, revolutionary propaganda, and revolutionary work among the masses to overcome their inertness, but, indeed, worked *against* the revolutionary instincts and aspirations which are always aglow deep down among the mass of the oppressed classes."[45]

Lenin's sermon implied that if he, rather than such as the Social-Democratic party chiefs of Germany, had been at the helm, things would have been different. Democracy would have acquired an international meaning. A German revolutionary army would have dominated Europe,but, as suggested above, would have managed in such a way that nations liberated, whether from Russia or Austria, would at least briefly have made their appearance as "independent" states, thus achieving their historic destinies in the prescribed Marxian manner. This was the idea which Lenin had tried to convey in his 1916 response to Piatakov[46] even as he strongly re-asserted his position that a dictatorial order would accompany the European revolution. But this immediately compelled him to explain why the dictator (never, of course, designating himself as the man on horseback) would not, like Napoleon, stamp out the rights of nations to become independent states, noting "that in individual cases by way of exception, for instance in some small country after the social revolution had been accomplished in a neighboring big country [Germany?], peaceful surrender of power by the bourgeoisie is *possible,* if it is convinced that resistance is hopeless and if it prefers to save its skin."

Lenin seems to suggest that a socialist revolution, once begun, would induce the sensible bourgeoisie and most nations of the continent to surrender without a struggle to avoid violence upon their persons. But, Lenin insisted, they retained the right to act out the historical process, including at least an ephemeral period of bourgeois republicanism followed by the civil war (class struggle) fought within the confines of a nations' ethnic boundaries. "If we demand freedom of secession for the Mongolians, Persians, Egyptians and *all* other oppressed and unequal nations without exception," Lenin went on, using even Africa and Asia to bolster his argument,

> we do so not because *we favor secession,* but *only* because we stand for *free, voluntary* association and merging as distinct from forcible association. That is the *only* reason! And in this respect the *only* difference between the Mongolians or Egyptian peasants and workers and their Polish or Finnish counterparts is, in our view, that the latter are more developed, more experienced

> politically than the Great Russians, more economically prepared, etc., and for that reason will in all likelihood *very soon* convince their peoples that it is unwise to extend their present legitimate hatred of the Great Russians, for their role of hangman, to the *socialist* workers and to a socialist Russia. They will convince them that economic expediency and internationalist and democratic instinct and consciousness demand the earliest association of all nations and their merging in a socialist society. And since the Poles and Finns are highly cultured people, they will in all probability, very soon come to see the correctness of this attitude, and the possible secession of Poland and Finland after the triumph of socialism will therefore be of only short duration.[48]

Lenin asserted that the more civilized the nation, the less urgently would it seek to become a bourgeois republic; all the more reason for extending the courtesy of choice to the advanced, if subject, nations as well as to the subject backward nations. "The incomparably less cultured Fellahs, Mongolians, and Persians," Lenin added, "might secede for a longer period [from the new revolutionary world empire] but we shall try to shorten it by disinterested cultural assistance, as indicated above. There is *no* other difference in our attitude to the Poles and Mongolians, nor can there be. There is *no* 'contradiction' nor can there be, between our freedom of secession and our firm resolve to implement that freedom when *we* are the government, and our propaganda for the association and merging of nations."

The references to the Russian empire in the foregoing comments clearly related to Lenin's polemic with Piatakov. But in speaking of secession followed by merging, Lenin ventured beyond the limits of that debate and encompassed the coming revolutionary European entity, of which *we* (i.e., Lenin and his following) would be the rulers. The non-European peoples seem thrown into the discussion for good measure, as though to suggest, that ignorance, marked by backwardness, might account for cases of resistance to a smooth and rapid surrender of national identity to the higher form of national denial. "For a Marxist, writing in, say German [a slap at Kautsky] it might be pardonable to overlook *this* peculiarity of Russia [the backward empire sitting on culturally advanced peoples]. For [Piatakov] it is unpardonable." Lenin continued: "The sheer absurdity of trying to discover some serious difference between oppressed nations and colonies in the case of Russia should be especially clear to a Russian socialist who wants not simply to *repeat,* but to *think.*"[49]

"We recognize," he went on, "and quite rightly—the predominance of the economic factor [Marxian determinism], but to interpret it [as Piatakov does] is to make a caricature out of Marxism." Lenin briefly restated his "discovery" of inequality in capitalist development as a basis for "explaining" that each nation would in its own way arrive at socialism, each "contributing something of its own" to the form of democracy, "to some variety of socialist transformations in the different aspects of social life."[50] This Utopian projection by Lenin is difficult to understand except as an attempt to intellectualize his rather clouded vision of things to come. Trying to unravel the twisted yarn of his ideas, however, only succeeded in further tangling the skein.

"There is nothing more primitive from the viewpoint of theory, or more ridiculous from that of practice, than to paint, in the name of historical materialism, *this* aspect of the future in a monotonous grey . . . . And even if reality were to show that *prior* to the first victory of the socialist proletariat only 1/500 of the nations now oppressed will win emancipation and *secede,* that *prior* to the final victory of the socialist proletariat the world over (i.e., during all the vicissitudes of the socialist revolution) also only 1/500 of the oppressed nations will secede for a very short time—even in that event we would be correct, both from the theoretical and practical standpoint, in advising the workers, already now, not to permit into their Social-Democratic parties those socialists of the oppressor nations who do not recognize and do not advocate freedom of secession for *all* oppressed nations. For the fact is that we do not know, and cannot know, how many of the oppressed nations will in practice requre secession in order to contribute something of their own to the different *forms* of democracy, the different *forms* of transition to socialism. And the negation of freedom of secession now is theoretically false from beginning to end and in practice amounts to servility to the chauvinists of the oppressing nations."[51]

Amid this flood of words, Lenin was, as ever, repeating his old refrain; that national self determination to the point of secession was an inseparable part of the Social-Democratic minimum program, being one of the essential "bourgeois-democratic" milestones marking the passageway of history to communism. At the same time Lenin was also describing his conception of how each national government, becoming historically obsolete, died off, blending into unity with the proletarian empire. That empire's (German) statist form would itself be growing ever more superfluous (if at a slower pace than that of any of the nations it had ingested) because of the inevitable and universal progress toward internationalism, i.e., communism. Thus he worked out the blueprint for a revolutionary superstate, and for its substates any of which, for a time, might exist in the form of transitory bourgeois democracies.

In the process of structuring this part of his revolutionary theory, Lenin, for reasons that will become apparent later, seized upon two letters of Engels, one to Kautsky, in 1891, criticizing the Erfurt program, the other, in 1875, to Bebel. The letter to Kautsky had sardonically attacked the "honest opportunism" of the Erfurt program for its failure to mention that a German democratic republic was essential as the "only" form of government through which "our party and the working class can attain power. Indeed, as the French revolution has shown, this is the specific form of the dictatorship of the proletariat." Engels acknowledged that the party could not legally have included mention of a republic *in its platform, but pointed out, at the same time, that this in itself* proved "how colossal was the illusion that a republic" much less a Communist society "might be achieved through peaceable means."[52] But conceding that pragmatism had necessitated omitting mention of a republic, he wondered why the program had omitted such items as could at least have served to indicate "that which could not be made specific; namely, a demand for complete self government in each province, in each county [*Kreis*] and in each commune [*Gemeinde*] through officals elected by universal suffrage? Could there not have been a demand that all state-appointed provincial and local officials be removed?"[53]

Lenin chose to interpret the above Engels comment of 1891 as the link between Marx, in 1871, and his own perception of 1916-1917. For, if Marx, in 1871, had referred to the bourgeois inheritance of the formerly monarchichal bureaucratic-military state apparatus, Lenin, noting its subsequent development under the bourgeoisie, could point to the natural expansion of its power in the epoch of imperialism, at which time the opportunist socialists had become a part of the machine. On the "authority" of Marx and Engels, therefore, Lenin went on to define the task of the proletarian revolution as that of "*smashing this machine and replacing it with the most complete self government from below possible, in the localities,* and by *direct* power of the armed proletariat, dictatorship, at the top."[54]

But how, asks Lenin "to go about unifying and organizing the *obshchina* [commune]?"[55] In translating Engels' mention of a unitary German republic as essential if the German socialists hoped to install the proletarian dictatorship, Lenin's use of the Russian word for "commune" was a tiny, barely noticeable, device of distortion. But it became of major historical importance—in fact one of the great turning points of history as things worked out—by enabling Lenin to weave his Russian experience and, of course, his person, into a prescription for curing the ills of German socialism. By using the word *obshchina,* which, derived from the Russian peasant *mir,* could thence be linked to the spontaneously formed workers soviets of 1905, Lenin had subtly shifted his semantical and hence his ideational ground. This made it possible for him to provide a "suitable" answer to the question of how to "unify and organize" the commune *or* unitary democratic republic, the two expressions having become interchangeable.

Although the anarchists offered "no way to unify and to organize," the bourgeoisie, Lenin pointed out, unified and organized the "commune" by means of its bureaucracy and "the military caste" (by which he meant the alliance between German bourgeoisie and Junkers). Lenin saw no structural difference between the dictatorship of the bourgeoisie and that of the proletariat. The difference lay solely in who did the "unifying and organizing," and that, according to Lenin's (out of historical context) reading of Marx and Engels should be "the union of the organized armed workers ('the soviets of workers' deputies.')."[56]

Referring to Engels' 1875 letter to Bebel, Lenin cites, as having "the *greatest possible* importance to the question of the state," the following passage:

> The free people's state is changed into the free state. Grammatically, a free state is one in which the state is free from restrictions of its citizens, that is, a despotic state. *One should drop the*

> *whole talk of a state,* especially *since the time of the Commune, which was no longer a state in the true sense of the word.* The 'people's state' has been endlessly thrown into our teeth by the Anarchists, even though Marx, attacking Proudhon, and later on, in the *Communist Manifesto,* says clearly that the state dissolves of itself and disappears with the introduction of the socialist economic structure. Since the state is therefore only a transitional phenomenon, used for the purpose of holding down one's opponents in the revolutionary struggle, it becomes pure nonsense to speak of the free people's state, so long as the proletariat still *needs* [Engels' emphasis being noted by Lenin] the state, not in the interests of freedom, but to restrain its opponents, and as soon as one can *speak of freedom,* the state, *as such, ceases to exist.* We would, therefore, suggest everywhere, instead of *state* [Engels' emphasis noted by Lenin] to use '*Gemeinwesen*', a good old German word which can easily replace the French '*Commune*'.[57]

Lenin then adds the following, highlighted by four marginal strokes and a fat NOTA BENE plus four exclamation marks:

> We [that is, Engels and Marx–although Marx did not sign the letter to Bebel] would suggest '*everywhere*' (in the programme) to use instead of 'state' the term '*obshchina*,' '*kommuna*'!!!![58]

It is clear from Lenin's entire train of thought that his enthusiasm for Engels' usage of the word *Gemeinwesen,* which he takes the liberty to render in Russian not only as *obshchina* but also as *kommuna,* could have risen only out of his intention of translating this motif from the French through the German into the Russian language. He did this in order to make the soviets of 1905 appear to belong in the Marxian tradition.[59] Lenin specifically made this connection on January 22, 1917, the anniversary of Bloody Sunday. The occasion was a lecture on the 1905 revolution at a meeting of young workers in the Zurich People's House. In a December 20, 1916 letter to Karpinskii, Lenin had requested literature on the subject of 1905 to help him prepare the talk.[60] Upon completing the written text, Lenin showed it to the director of the Zurich

Library for Revolutionaries, who described it as "lucidly structured in good German."[61]

Since Lenin took such pains to prepare a talk on 1905 for an audience likely to accept, without any question, whatever he might have to say on the subject, we can safely conclude that he considered the speech itself to be of greater importance than the occasion of its delivery. That such was indeed the case may be deduced from the fact that it contained Lenin's tactical instructions–speaking through the Swiss (for easy linguistic transmission) to the Germans–of how the German revolution was to be made. To arrive at this conclusion, however, we must keep in mind the elaborate tissue of words and ideas which Lenin had woven to link Engels' commune state, or *Gemeinwesen* (in a letter of 1891), to the soviets of 1905. The purpose of Lenins' speech to the Swiss workers was to present the events of 1905 in Russia as lessons for Germany in 1917.

Lenin began his lecture by reading some passages from the Petersburg workers' petition to the tsar, noting that his own reaction, in 1917, to the plea of "uneducated, illiterate workers, led by a patriarchal priest," was one of amazement because he was "struck by the parallel between that naive petition and the current peace resolution of the social pacifists." Such would-be socialists, he added, "are in fact only bourgeois phrasemongers." Lenin's analogy was far fetched but it had a didactic purpose. "The unenlightened workers of pre-revolutionary Russia," he explained, "did not know that the tsar was the head of the *ruling class* [Lenin was coloring reality to reflect rural Russia in a kind of Germany-like industrial light] precisely the class of large landowners, already tied by a thousand threads with the big bourgeoisie and prepared by every violent means to defend their monopoly, privileges and profits."

Having held up to the Swiss workers, who were hardly connoisseurs of Russia, an exaggerated image of the power of the Russian bourgeoisie in 1905, Lenin had established the basis for demonstrating the relevance of 1905 Russia to 1917 Germany.

"The [supposedly highly educated] social pacifists of today," he said, "do not know that it is as stupid to expect a 'democratic' peace from bourgeois governments that are waging an imperialist predatory war as was the idea that the bloody tsar could be induced by peaceful petitions to incline toward democratic reforms." But more than that, the largely hypocritical social pacifists deliberately make "meek proposals to divert the people from the revolutionary struggle." The uneducated workers of 1905, on the other hand "proved by their deeds that they were straightforward people awakened to political awareness for the first time." Lenin was making the point that whereas uneducated workers could be expected to behave as honest revolutionaries, the educated socialist leaders, being, in effect, members of the bourgeoisie, could not. The moral was that the revolution would emerge only after the masses had broken away from their leaders.

"Precisely in this awakening of the huge masses to political awareness and revolutionary struggle," said Lenin to the Swiss workers, "lies the historical significance of January 22, 1905."[62] He recalled sarcastically that Peter Struve, then leader of the Russian liberals, had written "just *two days* before Bloody Sunday that in Russia 'there was still not a revolutionary people.' So absurd did it seem to this 'highly educated,' haughty and arch-stupid leader of the bourgeois reformists that a revolutionary people could have arisen in an illiterate peasant country." And yet, said Lenin, within a few months "the hundreds of revolutionary Social-Democrats *'suddenly' grew* into thousands; the thousands became the leaders of two to three million proletarians," evoking fermentation among a hundred million peasants, giving rise in turn to revolts in the army and "to armed clashes between one section of the army and another. In this manner a colossal country with a population of 130 million went into the revolution. In this way dormant Russia was transformed into a Russia of a revolutionary proletariat and a revolutionary people."[64] Lenin was saying: If a dormant and largely agrarian people could within months become a mighty revolutionary force, then an advanced proletarian nation could even more speedily erupt into revolution.

Lenin's speech went on to stress the crucial importance of the strike, "a specifically proletarian means of struggle, precisely the strike having been the principal device for agitating the masses as well as the most characteristic phenomenon [in1905] associated with the wave-like cresting of decisive events." Providing statistics, Lenin was able to assert that no capitalist country in the world "even the most advanced, such as England, the U.S.A., or Germany," had ever matched "the grandiose Russian strike movement of 1905." But, as Lenin was suggesting, if a strike movement had been so effective in peasant Russia, its impact in an advanced country would be even greater; the more so since events in Russia did not "prove that the urban factory workers of Russia were more educated, or stronger, or more accustomed to fight than were their West European brothers. The very opposite is true!" The Western proletariat needed only to perceive "how powerful its dormant energy could become, which means that in a revolutionary epoch [brought on by the imperialist war] the proletariat *can* develop energy *a hundred times* greater than in usual peaceful times."

Russia, Lenin explained, had in 1825 experienced a revolution of nobles. Subsequently the heroic efforts of middle-class intellectual-led terrorists, although advancing the Russian revolutionary movement, had been unable to generate a people's revolution. Only the revolutionary proletariat had accomplished that end, using "the waves of mass strikes spreading over the whole country, strikes connected with the harsh lessons learned from the *imperialist* [my italics] Russo-Japanese war, and waking the broad peasant masses from their lethargic dreams."[65]

Lenin offered the example of the 1905 Russian strike movement to convince the German (via the Swiss) workers that they were likely to inspire other social groups by their militant actions. He thereby exposed his ignorance regarding the political impact of industrial conflict in Western countries. Such conflict was usually permitted to run its course within the framework of a struggle between capital and labor; the general public tending to remain neutral. Faulty, in addition, was Lenin's analysis of the Russian societal response to the waves of strikes. That response was due, in large part, to the lack of political outlets for opposition sentiment. It was that which brought great public support to the cause of the workers and concomitant concessions from the government; the soviets, for a short time, playing a quasi-revolutionary role. But such a result could scarcely have found its parallel in a West European country. One might wonder here whether Lenin, in stressing the revolutionary importance of spontaneous mass action, was not refuting his *What Is To Be Done?* call of 1902, repeated in articles written in 1905, for elitist party guidance over workers of limited political consciousness?[66] In that regard it should be remembered that Lenin's focus of the moment was upon a country which, unlike Russia, had no history of *intelligenty* militants infatuated with the people (*narod*). Moreover, Lenin, at this juncture, was especially intent upon persuading the German proletariat to break with its Kautskys, who had led them down the reformist road. None of this should be taken to mean that when and if the day came, Lenin and his associates would sit passively on the sidelines waiting to see how it all turned out.

In another "lesson" to the Germans, Lenin linked the spontaneous proletarian militancy of 1905 to the *imperialist* Russo-Japanese War. The mass strikes of workers, inciting widespread peasant rebelliousness, had sufficed "to shake the 'firmest' and last prop of tsarism," the armed forces. Their mutinous leaders, Lenin asserted, came "from *those elements* of the navy and army who had been recruited mainly from among the industrial workers, especially from among those, like the sappers, with the greatest technical knowledge."[67] Or, as Lenin was suggesting, a striking proletariat, besides fomenting revolution among the masses in general, could also, as the Russian experience indicated, produce revolt in the armed forces. This pattern of events, Lenin admits, had not been properly exploited in 1905 because the Russian masses were "still too naive, too good natured, and too Christian." They had failed to "follow up their advantage," lacking an adequate "perception of their task to enable them to understand that only the most energetic continuation of the armed struggle, only a victory over all the military and civil authorities, only the overthrow of the government and the seizure of power of the entire state could guarantee the success of the revolution."

Nevertheless, Lenin asserted, "the history of the Russian revolution, like the history of the Paris Commune [the linking of the two events by Lenin is significant as propaganda] teaches us the irrevocable lesson that militarism can under no conditions be defeated and destroyed, except by a victorious struggle of one portion of the popular army against the other part. It is not enough merely to fulminate against . . . and 'reject' militarism, to criticize it and show it to be harmful; stupid peacefully to refuse to render military duty. [This, in passing, was an attack on the pacifist and pro-disarmament elements in Switzerland and elsewhere.] The task is to maintain the desire for revolution among the proletariat and concretely prepare its best elements [the Bolshevik vanguard], so that, at the moment when popular ferment attains its peak, they can take their positions at the head of the revolutionary army."

Some industrial crisis, Lenin hoped, would, as it had in Russia, provide the spark to set off the German revolutionary explosion. "The everyday experience of any capitalist country teaches us [the lesson] that any strike is a minor crisis of capitalist society." To relate the lesson specifically to Germany, Lenin quoted the "famous pronouncement" of the Prussian Minister of Internal Affairs, stating that "every strike harbors the hydra of revolution." Lenin further tried to promote the idea that a strike was like a prelude to revolution even in the "most 'democratic' capitalist countries" when faced by a "really *big* crisis." And reverting again to 1905 Russia, Lenin summarized by saying he had tried to show how strikes "had stirred up the whole country" and had given rise to military risings.

But the Russian revolution had set another important precedent in its *Soviets of Workers' Deputies* [Lenin's emphasis] which "in several Russian cities began ever more to play the role of a provisional revolutionary government. Attempts were made to organize Soviets of Soldiers' and Sailors' Deputies and to unite them with the Workers' Soviets. Several cities in those days became something like small local 'republics,' the governmental authorities being ousted while the Soviet of Workers' Deputies actually functioned in the capacity of the new state power."[68] It is obvious that Lenin was establishing links between 1905 and Engels' comments of 1875 on the replacement of state officials by local self-governing bodies, apparently to create the impression that what had happened in Russia had been the fulfillment of Marxian prophecy.[69] But Lenin deplored the "all too brief periods" of local Soviet domination, their "'victories' being too weak and too isolated."[70]

Then Lenin spoke of the revolution among almost sixty percent of Russia's population "subject to national oppression," making particular mention of the Moslems and the Poles, among whom secondary school students demanded that schools be placed under control of the Soviet of Workers' Deputies, and the Jews, who "provided an especially high percentage of revolutionary leaders as compared with the total Jewish population." This led to pogroms "calling forth the disgust of the entire civilized world, by which I mean, of course, the truly *democratic* [my emphasis] elements of the civilized world, i.e., *exclusively* [my emphasis] the socialist workers, the proletarians." Once again Lenin had linked the concept of "proletarian" democracy to the notion that subject nations had the right to independence. This combination of motifs, as we have seen, loomed large in his vision of the German-led European revolution.

Lenin depicted the 1905 movement as a series of higher and higher mounting revolutionary waves which were met with ever more forceful armed reactions. It was "less like a spontaneous uprising against the government and more like a long drawn out *civil war,*" a form Lenin recalled that Kautsky had predicted in his 1902 *Social Revolution.* Although Lenin knew better by the time of his January 1917 talk, he found it expedient to profess that Kautsky in 1902 was still in the camp of revolutionary Marxism, the better thereby to authenticate the events of 1905 as following the orthodox model. "Undoubtedly," he went on, "that is what the coming European revolution will be like." He describes as the "high point" of the revolution the only episode of 1905 in which he had played a personal role. At the same time he mocked the term "Putsch" (quite accurately), used by "Professor Max Weber" to belittle the significance of the December rising in Moscow, workers taking the barricades against regular troops. Lenin, however, was careful not to omit Weber's mention of Lenin's part in that action, even though it was not flattering. "The Lenin group, writes this 'highly erudite and learned Herr Professor,' and some Socialist Revolutionaries had long prepared for this senseless uprising."

In sum, Lenin's lecture to the Swiss workers was a prescription designed to show how even a relatively minor industrial crisis in Germany could, under wartime conditions, mushroom into mass demonstrations, push aside the Kautskyite leadership of the party, incite conflict within the army and lead to the forming of local communes (or Soviets). In turn this would stir up national minorities in whatever countries the revolutionary German soldiers prevailed. Such events, as Kautsky (when still an honest revolutionist) had prophesied, would lead to a protracted series of civil wars rather than a single spontaneous uprising. This movement—Lenin juggling time and European territory about to suit his vision of the future—would gradually come under the leadership of the "Lenin group," which, on a previous occasion, had, through the December 1905 Moscow rising, re-enacted the passion play of the Paris Commune.

"Just as in Russia of 1905," said Lenin toward the end of his speech, "a popular rising against the tsarist government under the leadership of the proletariat attempted to achieve a democratic republic, so, in coming years, this rapacious war will cause the proletariat of Europe to lead popular risings against the power of finance capital, against the big banks, against the capitalists. And these upheavals can end only in the expropriation of the bourgeoisie and the victory of socialism."[71] Concluding his lecture, Lenin declared that "We, the old ones, may not survive to see the decisive battles of the coming revolution," a pessimistic comment, indeed, when contrasted to the exhortatory tone of the entire talk and the euphoric state to which Lenin had raised himself by the beginning of 1917. Krupskaia, remarking on that period, notes that her husband "was completely absorbed in theoretical work," using "every minute of the time the library was open" and being "positively certain that the revolution was impending. . . . Ilyich never for a moment doubted that there were such prospects. But as to how soon [the] coming revolution would take place—that, of course, Ilyich could not know." Krupskaia mentions Lenin's "rather wistful" words, concluding the talk of January 22. "And yet," as though apologizing for them, she writes, "Ilyich thought of nothing else, worked for nothing else but this revolution."[72] Krupskaia refuses to admit and possibly did not comprehend that Lenin, in his less euphoric moments, inevitably had to confront the simple fact that all of his hopes rested entirely upon his own "theoretical" projections. At the time of his January 22 lecture there was not a single indication of a revolution in the making anywhere in Western Europe. The question of an imminent revolution in Russia had long since ceased to occupy his serious attention, and in 1917 he referred to the revolution of 1905 as a "prelude to the coming European revolution." All of his hopes depended on what might happen in Germany.

CHAPTER V

THE IMPACT OF THE APRIL THESES I–DEFEAT IN JULY 1917

The March revolution was followed by a fortuitous offer from the German Foreign Office to transport Lenin and his associates back to Russia. This called for a hasty reshuffling of Lenin's ideological deck of cards. Russian-grown Marxist-Leninist ideas, adapted since 1914 to Germany, now had to be subtly retailored. Lenin, about to resume active captaincy of the Bolshevik party and to provide it with a programme, wanted, at the same time, to avoid interrupting his made-in-Europe plans. His hastily improvised programme, emerged, therefore, as a combination of his German-oriented position, plus material based on garbled news from Russia, and his ideas on the Russian peasants, formulated in the period 1905-1907.

In his April 8 "Farewell Letter to the Swiss Workers," Lenin, referring to the *continuation* [my italics] of his "revolutionary-internationalistic work in his own country,"[1] called attention to the already *seething* mood of the German proletarian masses, who, he said, had "given so much to humanity and socialism by their stubborn, unwavering and persistent organized efforts in the course of the long decades of European 'quiet' from 1871 to 1914." He went on to explain that "the objective conditions of the imperialist war serve as a guarantee that the revolution would not limit itself to its *first stage,* the Russian revolution," and, reminding anew where the heart of the revolution beat, stressed that "*the German proletariat,*" was "*the truest and most reliable ally of the Russian and the world-wide proletarian revolution.*"[2]

Lenin's five "Letters from Afar," reflect his view that the German revolution held primacy over the Russian, even though the less important of the two was already in progress. This made for a certain awkwardness. Lenin had, of course, been insisting since the early 1890s that Russia was a capitalistic country. Therefore he was free to explain that all capitalistic warring countries, Russia included, were ripe for revolution, and that if the eruption had first occurred in Russia, this was largely thanks to experience derived from the dress rehersal of 1905. But otherwise, as Lenin suggested, what had happened in Russia would soon be happening throughout Europe, since the war had bound the capitalists of the warring countries into a single "bloody clot." So, in Letter No 1 (March 20) Lenin asserted that an Anglo-French imperialist plot had motivated "Miliukov, Guchkov & Co. to seize power, in the interests of a continuation of the imperialist war"[3] in order to prevent a separate peace between Wilhelm and Nicholas. He further downgraded Russia's role in the European revolution, as compared with Germany's, by making much of her agrarian nature, calling, as in 1905, for a proletarian-peasant alliance, the creation of Soviets of Agricultural Workers and the introduction of class war in the villages.[4]

But in Letter No. 2, Lenin, as though compelled to admit that Russia was, after all, in the process of revolution (whereas Germany was not) proposed the establishment of a dictatorship of the proletariat in Russia (although he did not quite dare to call it that), referring instead to an "*organization* based on a *proletarian* militia, and an armed people under the leadership of the workers." In the same letter Lenin also obscured the peasant element in Russia, using, instead of "peasant," such words as "people" or "the poor."[5] Letter No. 3 (March 24) continues where Letter No. 2 leaves off and even provides details of how Russia's proletarian dictatorship should be structured. It refers to an exact number of Petersburgers (50,000) who might, every fifteenth day, perform citizen's police duty, and it demands a bottle of "good milk for each child."[6] But toward the end of the letter, the tone becomes less shrill, Lenin apparently becoming uncomfortable about prescribing for Russia a scheme which only a society like Germany could have put into effect. In addition, Lenin, "leader of Germany," could hardly present, as the seedbed of the proletarian state, a country so backward that the peasant directives he had designed for it in 1905-1907 were still applicable. So, backing away, he cautioned that the measures he had indicated did "not yet constitute socialism" and were merely concerned with "distribution of consumption and not the reorganization of production. They did not yet make up the 'dictatorship of the proletariat,' but only the 'revolutionary-democratic dictatorship of the proletariat and of the poorest peasantry.'" But since all of this went directly counter to the spirit of the letter's first portion, Lenin hedged by noting that theoretical classification was not of immediate importance, as if to say, "I was not mistaking backward Russia for advanced Germany."[7]

Beyond that, as though fearful that even the attainment of Soviet power might be too much to expect from Russia's primitive masses, Lenin, near the end of Letter No. 3, proposed that the revolutionary forces obtain the help of Finland, whose workers, he implied, owed a debt to the Russians. Finland, "left alone because of the revolutionary struggles in Russia from 1905 to 1917 had achieved democracy in a comparatively peaceful way and had brought the *majority* of the people to the side of 'socialism.'" Finnish support, he explained, could easily be gained, for if the "Russian proletariat" assured the Finnish Republic "self determination, including the full right of secession from Russia," then "the Finnish workers, who were better organizers than the Russians [Lenin here implying a higher level of Western-style proletarians] would help us to become organized and would, *in their own way,* advance the establishment of the socialist republic of Russia."[8]

Indeed, by the end of Letter No. 3, Lenin was rather firmly implying that eventual victory depended largely on the proletarian West. Russian revolutionary conquests "by the proletariat and the poorest peasants," aided by "Finnish organizational" talents, along with "the stimulation and development of the socialist revolution in the West," he wrote, will "lead us to *peace* and to *socialism.*"[9] This was pretty much the course of events which Lenin had foreseen in the period 1902-1905, with revolution in Russia serving as inspiration for the more significant European revolution. In his April 8 "Farewell Letter to the Swiss Workers," Lenin unequivocally places his hopes on Germany, stating that the Russian proletariat cannot with its own strength alone *accomplish* the socialist revolution," and that the "future belongs to that source which gave us Karl Liebknecht," founder of the Spartakus Society." Letter No. 5, written the same day, offered the Russian proletariat no choice other than an alliance with the peasantry.[10]

This guideline (stressed in Letter No. 1, obscured in Letter No. 2, then restored in Letter No. 3) went hand in hand with instructions to divorce the poorest peasants from their landowning fellows. This task of "extreme urgency," required immediate organization of "special Soviets of Workers' Deputies in the villages, i.e., Soviets of agricultural *wage* workers *separately* from the Soviets of other peasant deputies."[11]

In explaining why he thought this course of action to be of such "extreme urgency" Lenin re-stated his position of a decade earlier when he had argued for the nationalization of all the land, in order, thereby to convert the entire peasantry into wage workers. As natural allies of the factory proletariat, they would then join in the tasks of replacing the old state machine with revolutionary institutions and in introducing the revolutionary measures needed to control the production and distribution of goods. At the 1906 Unity Congress of the R.S.D.W.P, it will be recalled, Lenin had cynically supported the demands of 104 peasant delegates in the Duma, who, for what Lenin regarded as reactionary reasons, had demanded nationalization of the land. And on April 8, 1917, Lenin asserted "that the agrarian programme of the '104' remained in essence the agrarian programme of the *peasantry.*"[12]

So, in the little time he had before embarking on the "sealed train" journey, Lenin had patched together a "theory," which provided a place for the Russian revolution in his grand design. But throughout that eight-day trip his mind was principally occupied with his "future" in Germany. His refusal to speak to Wilhelm Janson, a minor event, entailing little risk of embarrassment, acquires major symbolic significance when it is kept in mind that Lenin could not possibly have been traveling–at the huge risk of being thought a spy[13]–except for the deal which he had made with the regime of archfoe Kaiser Wilhelm. Union leader Janson, representing the General Commission of German trade unions, boarded the train at Stuttgart and expressed his desire to deliver the greetings of the German unions to the Russian travelers. Fritz Platten, the man in charge of protecting the Russians against contact with Germans, put Janson off for the night, using as his pretext the Russians' extraterritorial status, and telling Janson that the travelers would refuse to speak to anyone while on German territory. However, Platten promised to discuss the matter with Lenin, knowing well that Lenin would refuse to grant an interview to a well known supporter of the *Burgfriede.* Platten was having fun at Janson's expense and his joke "evoked explosive joy among the travelers," who decided, after a brief discussion, neither to admit Janson to their presence nor even to respond to his greeting. But if Janson persisted on his mission, the discussants proposed "that force be used" to throw him out.[14] Lenin's overreaction to the attempt of a single German socialist to bring greetings was a form of propaganda. It meant to tell the world that he would rather deal with the Kaiser than soil himself by contact with a reformist socialist.

On the journey home Lenin had time to condense the ideas expressed in his "Letters from Afar," and their summary became the ten April Theses, reflecting Lenin's need to cloak Russia in a costume designed for Germany. Lenin attempted, the moment he arrived, to direct the course of Russian events so as to hasten the impending German-European revolution. Thus he asked his party comrades to oppose revolutionary defeatism and, startlingly, asked them to take the initiative in creating a third international. Furthermore, continuing (as he had in Switzerland) to envision the coming European revolution, Lenin demanded that his party oppose annexationism "in deeds, not merely in words," and offer each subject nation the right to secede from the Russian empire. The Theses also urged the Bolsheviks to aim for the establishment of a Soviet state—like the Paris Commune—having a "people's" police, army and bureaucracy. But he admitted, in effect, that such a scheme could have no immediate meaning in peasant Russia. Therefore, Lenin asked his party, while it was a minority within the "bourgeois democracy" to use only peaceful means and patient explanations, asserting that Russia was not yet ready for socialism but only for socially controlled production and distribution.

Having cautioned the proletarian party to avoid extreme revolutionary agitation, Lenin himself called for peasant violence to produce the social revolution that would ignite all of Europe. To become the shock troops of a European proletarian rising required militant action by the peasant poor, said Lenin, in effect, declaring that "the axis" of the Bolshevik program had shifted and that its "center of gravity" rested upon the Soviets of Agricultural Laborers Deputies, or peasant wage workers. "If the revolution is not decided by the Russian peasant," he added, "it will not be decided by the German workers." This statement clearly reveals a territorial shift in Lenin's mood. The peasants as a class, would, according to Lenin, confiscate all private holdings in the first stage of the agrarian revolution. Thereupon all the land would be nationalized and model communal farms created at public expense to be "managed by the Soviets of Agricultural Laborer Deputies."[15]

Menshevik Sukhanov, attending the initial April 17 meeting of Bolsheviks addressed by the returning leader, found himself shocked by "a purely anarchistic . . . , bankrupt and futile schema for a workers' dictatorship," lacking any analysis of "objective premises" or of "the socio-economic conditions for socialism in Russia." Nor could Sukhanov comprehend "how the Workers' and Farm-Laborers' Soviets, representing a small minority of the country, as the bearers of the proletarian dictatorship, against the will and the interests of the majority, were to construct socialism . . . , or of how, finally, [Lenin's] whole conception was to be reconciled with the elementary foundations of Marxism." Lenin had ignored "everything touching on what had hitherto been called scientific socialism," and had "just as completely . . . destroyed the foundations of the current Social-Democratic programme and tactics." Sukhanov, thinking he "*ought*, after all, understand what this was really all about," asked Kamenev and other Bolsheviks to explain Lenin's words. But they merely "grinned and shook their heads, without the slightest idea of what to say." Sukhanov left the hall feeling as though he had been "beaten over the head."

Later that day he attended a joint session of all three Social-Democratic factions (Bolsheviks, Mensheviks and Independents) which had been convened to hear Lenin. This time he noted that the Bolsheviks applauded vigorously while the rest of the audience seemed indignant as Lenin spat upon "the foundations of the Social-Democratic programme" and upon "Marxist theory." Bogdanov cried shame upon the "Marxists" (Bolsheviks) who applauded such "claptrap," and I. P. Goldenberg charged Lenin with seeking the "European throne . . . of Bakunin," adding that he had "raised the banner of civil war within [revolutionary] democracy." Such comments, Sukhanov noted, only served to intensify the public enthusiasm of Lenin's followers, but in private the "Bolsheviks made no bones . . . about Lenin's 'abstractness'" and "the Bolshevik sect," he reports, remained in a state of "bafflement and perplexity," only Kollontai, a recent Menshevik, supporting him "among his own disciples." In Bolshevik meetings the rationale of Lenin's position was, indeed, sharply challenged.[16]

At the April 21 session of the Bolshevik Petersburg Committee, Sergei Bogdat'ev, speaking for the majority, used kind words to introduce his attack upon Lenin's Theses. They were, he said, "theoretically correct but unworkable in practice." Bogdat'ev went on to remind Lenin that at Kienthal he had presented the socialist revolution as a general European but not as a national Russian phenomenon. He thus charged Lenin's new position with internal inconsistency, and, going straight to the heart of the matter, made the point that Lenin was trying to introduce styles appropriate to a commune state in an agrarian country. "Lenin now considers it necessary to complete the revolutionary transition from the old regime not with a bourgeois-democratic republic but with a proletarian-peasant dictatorship." Bogdat'ev further questioned the validity of Lenin's appeal for a bourgeois-free government based on the soviets, whose first task, according to Lenin, would be convoking a constituent assembly. But since this, by democratic necessity, would have to include bourgeois representatives, Bogdat'ev wondered why the Soviet could not be called "the parliament of a republic?"[17]

Six days later the Conference of Petersburg and All-Russian Bolsheviks had similar criticism and it was recalled that in 1905 Lenin had stipulated that a proletarian-peasant republic could follow only upon the completed bourgeois revolution. If, then, Lenin was asking for the establishment of a combined Paris Commune and proletarian-peasant republic even before the peasant revolution–an integral part of the bourgeois revolution–had taken place, was he not, Narodnik-fashion, trying to skip the capitalist stage on the road to socialism? And did this not imply a Blanqui-type attempt to seize power? Other objections concerned Lenin's proposal to take over the banks and his idea for an immediate change in the party's name to Communist. "I understand the feelings of comrades coming from abroad," said Kalinin, the principal speaker of the meeting, "for [in Europe] the designation Social-Democrat has been defiled. But that is not the case [in Russia]."[18]

Despite the skepticism of the party's leadership, Lenin's views soon became the party's official line; this because of pressures upon party activists from the masses (soldiers, sailors and workers) in and around Petrograd, attracted to the theme of class vengeance which the Theses conveyed.[19] So arose the paradox whereby Lenin's Theses became the channel of sentiment for an early overthrow of the Provisional Government, even though Lenin, barking louder than he intended to bite, was actually opposed to such an act.

The anger of the Petrograd mob toward the government's war policy was exacerbated when, two weeks after Lenin's return, Foreign Minister Miliukov sent the Allies a note reminding them that Russia continued to expect the acquisition of territorial spoils agreed upon in the course of the war. What could better have served to substantiate Lenin's charge that imperialism was a banker's international which used the workers as cannonfodder? Demonstrations in Petrograd early in May echoed the anti-war, anti-government and pro-Soviet motifs of the Theses. Miliukov and Minister of War, Guchkov, were forced to resign but the moderate socialist leaders of the Soviet, replacing the ousted "imperialists" in the new coalition government, found themselves trapped in the same foreign policy dilemma. Fearful of being abandoned by England and France, they promised that Russia's forces, long quiescent against the Germans, would go on the offensive.[20] Lenin, once again, was "proved" correct. Like the Kautskyite Centrists of Germany, the defensist socialists of Russia, seemingly justified the fatherland's war and the slaughter of the working class for imperialist profits.

The number of Bolshevik deputies in the Soviet increased and thousands joined the party.[21] Lenin, euphoric since all his predictions were materializing, was (even while asking his party to *convince* the masses to *vote* themselves into power through their soviets) reluctant to moderate the Theses' strident tone. Thus, even though ever-mounting numbers of demonstrators carried banners inscribed with Lenin's slogans–along with bayonets and pistols–Lenin, like a bemused but neutral observer, watched from the sidelines.

Immediately after the first demonstration, in May, Kamenev, heading the party conservatives, cautioned Lenin against rabble rousing. But Lenin, flushed with success, gave little thought to the limits or the nature of his suddenly acquired power. But uncorking the genie of mass militancy turned out to be much easier than a subsequent attempt to stuff it back into the bottle. When Lenin was accused of adventurism, he indignantly blamed the increasing turbulence upon poor party discipline. If party members employed incendiary rhetoric they were not following orders. (But given the sloppy party organization of that hectic time, the many new and inexperienced members, and the ambiguity of Lenin himself, did such a charge make sense?)

On May 5, Lenin himself, apparently a bit alarmed, termed the slogan "Down with the Provisional Government," which had been used in the demonstration, as adventuristic, so long as the majority of the people were not behind it. "Only then," he pontificated, "will we be for a taking of power into the hands of the proletarians and semi-proletarians [peasants], when the Soviet of Workers' and Soldiers' Deputies stands on the side of our policies and wants to take power into its hands."[23] The party approved Lenin's statement but who else was paying much attention to his words of caution?

There was no doubt that the Bolsheviks were leading the masses, but they could lead them only in one direction–forward–toward a seizure of power.

By scheduling an early offensive, the second Provisional Government incited certain elements of the armed forces beyond the point at which they could be controlled. This circumstance probably gave Lenin *carte blanche* to take the reins in Petrograd as early as June, but he was not thinking along such lines. Nevertheless, a situation was created whereby a rising in his name could (and did) occur, whether or not he sanctioned it. It is understandable that Lenin did not want to dampen the ardor of those restless forces that made him a political Titan. However, since he opposed an early seizure of power, one might ask why he remained so seemingly oblivious to the likelihood of a spontaneous rising? And why, even while preaching caution and patience, did he incessantly pour kerosene upon the flames?

The only sensible answer to this is that Lenin above all desired to impress the West (Germany) with his success in calling forth anti-imperialist revolutionary forces–the very thing he had sought to bring about at Zimmerwald. Also, Russia had become the ideal place from which he could project the image of himself as leader of an all-European revolution. Straddling two worlds–his body in Russia, his soul in Germany –he did not want to dilute the impression, created by all the excitement, that, unlike Europe's, and especially Germany's, Marxists he had remained true to his slogan that the defeat of the fatherland was the least of all evils.

On June 17, at the 2nd Session of the First All-Russian Congress of Soviets, Lenin proclaimed the Bolsheviks' readiness to take power "at any minute." On the same day, his speech at the Congress, in effect, called for a seizure of power by the Soviet of Workers and Soldiers. On June 22 Lenin declared that Europe would laugh at the people of Russia because, having alone of all peoples established organizations truly representing them, they should be holding power. Instead, their soviets, despite possessing arms, were sending socialists into the ministries, who were giving power back to the banks, thus allowing them to continue their predatory schemes. But on June 24, after having on June 22 found it necessary to call off an armed demonstration, Lenin, in *Pravda* ridiculed the "perplexed and frightened" Mensheviks and SRs for suspecting the Bolsheviks of plotting a coup d'état.[24] However, Lenin's very statement, even while denying any secret Bolshevik schemes, nevertheless continued to associate his party with the idea of a seizure of power.

Another explanation for Lenin's ambivalence may be found in his inability, once having formulated a policy (which he called a revolutionary theory) to scrap it until it had proven to be wrong in practice. Since he considered his April "theory" successful, he was unable, until confronted by a roadblock, to contemplate a change of course, or even to recognize that peaceable and violent components could not co-exist in the same program. It was important to Lenin that Soviet Power should be attained only at such time as the workers and peasants became conscious of the fact that all they had to do was to take over. And since Lenin regarded the attitudes of the Petrograd (soldier and sailor) peasants and workers as mirroring the sentiments of all of Russia, Lenin did not think the people of Russia to be with him—that is, conscious of their power—as long as the Soviet majority was not yet dominated by Bolsheviks. On June 18, for instance, Lenin, having learned from Ivan Flerovskii, a Kronstadt activist, that the sailors wanted action instead of meetings and resolutions, he replied that "the impatience of your masses is legitimate, natural. But Kronstadt and Petrograd are not the whole of Russia. For Russia it is still necessary to struggle."[25] Lenin's lack of clarity at this point can also be understood in terms of the world revolutionary general's play-it-safe mentality. So long as he was not sure of a majority backing throughout Russia, he wanted no seizure of power in the capital which might have thrust Lenin into a position uncomfortably similar to that suffered by the Communards of 1871.[26]

Lenin's dilemma between April and July, in sum, lay in his hope that a German revolution might lead the way, even as he was gaining a sense that Russia might actually be first to establish a proletarian, or rather a proletarian-peasant dictatorship. Also, compared to what he perceived as an ignominious rejection by Kautskyite Germany, Russia had given him the treatment of a prophet-hero. Gazing expectantly toward Europe, from atop the smouldering Russian volcano, Lenin found himself completely baffled when suddenly confronted by a demand for decisive action.

Two weeks after the start of the July 1 offensive, the atmosphere in the garrisons reached the breaking point. The Bolshevik leadership, under restraints imposed by the vacationing Lenin, could decide only to take part in the July Days' rebellion for the purpose of "giving it a peaceable and organized character," so that it should not become "an armed seizure of power."[27] Various military contingents, meantime, were certain that Lenin was ready to lead them. Having received nothing but discouragement from the Soviet, in response to their demands that it take power, these troops, on July 17, marched directly to Bolshevik headquarters. Power in Petrograd was Lenin's for the taking, but, told earlier that day, in his Naivol, Finland vacation spot, that serious things probably had begun, Lenin said only that such a development "would be altogether untimely."[28] Having no plan to use the military strike force which his own words had brought into being, Lenin poured ice water on the 20,000 Kronstadt sailors who appeared beneath the balcony of Kseshinskaia Palace on the afternoon of July 17 to get their marching orders. Lenin spoke briefly, complained of illness, and expressed the conviction that the slogan "All Power to the Soviets" would sooner or later became a reality "despite all the zigzags in the path of history."[29] At the moment the zigzags were in Lenin's mind. Denied leadership, the impressive July revolution floundered aimlessly about Petrograd and soon disintegrated.

The advent of loyal troops, enabled the Government to attack the Bolsheviks. Using forged documents, it denounced Lenin as a German agent. Various Bolshevik leaders were arrested, Lenin himself barely escaping, eventually fleeing to a hideout in Finland, from which he did not emerge until months later. One day leader of a growing force and master of Petrograd, Lenin was the next day an outlaw with a price on his head. This dramatic turn of events shocked Lenin into a clearer perception of the state of affairs. He realized how wrong he had been in trying to coordinate the pace of the existing Russian revolution with events in Germany completely beyond his knowledge or control. In any event, by late July and August 1917, Lenin found himself compelled to think first and foremost of his own physical and political survival. The attainment of power in Russia, therefore, became his first order of business. But before proceeding to practical political action, Lenin, as always, had to produce its "theoretical" justification. This explains the conversion of his collection of Marx-Engels writings on the state into *State and Revolution; Marxist Teaching about the Theory of the State and the Tasks of the Proletariat in the Revolution.* In an obvious reference to the intended *coup d'état,* the book's preface described the revolution (the time was August 1917) as "evidently completing the first stage of its development." The revolution in its entirety could be understood "only as a link in the chain of socialist proletarian revolutions called forth by the imperialist war." Therefore, since the masses of Europe as well as Russia would soon be overthrowing capitalism, "the question of the relation of a socialist proletarian revolution to the state" had acquired immediate practical significance.[30]

Lenin was justifying an impending bid for power in Russia by saying it would soon become incorporated within an impending all-European revolution. Lenin's completed book, hastily scissor-and-pasted together, remained true to its origins, a tract primarily applicable to Germany. But with its help, and some references to recent events in Russia, Lenin now intended to press for an early seizure of power in his own country.

In Chapter III of *State and Revolution* Lenin citied from a letter of Marx written to Kugelmann, April 12, 1871, the time of the Paris Commune. Marx wrote:[31]

> If you look at . . . my *Eighteenth Brumaire,* you will see that I declare the next attempt of the French Revolution to be: not merely to hand over, from one set of hands to another, the bureaucratic and military machine—as has occurred hitherto—but to *shatter* it; [the italics, Lenin points out, are Marx's] and this is the pre-condition of any real people's revolution on the Continent. This exactly constitutes the attempt of our heroic Parisian comrades.

After noting Marx's insistence upon violence and the distortion of this view by the "prevailing Kautskyan 'interpretation' of Marxism," Lenin went on to draw further and far less warranted conclusions from the citation.

> Secondly, . . . this extremely profound remark of Marx deserves particular attention in that it states that the destruction of the bureaucratic-military state machinery is "the pre-condition of any real *people's* revolution." [It is most important to note that the italics are Lenin's, not Marx's.] This concept of a "people's" revolution seems strange on Marx's lips. And the Russian Plekhanovists and Mensheviks, . . . who wish to be considered Marxists, would probably explain this expression as a slip of the tongue. To such a crippled program of liberalism have they distorted Marxism . . . .
>
> On the Continent of Europe, in 1871, the proletariat did not in a single country constitute the majority of people. A "people's" revolution, actually drawing the majority into the movement, could be such only if it included both the proletariat and the peasantry. Both classes then constituted the "people." Both classes are united by the circumstances that the "bureaucratic-military state machinery" persecutes, oppresses, and exploits them.
>
> To *shatter* this machinery, *to break it up*—this is the real interest of the "people," of its majority—the workers, and most of the peasants—this is the "pre-condition" of a voluntary union of the poorest peasants with the proletarians; while, without such a union, democracy is shaky, and socialist transformation is impossible.
>
> Toward such a union, as is known, the Paris Commune was striving, but it did not attain its end for reasons internal and external in nature.
>
> Consequently, when he used the phrase "real people's revolution," Marx by no means forgot the peculiar character of the petty bourgeoisie [he spoke of it much and often], and was very carefully taking into account the actual relationship of classes in most of the Continental European states in 1871. From another standpoint, also, he laid it down that the "shattering"

> of the machinery of the state is demanded by the interests both of the workers and of peasants, unites them, places before them the common task of destroying the "parasite" and replacing it by something new.

From the letter's use of the word "people" Lenin drew the inference that Marx had had in mind a union of proletarians and peasants. From the mere word "continent," by which Marx meant France, Lenin derived all of Europe, including Russia. In short, Lenin was saying that Marx would have given his blessings to a revolutionary dictatorship in Russia, based on the proletarians and peasants. So much for theory. But on what force would Lenin's projected seizure of power depend? The July Days had led to a dispersal of the Bolshevik leadership; Lenin, Zinoviev and others going underground, while such party luminaries as Kamenev and Trotsky sat in jail. Numerous rank and filers were quitting the party, other persons were withdrawing their applications to join. Defection of dues-paying members spelled depletion of funds. Those remaining in the party suffered baitings and beatings, *Pravda* was wrecked by hostile elements as were party organs throughout Russia. Regiments which had displayed pro-Bolshevik tendencies during the July Days were either disarmed, as were many factory workers, or sent to the front.[32] In late July and early August things seemed bleak for the Bolshevik cause.

However, Bolshevik fortunes improved rapidly, and it soon became possible for Lenin to think seriously of making a bid for power, and he hastily called upon the August Party Conference to aim for a *coup d'état.* At the same time he began to think up all manner of explanations (actually lame excuses)[33] for his failure of leadership in the July Days, obviously hoping to re-energize the now demoralized XIIth Army militants and the spurned Kronstadt sailors. However, the party rejected his appeals for decisive action and no Petrograd military forces showed signs of being prepared to risk another fiasco.

CHAPTER VI

THE IMPACT OF THE APRIL THESES II–TRIUMPH IN NOVEMBER AND BEYOND

At that juncture, in ways Lenin did not anticipate, there appeared a *deus ex machina.* It came in the form of a military force that was to give practical meaning to the theoretical projection which a desperate Lenin had shot like an arrow into the air. As we shall see, the very April Theses which, in July, had almost torpedoed Lenin, would, ironically, be a principal key to his success in November. This happened thanks to the Latvian Rifle regiments, or *strelki,* organized in 1915 to fight as a national force, within the Imperial Russian Army, against the German invaders of Latvia. In November they acted, in Solzhenytsin's words, as "the midwives of the revolution." But well before that time, that is, within weeks after Lenin's return to Russia, the *strelki* stood ready to give their all for his cause.

The emotions, underlying Latvian pro-Lenin zeal, besides the "natural" Bolshevism of the Latvian peasantry, dating from around the turn of the century,[1] may be ascribed to an anti-Russian spirit which mounted rapidly within this crack troop in the course of 1916. From its very beginning, this sole national minority unit in the Russian army was tremendously disturbed by the German occupation of Courland. In guarding the Riga front the *strelki* were protecting the northern half of their homeland. From the vantage point of the Russian General Staff, however, the Riga sector, although certainly considered of major importance, was just another square on the military chessboard which had to be fitted into the war's total strategy. In March 1916, for instance, the Russian staff ordered an offensive on the initiative of the Verdun-pressured French. But the troops sent forward on the Riga front consisted largely of men whose interest lay in driving the Germans not out of France but out of Latvia. Fighting ferociously, the *strelki* angrily observed how the Siberian forces fighting beside them were busily emptying the pockets of fallen Germans or were quickly raising the white flag of surrender. Although breaking the German lines in three places, therefore, the Latvians found it necessary to withdraw with heavy losses.[2]

A similar pattern resulted when Latvian and Siberian troops were coordinated with the forces of the Southwestern Front in the July 1916 Brusilov offensive. The Latvians hoped to take Mitau. Their Russian chiefs, however, considering the Riga front to be passive, had no desire to lengthen it and thus increase its vulnerability. The sole Russian purpose for the offensive was to prevent a German move southward. The Siberians again fought poorly, once more enraging the Latvians, who thenceforth began to assume that the Russian generals, for purely political reasons, were using them as cannonfodder.[3] In December 1916 two Russian generals described Riga as a "center of revolutionary propaganda,"[4] and anti-Russian hostility was spurred to even greater heights by the "Christmas Battle" of early January 1917.

In fact, the Russian staff had no plan for supporting that disastrous bloodletting. The Latvians had themselves initiated it because of the falsely encouraging comments by a single general. Still, the *strelki* felt sure that they had once again been badly abused.[5] By the time of the March Revolution, the almost 50,000 Latvian soldiers may well have been the most embittered men in the Russian army. Opposing the Russian-designated governing authority in Riga, they immediately lent armed support to the Bolshevik-leaning Riga Workers' Soviet, an early display of soldier's distrust of the Provisional Government.[6]

Inevitably the *strelki* became a foundation for the rapid revival of a Bolshevik-dominated Social-Democratic Party in Latvia which the war had all but destroyed. In turn this helps explain the phenomenal success of the 436th Novaladozhskii Regiment (stationed near Riga) in organizing "the most successful propaganda enterprise in the Russian army," the soldier's paper *Okopnaia Pravda.* In March, then, even before Lenin's return, the Russian Bolsheviks, who had taken control of the regimental committee of the 436th Novaladozhskii Regiment, became an effectively dissident nucleus within the Menshevik-controlled Twelfth Army and had established cooperative relations with the Latvian Social-Democrats. This provided a vital channel of communications between Russian and Latvian Bolsheviks.[7]

All in all, the Latvian radicals were primed to support the most militant directive of the day and the April Theses was clearly that. In addition, and by purest coincidence, the Theses contained ideas and even certain words which seemed tailor-made to fit the condition of the Latvian army. As a result they rallied around Lenin, willing to follow wherever he might lead.

The April Theses were transmitted to the *strelki* through the 13th Conference of the Latvian Social-Democratic party which met in Moscow, May 2-5, just after the April Theses had been adopted as the party program by the Petrograd All-City Conference. The fact alone that the April Theses dominated the agenda of the 13th Conference tells of their special importance to Latvians.[8]

This does not mean to suggest that every single item in the Theses suited the Latvian Bolsheviks' political needs of the moment. For the most part, however, the Theses seemed as though written to their order. The 13th Conference hailed Lenin's proposal for a Third International. The new International, it asserted, ought to admit only such revolutionary organizations as rejected "any kind of nationalism," adding that the Third International ought not to bc "a bloc of separate socialist parties but a party of international revolutionary social democracy" and "that the Third International should be brought to life at the earliest possible moment and be organizationally cemented and actively led from the center of these internal forces."[9]

In Thesis No. 1, Lenin justified "revolutionary defensism, only on condition of the transfer of all power into the hands of the proletariat and the poorest sections of the peasantry joining it."[10] The Latvian Rifles, for the very best of reasons–their own peculiar role in the fighting–regarded the war precisely as a revolutionary defensist war fought by the "poorest sections of the peasantry" against an invader, who if victorious, would preserve intact the estates of the German Baltic barons. "Fraternization," the single word paragraph which concludes Thesis No. 1, was, of course, also attractive to the war-weary Rifles, especially as interpreted in the revolutionary-internationalist sense of the term. Deep-rooted as was their hostility toward the German *Herrenvolk,* they understood very well, being Marxists–many of them literally since their kindergarten days[11]–the difference in class between their baronial landlords and the *feldgrau* proletarians confronting them in the trenches near Riga.

Besides, it was the Germans who, in April, had initiated fraternization attempts by distributing leaflets in the Riga area. These referred to the enemy as "Brothers" and stressed the common desire of troops on both sides for democracy and representative government.[12] But two weeks after the German offer had been made, a Latvian congress of *officer* and soldiers' deputies of the 2nd, 3rd, 4th Latvian Rifles regiments, the 4th Siberian *strelkovoy* artillery brigade and the 2nd Siberian artillery division had countered with a detailed plan for disseminating printed and oral revolutionary propaganda among the Germans. The plan for the so-called "agitational offensive" called for sending elected teams–one agitator and one assistant–equipped with leaflets, into battle zones in which opposing trenches were the shortest distances apart. Artillery covering such areas and those adjoining them was to be given a signal to cease firing for a designated half-hour, it being specified in the plan, signed by a Captain Donvarov, that the agitational effort must not exceed "half an hour."[13] That this incident was quite in line with the mood of the Latvian forces in general is proven by the fact that the entire Latvian contingent, on a subsequent occasion, passed a resolution to end the war by fraternization.[14]

Theses No. 1 also contained Lenin's demand for "a rejection of all annexations in deeds, and not only in words."[15] Lenin had used Courland to illustrate what he meant by an annexed land, going on to describe that then German-occupied portion of Latvia as having "always been annexed to Russia." His use of Courland in this context seems to have risen entirely from the circumstances that he was polemicizing with the Kadet paper *Rech,* which happened to have hit upon Courland to illustrate *its* point on the subject of annexation.[16] Lenin might just as readily have used Finland for his own argument–as indeed he did on a later occasion–or he might have mentioned Poland or the Ukraine.[17] In any case, it was Courland he mentioned in his example and to Latvians offering their lives on the Riga front to save their Fatherland, and to the half million who had been driven from their homes in Courland, Lenin appeared to be focusing attention on their particular plight, highlighting the heroism and the suffering of tiny Latvia.[18]

Thesis No. 2 defined the "present moment in Russia as a *transition* from the first stage of the revolution," which, because of inadequate organization and class consciousness of the proletariat, had allowed power to fall into the hands of the bourgeoisie, "to its *second* state, in which power would rest in the hands of the proletariat and the poorest strata of the peasantry."[19] To the Latvian peasants, in or out of uniform, it may well have seemed that Lenin was making pointed reference to that which, unique within the Russian Empire, had taken place in southern Livonia in the period from March to early May. The sensationally bold initial attempt made by the landless peasantry to challenge the domination of those who held land, had failed at that time only because of eventual loss of nerve or, what might be called, inadequate class consciousness. And so, instead of taking political power, as they could easily have done, the landless, in the end, meekly consented to join with the propertied peasants in the Zemel'nyi Soviet of Southern Livonia. Despite their five-to-one numerical preponderance over the landed, the landless settled for 45 votes in the chamber as against the former's 48.[20]

In Thesis No. 3 Lenin asked his party to deny all support to the Provisional Government, demanding a "complete exposure of all its lying promises."[21] Once more this could be interpreted as exhibiting Lenin's particular interest in the Latvians, as, viewed in retrospect, he seemed to be giving his stamp of approval to the ultra-militant stance taken by the Riga Soviet of Workers' Deputies on 18 March. On that date, the Bolshevik-dominated Riga Soviet, supported by machine-gun units of the Latvian Rifles (placed on strategic heights surrounding the city) had passed a resolution of no confidence in the newly appointed provisional governor of Livonia Guberniia, Andrejs Krastkalns, the former mayor of Riga.[22] The Soviet had also called upon the Council of Social Organizations—Latvian bourgeois groups supporting the Provisional Government—to act swiftly in taking the place of "the Riga German reactionary duma," to institute a people's militia, to oust the existing school Soviets, and so forth. In short, even before Lenin had reappeared in Petrograd, the Latvian Bolsheviks, in marked contrast to the Russian Bureau of the Central Committee, had gone on record as opposing the Provisional Government, which they associated with the probable continuation of German predominance.[23]

Thesis No. 6 carried a message that had no relationship to agrarian conditions in most of the Russian Empire but was written as if to please the bulk of Latvia's peasants. Lenin asked that the agrarian program of Social-Democracy be based upon "nationalization of *all* lands in the country and management of such lands by local Soviets of Fieldhands and Peasants' Deputies. A separate unit of Soviets of deputies of the poorest peasants was to be created and placed in charge of model agricultural establishments (about 100 to 300 desiatins) to be carved out of large estates, as local conditions premitted, and upon the determination of local institutions. This was to be done at public cost."[24]

As noted above, N. N. Sukhanov's recounting of the very first reading of Lenin's Theses, records his astonishment at Lenin's denial of the need for a "parlimentary republic" or a "bourgeois democracy." Lenin said: "We don't need any government except the Soviets of Workers', Soldiers' and Farm-Laborers' deputies!" But what further struck Sukhanov about this comment and probably no others in Russia but the Latvians, was that "Lenin didn't speak of *Peasant Soviets* . . . ." Sukhanov emphasizes the word "Peasant" because he instantly understood the startling significance of this word's omission from Lenin's statement–Lenin having, as it were, erased the real life *muzhik*. Sukhanov continued, "and there were no *farm-labourers'* Soviets, nor could they be formed–as must have been clear to anyone at all equipped for a 'polemic on the agrarian question.'"[25]

Sukhanov, listening carefully to Lenin's speech, had astutely caught the bizarre erasure of the vastly predominant peasant spectrum and its replacement by a class ready to be organized into Farm-Laborers' Soviets but for which, in fact, there was no special basis. What, indeed, was Lenin up to? Why was he presenting to his bewildered party comrades, as though it was something brand new in 1917, his agrarian program exactly as he had drawn it up a decade earlier? The answer to this necessarily spans the passing of the decade in question. As I have explained elsewhere,[26] Lenin's agrarian program, having evolved to its apex in the period 1905-1907, was predicated upon a "semi-proletarian" peasant, who in all respects greatly resembled the Latvian landless peasant, the creature of an advanced agricultural economy, quite different from that of Russia as a whole. But in Russia, what Lenin chose to call a "semi-proletarian" peasant was virtually non-existent. That did not prevent Lenin from believing such a being to exist, if only because his wish-fulfillment world of the future required that it be so. Essentially, Lenin's need to manufacture a mythical peasant type for Russia around 1907, undoubtedly arose out of his need to keep alive for some future date a more successful recreation of the revolution that had failed. And now, in 1917, the time had come, and the propaganda and tactical needs of the moment made it more urgent than ever before that Lenin conceive of and convey through propaganda the idea that Russia teemed with "semi-proletarian" peasants.[27] Admittedly, Russia's agrarian conditions had changed considerably in the decade of Lenin's absence. But the changes did not match Lenin's estimate of the peasants' situation, nor could they have since Lenin had not reexamined the peasant problem in the decade after 1907. And although by 1917 his 1907 depiction of the semi-proletarian (actually proletarian) peasant, familiar with machinery, had some approximation with reality in the Russian Empire as a whole, his analysis of 1907 was still, in 1917, most appropriate to peasant conditions in the Baltic Provinces.

This is not to say that the ideas suggested above ran through Lenin's mind, as, in a fever of excitement, he proclaimed the April Theses. However, he was making his debut in Petrograd as the Marxist leader of a German-inspired European revolution which he expected at any time to be set off by the war. From what has gone before it is clear why he had to camouflage as a capitalistic society that land into which the Messiah of international socialism (Lenin) had just arrived. There was no possibility, in Russia, that Soviets of Farm-Laborers Deputies could be organized. Sukhanov, as mentioned, had instantly perceived this fatal flaw—and many others as well—in the prophet's homecoming address. But in Latvia, whose agricultural methods, as noted, had remained uniquely advanced within the Russian Empire, the bulk of the peasantry (as in 1905) and unlike their Russian fellows, still enjoyed no stake at all in land ownership. That fact alone made Thesis No. 6—proposing that field-hands take over all the land—sound like sweet music to the landless peasants.

But there was more. In preparation for the Seventh All-Russian Conference, Lenin wrote a lengthy elaboration of the April Theses as a draft for the party platform. Captioned "The Tasks of the Proletariat in Our Revolution," it was completed on April 10. Several copies were typed and distributed among party members, and it is safe to assume that one copy, at least, found its way to the Thirteenth Conference of Latvian Social-Democrats. In the draft platform, sections 13 and 14 were jointly titled "The Agrarian and the National Programs." These sections, linking the agrarian program as we shall see, to internationalism, asked the proletarian party to support nationalization of the land and its disposition "totally and exclusively" through "*oblast'* and local *Soviets of the Peasants' Deputies.*" Within those bodies "the party of the proletariat must make clear the need for organizing special Soviets of Fieldhands Deputies and special Soviets of Deputies from the poorest (semi-proletarian) peasants," whose function it would be to control the large model estates made up of land confiscated from landlords. Lenin stressed "above all" the promulgation and immediate attainment of complete freedom of separation from Russia for all nations and peoples who were oppressed by tsarism and forcibly united to Russia and forcibly retained by her, i.e., annexed."[28] From the use of such language, it was only natural that the landless peasants should have received something like the following message: "Lenin wants us poor Latvians to resolve our land problems by ourselves. And, by telling us that we have the right, if we wish, even to separate our nation from Russia, this saintly man is trying especially to assure us that he will no longer tolerate the perennial interference by Russian bureaucrats into the affairs of the Latvian people."

In substance, then, Lenin's Theses came like a Zionist manifesto to a Latvian peasantry, or peasant-proletariat, oppressed by foreigners in their land since time immemorial, until—as destiny's most recent jolt—the war had come to blow them out of their country, dispersing them among the Russian industrial centers. "The Lettish Bolsheviks," writes Trotsky, "torn away from their home soil and wholeheartedly standing in the soil of the revolution, convinced, stubborn, resolute, were carrying on day-by-day and all day long a mining operation in all parts of the country. Their angular faces, harsh accent, and often their broken Russian phrases, gave special expressiveness to an unceasing summons to insurrection."[29]

At the beginning of May, immediately following the Thirteenth Conference of Latvian Social-Democrats in Moscow—in actual fact, a conference of Bolsheviks—*Cina,* the newspaper of those who had been dispersed, returned from its foster home in Petrograd to Riga.[30] At the same time its editorial board, henceforth to be dominated by Bolsheviks, ousted the Mensheviks Skujenieks and Menders. A further indication of the powerful influence of Bolshevism in Latvia was the joint action taken by the Riga Soviet of Workers' Deputies and Latvian Rifles Regiments on May 17. They adopted a resolution favoring solidarity with the Seventh All-Russian

Conference of Bolsheviks. Among the Rifles' deputies present, who had attended the Moscow Concerence, 200 voted for the resolution, one was opposed and eight abstained.[31] Judging from this, the Latvian Rifles, as a unit, had at the time, already decided to back Lenin to the hilt. As Stučka, the leader of the Latvian Bolsheviks, wrote June 4, in a *Pravda* article, "The news that the Latvian Rifles had gone over to the Bolsheviks gave the entire [Latvian] bourgeoisie a jolt such as their class had experienced nowhere else in Russia. And the entire [Latvian] bourgeois press hurled itself upon the Rifles with even greater rage than did the Petersburg bourgeois press against the Kronstadters. . . . At least one Latvian bourgeois paper demanded as early as May 31 that the Rifles should cease being supported and another cried: 'Not a single paper mark to the Bolshevik Rifles.' "[32]

"By June 1917," as Andrew Ezergailis has noted "Latvia was in the hands of the Bolsheviks." If one thinks of the Latvian peasantry of 1917 as being in a condition similar to that of the Hebrews in biblical Egypt, Lenin seemed like the Moses who would lead them out of slavery and through the desert. And in that sense, poetic license being forgiven, Lenin's ten April Theses played a role somewhat like that of Moses' Ten Commandments. Indeed, a year after the event, Stučka, remarking in an article on the first rendition of the Theses by Lenin, referred to them as having greater historical importance than Martin Luther's "famous theses posted 400 years ago (1517) on the doors of the Wittenberg church." Emphasizing particularly the Latvian reaction, Stučka went on to declare that "The Theses opened our eyes to that which the slogan 'All Power to the Soviets of Workers' and Peasants' Deputies meant in actuality and which we ourselves [probably referring to the previously mentioned radical ferment which occurred as early as March in Riga and environs] had realized in practice. The Theses above everything else that happened in Russia opened our eyes to the fact, that the *Soviets themselves* were in fact nothing but [the resurrection of the Paris Commune]. From that moment on we began to see clearly."[33]

The foregoing allows us to understand why, in mid-September of 1917 the Latvian Rifles Regiments joined a Lenin-centered clique of Russian Bolsheviks in a plot to seize power in Petrograd. The *strelki,* as we have seen, attached themselves to Lenin's April program mainly because of its stress on national determination and on the management of collective farms by landless peasants. Most Latvians were landless peasants and in early 1917 a half million of them were refugees from Courland, living in one or another part of the vast Russian empire. Lenin's preaching of an international state, therefore, rather than frightening, encouraged them. They interpreted his views on internationalism, coupled with his promise of national self-determination to mean they would finally acquire control over the agricultural soil of Latvia—after centuries of deprivation—and be rid of both German baronial and Russian imperial domination.[34]

On May 30, 1917, the 48,000 *strelki*—by that time probably the best fighting corps in the rapidly failing Russian army—pledged their loyalty to Lenin and soon thereafter supplied the armed power for the Bolshevik takeover (by July) of unoccupied Latvia. The rapidly leftward acceleration in Latvia of the *strelki* and the landless peasants was matched by their compatriots in Russia, and Smilga of the Russian Bolshevik Central Committee and Latsis of the Petersburg Bolshevik Committee tried vainly, in June and July, to force Lenin's hand in a move to take power. But, up to July, as noted, Lenin had hoped unrealistically to keep the revolutionary current flowing within the peaceable democratic channels of the Soviets, and although he expected ultimately to take power, he wanted to achieve it without resorting to a coup.[35]

The July Days destroyed the delicate timing of Lenin's plan, besides driving him underground. But soon thereafter, deprived of his normal propaganda channels, Lenin opted for a seizure of power as a last ditch hope for recouping his fortunes. However, the Sixth All-Russian Party Congress, which met in late July and August, refused to go along with him.[36] Thwarted by his party, Lenin did not change his plans; indeed he became increasingly impatient to seize power after the Germans captured Riga and, days later, Kornilov tried to become master of Petrograd. Lenin believed the two events to be linked in a government plot to surrender the most radicalized corner of the Russian empire to the Germans. On the other hand, if he could take power before the Germans entered Petrograd, enabling him to make a separate peace with the Germans, this would keep alive his hopes of eventually moving to stage center of the German-European revolution.

The Latvians, needless to say, had borne the bloody brunt of the successful German assault on Riga, which fell September 4. Already suspicious of the Russian government and generals, they viewed Riga's fall, along with Kornilov's coup, exactly as did Lenin, i.e., as a deliberate design to surrender the Baltic Coast to the Germans whom they so passionately hated.

It is further important to understand that by losing Riga the Latvian Bolsheviks had lost what Petrograd was to Lenin: their political power base. That loss was especially painful because in late August the Latvian Bolsheviks had won control over the Riga Council in municipal elections, so that the Latvian capital had actually become Red Riga. (This election was accompanied by a great deal of street fighting–in a sense paralleling the Kornilov episode that was soon to follow.)

In the meantime, Lenin's increasingly urgent appeals for a seizure of power were getting no response in the Bolshevik Central Committee. It was only natural then, that he should throw in his lot with the group most eager and best able to serve his purposes. The Latvians not only were his zealous supporters and willing out of self-interest to resist the German advance, they happened also to be the only force that could, for a time at least, prevent the Germans from marching on Petrograd. Lenin also sought help from other military forces in Petrograd's vicinity, and, of course, he wanted the Central Committee to approve of the plan to seize power. But, as things stood, Lenin could count neither upon an armed group of any significant size, except the Latvians, nor upon a favorable consensus from the Central Committee. So, as a result of necessity, a Lenin-Latvian axis began to take shape. Early in October, Semyon Nakhimson, a Latvian-Jewish intellectual and a member of the Petrograd Military organization, who knew both the Russian and Latvian languages, was selected to effect a coordination between Lenin's clique among the Bolsheviks and Latvian Bolsheviks, led by Stučka. Designated as Commissar of the Latvian Rifles, he also became part of the collective that issued their newspaper, and was given veto power over the collective's decisions.

Initally the plot centered around the Helsinki military base, a logical choice because it was controlled by Smilga, a Latvian Central Committee member. Around October 10, Smilga received two letters. One from Lenin urged him to prepare for a coup, using the forces at his disposal in Finland. Another letter from the *strelki* committed their support to such an effort. A Congress of Northern Soviets, scheduled to meet at Helsinki, was thereupon relocated in Petrograd by Smilga. Thus, on October 24 the deputies of all the militant groups stationed near the capital, had been concerted for action, and at the Congress, *Strelki* Secretary Petersons announced that 40,000 Latvian bayonets, dwarfing all other contingents, stood ready to participate.[37]

At the Central Committee meeting of October 23, Lenin appeared in person to convince the party leaders to vote for a rising. Such a vote was intended to be the green light for the Northern Congress (then convening) to set in motion the deputies of military units representing Narva, Pskov, Helsinki, the Baltic Fleet and the Latvian Rifles. The plan, judging from the way it was eventually carried out, called for 1) a *putsch* in Petrograd, however unsubstantial, compelling 2) Kerensky, as he had in July, to call for help from loyal units of the XIIth Army, at which time 3) the Latvians would take over the XII Army, deciding the issue.

But a crimp was put into the Lenin-Latvian plan. The ambivalence of the Central Committee, although pressured by Lenin and Sverdlov on October 23 to vote for a rising, was not effectuated. An expanded Central Committee meeting was to discuss the question further on October 29, but on October 24, Zinoviev and Kamenev publicly disapproved of the prospective coup, and it is clear that their sentiments were shared by the Central Committee's majority. Therefore the Northern Congress, having received no signal from the Central Committee, did not press forward. However, the plan did not die and the Lenin-Latvian scheme continued to develop further on Latvian soil.

When, on October 29, Lenin again persuaded his still skeptical Central Committee to vote for military action (a much larger group being present than on October 23) the Committee did not know that the preparations begun at the Northern Congress on October 24 (of which the Latvians were a predominant force) had continued to mature. So, the Central Committee had no clear idea of how to proceed, not knowing what personnel it could count on to perform the *coup d'état* and not knowing that the Latvian Rifles stood outside the city awaiting their signal to move.[38]

The Latvians still had certain doubts regarding their course of action. 1) If they moved northward, might not the Cossacks attack them from the rear? 2) Would their drive into the Petrograd region not be viewed as a Latvian intervention in Russian affairs? 3) Would they not, by attacking Petrograd, risk denuding Latvia to Germans, since, if they left the front, might the Siberian troops not desert? But despite these concerns, the task of providing the armed power behind Lenin firmly remained the Latvians' purpose.[39]

Antonov-Ovseenko became assured of this after a visit to Latvia on October 29. He had gone there on Lenin's urgent request to check on the exact mood of the *strelki,* for Lenin had received information making support from the navy highly questionable. Sverdlov had told Antonov-Ovseenko to make sure that the largest possible number of fighters should be ready to take part in the *coup d'état.* Amid ostentatious displays in his honor, Antonov-Ovseenko informed the Latvian party conference at Valka that "revolutionary Petrograd" awaited Latvian help. He discussed tactical details with the leading cadres of the Latvians and was impressed with their enthusiasm, marked by such comments as "We consider ourselves to be the protectors of Petrograd," and predictions that there would be no difficulties in "getting Latvians into action." The anxiety about leaving Latvia defenseless, in view of the possible Siberian desertion was expressed. Even so, the Latvians gave assurance that several regiments would be "ready for Petrograd within a week." Antonov-Ovseenko left Latvia "feeling satisfied that the precise date of troop movements had been set."[40]

The decisive role played by the *Strelki* in the seizure of power seems beyond dispute. At the November 7 meeting of the Second Congress of Soviets, Petersons ("I speak for the Second Lettish Rifles") was greeted with wild cheering when he said: "No more resolutions! No more talk! We want deeds–the power must be in our hands. Let those imposter delegates [professing to represent the army] leave the Congress. The Army is not with them!" On November 12, General V. L. Baranovsky phoned General N. N. Dukhonin at the Staff Headquarters to tell him that the Latvians, all acting "like Bolsheviks" had crushed all military attempts to save the Kerensky government. That same day, John Reed credited the victory over Kerensky in part to the support given the "leaderless," "aimless," "disorganized," "foodless," "artilleryless," and "undisciplined Red Guards" by the "valiant Lettish Riflemen" who had "taken up a position in the rear of Kerensky's bands." This was enough to impel Kerensky's staff to order a retreat which "speedily assumed a disorderly character." On November 13, General J. D. Iuzefovich reported that the Latvian troops were *"completing an organized plan to seize power"* (my italics) and take over the most vital centers. Iuzefovich and members of the General Staff so little understood what the Latvians were up to that they arrived at the conclusion (fantastic in light of the Latvians' hatred for the Germans) that the actions of the *strelki* were undertaken at the behest of the German Army. But aside from suspecting some German plot the generals correctly perceived that the Latvians were following an organized plan, and the *strelki* did take control of vital railway centers, thus preventing the scattered pro-Kerensky forces from reaching Petrograd. On November 28, the Bolsheviks took over *Iskosol* (Executive Committee of the Soviet of XIIth Army).[41] This tied the final knot in the Lenin-Latvian scheme to seize power, which, as far as the Latvian Bolsheviks were concerned had been their objective from almost the moment they had learned of the April Theses. Lenin, as we know, waited until after the July Days to jump aboard the locomotive of history which completely unpredictable circumstances had fortuitously placed at his disposal.

Soon after the coup, fiery Latvian M. Latsis, a founding father of the Cheka, declined the Commissariat of Internal Affairs which Lenin offered him. Stučka, however, accepted the Commissariat of Justice and other Latvian Bolsheviks assumed key positions in the executive organs of the Russian Army in Finland. A contingent of *strelki* became the proletarian guard of the revolution.[42] Smolnyi Commandant Malkov credits the "courageous" Latvians, along with some other contingents "forever half starved," with carrying out "difficult military assignments" during the "harsh winter of 1917-1918."[43] The *strelki* eventually became the nucleus of the Red Army when resistance to Lenin's dictatorship ripened into civil war, General Vacietis of the Rifles being appointed Commander-in-Chief of the Red Army. It can safely be said that the Bolshevik regime would not have survived its first year but for the Latvians' unflagging zeal in Lenin's cause.

A brief sketch of the peripatetic role they played in 1918 will help to illuminate an important link in the chain of events with which this book is primarily concerned. Initially less than 3,000 *strelki* were available to man Lenin's bodyguard at his Smolnyi Headquarters, to staff key positions of the Cheka, and to put down anti-governmental disturbances.[44] The bulk of the *strelki* contingent remained in Latvia until Feburary as a bulwark against the Germans despite the peace negotiations which had been in progress since November-December. (The armistice talks were concluded in November.) That a mere 3,000 could carry out such varied and difficult assignments was a tribute to their sense of discipline, their esprit de corps, which set them apart from the rest of the defeated and demoralized Russian army. The tsarist officers, later to become the counterrevolutionary spearhead, remained politically neutral for several months after the revolution. Within that honeymoon span of Soviet power, the Latvian Rifles put down a demonstration of support of the "one day" Constituent Assembly meeting, crushed a rising of Polish troops under General Dovbor-Bussinski and defeated a group led by General Kaledin.[45]

In February, after Latvia and Estonia had been completely overrun by the Germans, the Latvian troops retreated into Russia proper, where they closed ranks with the 3,000 previously engaged in protecting Lenin's regime. Assuming that Germany would be defeated in the West, the Latvians decided to remain united, in order "at the first opportunity" to return to Latvia "and establish a worker's government." It was thus, in March, that the *strelki* became the foundation of the nascent Red Army. Although groups of Latvians were soon thereafter shipped to many areas of Russia where danger threatened, the Latvians remained organizationally united "telling themselves that the time would come when with their small numbers they would do big things."[46]

And so they did. In April, on orders of War Commissar Trotsky, they eliminated the Anarchist nest of Moscow. Early in July, shortly after the Fifth All-Russian Soviet Congress, guarded by Latvian Riflemen, had met in Moscow and the Left SR's had bitterly attacked the Brest Treaty, Spiridonova expressing her wish that Lenin die, the Latvians, led by Colonel Vacietis, crushed the July 6 revolt in the capital. That Left SR rising had its parallels in various cities along the Volga. In Iaroslav, Military District Commissar Nakhimson, former political commissar of the *strelki* was executed. General Muraviev attempted from Simbirsk to send troops against Moscow, announcing that the Bolshevik government had been overthrown. The Latvians, who had one battalion, one battery, and one cavalry squadron in Simbirsk refused to obey his order. When Muraviev appeared before them to dissuade them of their obstinacy, he was shot as he spoke.[47] Vacietis was then named commander of the Volga forces in Muraviev's place. On July 10, units of the 1st and 3rd Latvian Rifles regiments were sent from Moscow to put down the rising in Murom.

Latvian contingents dispatched from St. Petersburg, Moscow and some Volga cities joined to crush the Iaroslav revolt within sixteen days.[48]

Referring to the condition of the Red Army in July 1918, Trotsky describes its resistance strength as "minimal," noting that city after city, "in the summer of 1918, was falling into the hands of the Czechoslovaks and the Russian counterrevolutionaries who joined forces with them. Their center point was Samara. They conquered Simbirsk and Kazan. . . . After crossing the Volga they were preparing their advance on Moscow."[49]

Because of the lack of effective Russian forces, the *strelki* were sent to troubleshoot the length and breadth of Soviet Russia, and, as Vacietis notes, always fought "hard to maintain Soviet power."[50] Quite logically, then, it fell upon the Latvians to stop the Czechoslovak Legion. The latter was the sole body of troops, besides the Latvians, to retain its discipline after the military debacle of 1917. Ironically, they, like the Latvians, had also been offered the opportunity to become the core of the formative Red Army.[51] However, when the Czechoslovaks unexpectedly turned against the Bolsheviks,[52] to become for a time the most dynamic force among the White and interventionist troops in Siberia, they found themselves pitted against Latvians in the struggle for Kazan. Thus, rather strangely, two non-Russian contingents battled to help (in large measure) decide the outcome of the Russian Revolution. The *strelki* victory at Kazan, Vacietis writes, "made a great impression on the whole country. In Moscow the air became more purified. . . . It was cause for rejoicing."[53] By August the Latvian Rifles had become the bastion of the Bolshevik Eastern Front. But when soon thereafter the Southern Front was menaced, it was again a shock troop of Latvians that was sent to the region of the Povorino Station. By November, the *strelki* exposed to endless bloodshed, had been reduced to 18,000 men. However, their sacrifices to save Soviet Russia had, at last, seemingly brought its reward as the *strelki* were sent to occupy Latvia in the wake of the retreating Germans. The same Latvian land which had provided the incentive for their aid to Lenin in 1917 was a year later, as we shall see, again a useful tool for Lenin's schemes.[54]

CHAPTER VII

LENIN LOOKS WESTWARD

Lenin's April program was initially rejected by the Bolshevik leaders because they believed it made no sense. They were right. The April program foundered in July upon its internal contradictions. The same leaders rejected Lenin's post-July call for a *coup d'état.* That also made no sense to them; it seemed a risky venture for which there was no need, especially since Bolshevism was every day gaining popular strength. If, in 1917, Lenin's sharp tactical turns baffled his comrades, that was so because he could never even offer a hint that it was his desire, personally, to take over the German-European revolution. The Brest-Litovsk peace talks, for the third time within the span of a single year, presented the party's leadership with their typical enigma: they could not understand what Lenin was doing. (This, however, did not prevent a Central Committee opportunist like Stalin from voting with Lenin for a separate peace with the Central Powers, although he was completely in the dark about what was actually motivating Lenin.)[1]

The very process of undertaking negotiations with the Kaiser's diplomats and generals was morally unacceptable to the "idealists" of the party, led by Bukharin, who opted for revolutionary war rather than accept the terms of the Central Powers. But Lenin argued passionately for giving up the non-Russian fringe of the empire as well as the Ukraine for the sake of what he called a Tilsit Peace. This, to the "left communists" seemed a betrayal of anti-imperialism, one of the revolution's *raisons d'étres,* and it also flew straight into the face of Lenin's much heralded devotion to national self determination. Lenin's insistence upon peace at any price was obstinately opposed by many of the party's Central Committee, and, in defending his position, Lenin was, as ever, unable to hint at that which would have made his motives seem sensible.[2]

In the party councils, Lenin even went so far as to deny the imminence of a German revolution. "Our Russian proletariat was not at all to blame for its delay," he said. He thus obliquely criticized the German proletariat at the same time continuing to woo it with assurances that revolution in Germany would sooner or later occur. Meantime, "for us" Russians, the best strategy was to "gain time."[3] Thus Lenin directly contradicted his arguments of a year earlier, describing the Russian revolution as an integral part of a forthcoming German-led European revolution, also sweeping from its foundations his claims of early 1917 that the Russian revolution was an inevitable outgrowth of the "imperialist war." Principles of a bygone era were easily sacrificed to Lenin's desire, above all, to secure the then shaky existence of his regime. (The notion of an eastern reserve army of revolution may conceivably have shaped his thinking.) During the Brest negotiations Lenin was willing to accept help from the Allies *against* the Germans; anything to assure the survival of his Russian base of power.[4] Allied help, however, failed to materialize, still Lenin managed to bring home the "separate peace." It was ratified by Vtsik, March 16, despite bitter protests from Left Bolsheviks and the Left SR's with whom the Bolsheviks then still shared a coalition government.

The vast territories surrendered by the peace, infuriated elements hitherto neutral to the political settlement of 1917. This greatly amplified the civil war's scope as various mutually hostile factions were able to join forces against the traitorous Bolsheviks. The thrust of the White armies soon gravely threatened Lenin's power, but from the point of view of his West-oriented aims the initial effects of Brest-Litovsk were immensely beneficial.

A Soviet Russian embassy was opened in Berlin to become the source of money and advice to the leftist press and parties. Lenin had gained his long-sought opportunity for making direct contact with the German workers. He could finally propagate Bolshevism from within Germany, through the Soviet embassy. Besides buying information from officials of German ministries, the embassy also sent out "anti-war and anti-government literature to all parts of the country and to the front," and spent large amounts to arm revolutionaries.[5] In addition, events in Europe generally, after Brest-Litovsk, seemed to justify Lenin's policy of peace at any price. By the late summer of 1918, Lenin, despite the razor's edge on which his power tottered, was predicting the "unconditional and inevitable" approach of the German revolution. September headlines in *Izvestiia* proclaimed "the collapse of World Imperialism" and early in October, Lenin declared that the "barely begun" German crisis would "inevitably culminate in the transfer of power to the German proletariat."[6] Lenin's ardent aspiration to lead that revolution seemed within reach and his chances for success appeared to be enhanced by a development which, a year earlier, he could not have anticipated. The Russian Soviet state, history's first socialist regime, had begun to inspire the founding of additional soviet governments. All of these were as yet within the confines of the former tsarist empire, but each was being prepared, for unison with the RSFSR via a regime which would metamorphose from a status of nominal independence through one allowing for federation, leading, of course, to "fraternal" working class unity. In short, Lenin's revolutionary machine–the army of a "Marxist" government exporting the revolution to other countries in "democratic" fashion–was actually in progress. However, Lenin had not foreseen that the process would occur in the way it did.

In November 1918, Commissar of Nationalities, Stalin, wrote a *Pravda* article, whose very title, "The October Revolution and the National Question," encapsulates, *in toto,* Lenin's masterplan. The revolution, "besides giving land to the peasants and the factories to the workers,"–the dictatorship of the proletariat–had proclaimed "self determination for the laboring masses of oppressed peoples." The "genuinely *socialist*" revolution which Stalin went on to elucidate, was simply what might be called "Lenin's Law," i.e., the establishment of the proletarian dictatorship in a single country is followed by the expansion abroad of revolutionary power.

Writes Stalin: "The revolution which started in the centre. . . was bound to spread to the border regions [of the former Russian empire]." This is a major historical distortion because within each of the minority peoples the revolution's course was determined by each country's peculiar features. The "bourgeois-nationalist" elements were, of course, both anti-Russian and anti-Socialist, but even the Marxists of most nationalities were largely anti-Bolshevik as well as anti-Russian. The Georgian Mensheviks, for instance, took power in their country and held it for two years. The way things actually happened, however, did not prevent Stalin from envisioning a "revolutionary tide" washing "from the North all over Russia." This tidal wave encountered dams "in the shape of the 'National Councils' and regional 'governments' (Don, Kuban, Siberia) which had been formed prior to the October Revolution." This misrepresentation of the course of events certainly reflected the image which Lenin wanted to convey. Stalin glibly writes that the bourgeois national governments had allied themselves to "imperialism," when, in truth, they were desperately clutching at any straw in the hope of preventing their countries from reverting to the status of Russian colonies. As Stalin tells it, they attracted to themselves "all that was counter-revolutionary in Russia,"–i.e., help where they could find it–to become whiteguard "national" regiments.

Besides the "national governments," as Stalin has it, there were "in the border regions national workers and peasants," (note this cumbersome phrase to distinguish the heroes from the villains) who had "organized even before the October Revolution in their revolutionary Soviets patterned on the soviets in the centre of Russia." With that statement Stalin admits that the revolution split each nation of the Russian empire along class lines, which, in turn, destroys his story of occasional dams resisting the revolutionary tide. It really makes no sense to designate the nationalist elements who elected to resist Red Army-supported native Bolsheviks ("national workers and peasants") as alien or artificial phenomena. After thus contradicting himself, Stalin concluded his article as though it had proven that "a socialist alliance of the workers and peasants of Russia" had been formed "against the counter-revolutionary alliance of the bourgeois national 'governments' of the border of Russia."

Stalin had twisted the concept of centralization into self determination; but then this, in essence, had always been Lenin's way of dealing with the subject. Stalin justified his definition by asserting that it was false to describe "the fight of the bourgeois governments as a struggle for national emancipation against the 'soulless centralism' of the Soviet regime" because "no regime in the world [prior to Soviet Russia had ever] permitted such extensive decentralization" or had "ever granted to the people [of the Russian empire] such complete national freedom." Therefore, the resistance of the border governments was nothing less than "a fight of bourgeois counter-revolution against socialism."

As though attempting further to solidify his contention, Stalin observed that the "national" and "regional" governments could not bear the brunt of the twofold attack from outside "by the Soviet power of Russia and from within by 'their own' workers and peasants." This statement, naively boasting of Soviet intervention against so-called "bourgeois-nationalist" governments, fully exposes Lenin's "self determination" as a fraud. The same doctrinaire "Lenin-think" allowed Stalin to charge the "national governments" with being "obliged" to seek assistance against "their own" working classes from Western imperialists, "the age-old oppressors and exploiters of nationalities of the world." With such absurd reasoning, Stalin blamed the Western imperialists for Russia's oppression of the Baltic peoples, the Poles and other East European nations.

Since the October Revolution had expanded from its Russian center to "embrace a number of border regions," Stalin predicted that it would cross beyond the borders into "the enslaved East and the bleeding West." The latter, torn by war, would be first to welcome the winds of revolution emanating from Russia, as was indicated by the worker-soldier risings in Austria-Hungary and Germany and by "the formation of Soviets of Workers and Soldiers Deputies" in those countries. "The mortal sin of the Second International and its leader Kautsky," Stalin went on, applying Lenin's world war lingo to Soviet imperialism, "consists, incidentally of the fact that they have always gone over to the bourgeois conception of national self determination, that they have never understood the revolutionary meaning of the latter, that they were unable or unwilling to put the national question on the revolutionary footing of an open fight against imperialism, that they were unable or unwilling to link the national question with the question of the emancipation of the colonies. The obtuseness of the Austrian Social-Democrats of the [Renner and Bauer type] consists of the fact that they have not understood the inseparable connection between the national question and the question of power."[7] The last sentence reflects not only Lenin's attempt to connect "inseparably" the idea of proletarian dictatorship to that of self determination but also Stalin's desire to link his 1913[8] pamphlet on self determination to what it had become in practice: the official manual of the westward moving Russian revolution.

The connection between events in the Russian empire and the supposedly parallel occurrences in Central Europe is also stressed in Stalin's *Zhizn' National'nostei* article of November 17, 1918. Captioned "Partition Wall," Stalin refers to constantly multiplying "proletarian uprisings" in Germany and Austria-Hungary, in Finland, Estonia, Latvia, Lithuania,

Belorussia, Poland, Bessarabia, the Ukraine and the Crimea.[9] The first two on that list, hardly by accident, are quite casually placed in the same basket with the Russian empire nationalities.

The word "soviet" was indeed being used among retreating and rebellious German and Austro-Hungarian troops. But occurrences outside the Russian empire were not of the same order as those taking place inside it, where Russian Bolsheviks and/or Red Army contingents had a direct part in shaping events. Still, in the mere fact that Soldiers' Councils were springing up and had begun to attract the peoples of Central Europe (if only because they associated the term "soviet" with the idea of peace) had to bring joy to Lenin. For if he had really sold Europe on the notion that the soviet, risen on Russian soil and out of Russian conditions, was actually a continuation of the Paris Commune, as he said it was, and therefore equated to "proletarian dictatorship," such an interpretation in the West could only help authenticate his qualifications for assuming the leadership of the German revolution.

The increasing popularity, in Germany, of the Russian-style soviet, prompted Kautsky, in August 1918, to write a pamphlet[10] attacking Lenin's "proletarian regime" for being undemocratic and, therefore, neither socialistic nor Marxist in nature. Kautsky also derided Lenin for advertising his regime as being the kind of proletarian dictatorship Marx had had in mind. Kautsky explained quite properly that Marx had nowhere made it clear what the phrase meant in practical application.[11] Lenin enragedly counter-attacked. In *The Proletarian Revolution and the Renegade Kautsky,* he again explained that "the proletarian dictatorship" was "the heart of Marxism" which Kautsky and other "vulgarizers" had "deliberately ignored." Lenin used the debate to take the ideological offensive and to let the German workers know that it was specifically Bolshevism, i.e., Lenin's creation, which had consistently been "correct" in defining "the revolutionary situation in Europe." Bolshevism had become "world Bolshevism, with an idea, a theory, a program and a tactic that distinguished it completely from social chauvinism and social pacifism [that is, from Right wing and Centrist German socialism.] " Bolshevism, Lenin boasted, had "created the ideological and tactical foundation of a . . . truly proletarian and Communist International." Bolshevism had "popularized throughout the entire world the idea of the 'dictatorship of the proletariat'" and had "translated these words from the Latin first into Russian, and then into *all* the languages of the world" and had demonstrated its ability (Lenin's argument here was actually counter-productive)–even in a backward and besieged country to enable the workers and peasants to hold out for a whole year while battling the entire world. At the same time it has been creating "a democracy immeasurably higher and broader than all previous democracies" thus providing the incentive for "tens of millions of workers and peasants to move toward the actual attainment of socialism."[12] Lenin's pride in Bolshevism's ability to survive what Russia went through is testimony to his indifference toward the sufferings of millions as long as his personal image was enhanced. The bold and reckless ventures so characteristic of Lenin, (which so often mystified his closest associates) grew out of his total concentration on attaining his goal of the moment.[13] Such a goal, of course, was always proclaimed as meant to benefit the world's toiling masses.

Only the disparity between Lenin's real and his pretended purposes can explain Lenin's January 1918 proposal that socialism be introduced in Soviet Russia within months. Shortly after Lenin's death in 1924, Trotsky tried to make this bizarre notion seem reasonable. "Now," he wrote, "these words seem quite incomprehensible. Is it not a mistake? Are not decades or years meant? But no, it is no mistake . . . . I remember very well that in the [early] sessions of the Council of People's Commissars at Smolny, Ilyich repeatedly said that within half a year socialism would rule and that we would be the greatest state in the world. The Left Social Revolutionaries [then still part of the ruling coalition] and not they alone, [i.e., Bolsheviks as well] raised their heads in question and surprise . . . but were silent."

By means of such a startling proposal, Trotsky explains, Lenin was attempting to shock the ruling oligarchy to think in terms of the new society's "socialist structure," a mode of perception still completely foreign to them.[14] Trotsky could, of course, only hazard guesses as to what had been on Lenin's mind, and a eulogy, in any case, deals gently with the departed. But unless he was insane, Lenin could not really have believed possible such a swift transition to socialism of a technologically underdeveloped country, which, moreover, had just gone through catastrophic dislocations. But why did Lenin keep proposing the impossible? The answer to this question must center around Lenin's inability to admit his true motives. Lenin's personal goals required him to create the impression, counter to all reality, that socialism was actually becoming the Russian way of life. Then, when the German revolution occurred, its would-be leader, Lenin, could claim not only to have led a successful revolution which had brought to life the dictatorship of the proletariat, but he could also serve up the building of a planned economy as proof of the Marxian nature of the Russian revolution despite the fact that it had risen in an agrarian society.

From November 1917 to the Fall of 1918, a year marking the collapse of Imperial Germany, Soviet economic policies changed rapidly from initial socialistic gestures (including calamitous worker-run factories and a few state farms) to an ephemeral (April-May 1918) experiment with "state capitalism" anticipating NEP, to the introduction of "War Communism,"[15] a euphemism for total state control, made necessary by the growing White menace.[16] During these periods, each an experimental accommodation to urgent needs of the moment and certainly not carefully thought through, Lenin invariably described the Soviet economy as advancing along the road to socialism. Around May 1, 1918, he wrote that the task of organizing the economy "for the purpose of a new and higher level of production and distribution of products on the basis of socialized large scale machine (labor) production" was what constituted "the main content–and the major condition for the complete victory of the socialist revolution, which began in Russia on November 7, 1917."[17] Again, at the July 29 session of Vtsik, he remarked that Soviet Russia, despite the burdensome peace treaty, had "won freedom to carry on socialist construction at home, and that our advances along this road *now becoming known in Western Europe, constitute elements of propaganda* [my italics] infinitely more effective than any previous ones."[18]

Lenin wanted it on record, particularly for the world outside, that Russia was not merely headed toward but was already living under socialism. It was, then, as a defender of something not yet in existence that Lenin wrote his reply to Kautsky. And who can display greater fury than one who must cover over with words what is lacking in fact? According to Bonch Bruevich, Lenin was "literally aflame with rage," and "working whole days, till late at night, writing this stupendously powerful work."[19]

Although socialism, as Lenin well knew, was light years away from Russia, he was on solid ground when he challenged Kautsky to deny that

Bolshevism "more effectively than any party in any country" had "helped the development of the proletarian revolution in Europe and in America" and that "the victory of the proletariat in Russia had given a boost not only to the European but also to the world revolution." Resting his case, Lenin added, "A single country could not have done more."[20] Lenin was not trying to praise Russia. He was praising Bolshevism, thereby shouting out that the triumph in Russia had been his work. This implied that he could do as much for other countries.

Kautsky's pamphlet, designed to prove to Germans that the Soviet form did not apply to them, delivered especially telling polemical blows by ridiculing the agrarian foundation of Lenin's "proletarian dictatorship."[21] Only through vilification and obfuscation could Lenin parry this powerful and literally unanswerable thrust.[22] However confused Lenin's argument, the course of events and, above all, the collapse of Germany was on his side. Regardless, therefore, of his pamphlet's lack of logic, he was able to conclude it with an exultant note.

> P.S. The above lines were written on November 9, 1918. On the night of the ninth-tenth came the news from Germany of the beginning of a victorious revolution, starting in Kiel and other northern towns and ports where the power passed into the hands of the Soviets of Workers' and Soldiers' Deputies, then in Berlin, where power also passed into the hands of a Soviet. The conclusion which I still had to write to my pamphlet on Kautsky and the proletarian revolution is now superfluous.
>
> November 10, 1918.[23]

Power in Germany was falling into the hands of the Soviets. Had not the German proletariat itself refuted Kautsky? Had it not accepted the Leninist-Bolshevik formulation of the dictatorship of the proletariat despite its Russian origins? Lenin was obviously euphoric about the prospect of leading the German proletariat in the task of spreading Soviet socialism throughout the world. The final step along the road would, of course, have to be the actual establishment of the Third International. This would make Lenin's transition from Russian to German world leadership a simple matter of transferring his headquarters from Moscow to Berlin, since national boundaries would have ceased to exist except as lines on a map.

Lenin bent every effort to bring the Third International to life at the earliest moment. He regarded extreme haste as urgent for two reasons. One was the war's end which had reopened direct contact among European socialist parties so that efforts were in progress to reconstruct the Second International. Lenin did not want the European and especially the German proletariat to be distracted from his plan to form a new international, especially at the moment when everything seemed propitious for him to become its acknowledged founder and leader. Late in December 1918, therefore, Lenin, through the Bolshevik Central Committee, sent a radio-telegram to "all those standing on the position of a Third International."[24] Early in January 1919, after a meeting attended by Lenin, Chicherin and two others, an actual invitation was drafted, inviting "all parties opposed to the Second International to come to a Moscow founding congress of a third international."[25] Lenin was obviously trying to focus attention upon his particular role in galvanizing communists of all countries to rally to the support of the "already practically existing international," at the same time as he was trying to provide opposition to "the international of betrayers which is formed with the obvious aim of creating a stronghold against the rapidly developing world proletarian revolution."[26]

An equally important reason why Lenin wanted a Communist International to be founded at once was that Allied intervention against the Bolshevik regime, supposedly initiated to restore the Eastern front against the Central Powers, continued unabated despite the latter's surrender. Lenin was certain that the interventionist governments would try to fill the newly-created East European power vacuum with anti-Bolshevik bastions, and would, to that end, not hesitate to ally themselves with the Germans.

On November 6, 1918, Lenin predicted "that the Anglo-French capitalists" were about to join forces with former foe Wilhelm "to try to strangle the Soviet Socialist Republic, having realized that it has ceased to be a socialist experiment, but has become the actual nucleus of the world socialist revolution."[27] Lenin's reasoning–an echo of similar views expressed on the eve of the November seizure of power[28]–was still based on the simplistic notion of capitalism as a bloc of interventionist bankers. In truth, the French and British, after all the bloodshed, were far from ready to embrace the Germans. However, because the Allies had no way of sending troops to protect the small nations of Eastern Europe from Bolshevik inundation, Article XII of the November 11 Armistice Agreement demanded that German troops remain in all former Russian territory until such a time as the victors deemed the situation suitable for complete withdrawal.[29]

The "understanding" between Allied and German governments concerning "former Russian territory" grew to major consequences in Latvia because only in that country was Bolshevik power strong enough to hold on for an extensive time. Also, because of traditional German roots in the Baltic countries and a well-developed German plan to colonize that area,[30] Latvia became the nucleus of a design to resume the German invasion of Russia, using as a pretext the fear that Bolshevism would spread to Western Europe. Representing the Republican German government, trade union leader and ardent pan-German, August Winnig, arrived in Riga, in late October 1918, and was designated Plenipotentiary of the Reich for the Baltic Lands. It was Winnig's belief that the traditional German *Ostpolitik* should continue to be pursued, securing German influence in the Baltic and keeping open the German path to the East.

The task at hand was to keep the Bolsheviks out of Latvia, and in this immediate aim, Winnig coincided with the Latvian Democratic Bloc and the Latvian National Council, the two groups then about to coalesce into the Government of the Latvian Republic. As Plenipotentiary of the Reich his first official acts, promulgated three days before the proclamation of the Latvian Republic, were designed to strengthen all Latvian parties against the Bolsheviks. Thus, he released from prison all political offenders but the Bolsheviks, an action supported by the Latvian Socialists, and on the same day, November 15, he called off the censorship of the press and the rule against public meetings. However, the prohibition against publishing newspapers without German permission remained in effect. Winnig permitted the Socialists to publish their paper and supplied them with the means to do so. He denied the Bolsheviks the same privilege and turned down most of their requests to hold public meetings.

At one of the Bolshevik meetings, Winnig took it upon himself to attempt a mass conversion; to explain that history showed the most important revolutions to have been the least violent, whereas bloody upheavals had often proved needless and of no great historical importance.

"And so," he relates, "I spoke as though to workers in Leipzig or Hamburg. These people listened attentively enough, but when I had gone they ridiculed me." A report described what had occurred at the meeting after he had departed.

> A voice from the assemblage: "Why was the German Menshevik allowed to speak?"
>
> The chairman: "He would otherwise not have permitted us to hold this meeting."
>
> Voice: "We have been insulted."
>
> Chairman: "You should have told him that when he spoke."
>
> Voice: "We shall still tell it to him. We shall yet wade in German blood up to our ankles."
>
> Chairman: "That is our hope but we may not speak of it yet. The Menshevik has the power at present."[31]

Judging by what happened shortly thereafter, the above bit of dialogue makes it clear that the Latvian Bolsheviks, whose strength was centered in Riga, knew that a *strelki*-headed Red Army invasion was on its way. Such a concentration of a Bolshevik strike force in Latvia, as we shall see, was the starting point for Lenin's hoped-for conquest of Germany and, after Germany, the world.

The Foundation of the Comintern, March 1919

In expressing his contempt for the leadership of German Social Democracy throughout the war, Lenin, by not exempting the left socialists from attack, implicitly included the entire party membership in his criticism. Lenin's growing animosity toward the procrastinating German Marxists, already quite evident in his October 1918 "renegade" Kautsky diatribe, was further indicated in December, when he invited delegates to a meeting of "an already practically existing international." That such an important step—the prospective creation of a third international—could be taken without Lenin's even attempting to consult such personages as Liebknecht and Luxemburg, proves that Lenin was spitting on all German leaders, who would soon be replaced by himself. Such an interpretation of Lenin's thinking is given even greater substance when it is remembered that the Red Army, at the very time the radiogram invitation went out, was replacing the retreating Germans in Estonia, Latvia and Lithuania (as well as in Ukraine and Belorussia) and that *Izvestiia* on December 25, announced that the impending conquest of the Baltic countries was the prelude to Russia's "red proletariat" influencing "the revolution in Germany."[32]

The Lenin-Latvian Bolshevik plotting of November 1918, had, as we recall, been preceded the year earlier by the successful plot to use the Latvian *strelki* in the November seizure of power. In 1918, in a far from unrealistic plan, the *strelki* were being cast in the role of spearhead for a march into a Germany, torn, economically chaotic, demoralized by a lost war, and in many respects resembling Russia of 1917. Out of that invasion, it was no doubt hoped, there would come the seizure of power in Berlin by pro-Bolshevik forces. The obvious political concomitant to such a military-revolutionary action in the heart of Europe was Lenin's attempt, at about the same time, to found the Communist International.

It should be noted that an essential feature of the export of Sovietism to thc West would be exactly that which Lenin, a year or so earlier, had expected the eastward driving Germans to accomplish, i.e. to allow each conquered nation, rolled over by the victorious revolutionary army, a brief period of showcase independence. That was to be followed by a "popularly determined" union of its working class with that of other nations, notably with that of Russia.

In the light of this scenario, Latvia was the most important square on the geopolitical chessboard. This the most westward lying nation of the Russian empire, could not be confused with ethnic Russians (like sovietized portions of Belorussia and the Ukraine) and could, therefore, be held up to the world as a European soviet republic. If the first act of the play was the concentration, in November, of the *strelki* in the Red Army along the Latvian frontier (news of this, as we know, had swiftly filtered into Riga) the next move, early in December, was the founding of an "exile" Soviet Latvian Republic in Russia to counter the previous month's formation of a Latvian "bourgeois" republic. Stučka headed the "exile" government and announced with great assurance that the First Congress of Latvian Soviets would convene in Riga on January 13. Again, as on the occasion of the Lenin-Latvian collaboration in 1917, Sverdlov was closely in touch with the situation (as, of course, was Lenin) and it is no surprise to learn that Sverdlov was "invited" by Stučka to attend the festive occasion.[33]

"Slowly but surely," wrote Stalin on December 15 in *Zhizn' Natsional'nostei,* "the tide of the liberation movement is rolling from East to West, into the . . . regions" occupied by Germany and Austria.

"Slowly but just as surely the 'new' bourgeois republican 'governments' of Estonia, Latvia, Lithuania and Belorussia are receding into oblivion and making way for the power of the workers and peasants. *The partition wall between Russia and Germany is crumbling.*" (My italics. The phrase "partition wall" was also used to caption Stalin's November 17 article and suggests an imminent breakthrough to the West.) The article briefly reviewed the "liberationist" activities of native Bolsheviks, aided by the promise of support from the RSFSR in the areas of the Russian empire from which the occupation troops had recently withdrawn. Such "support" included the passing of Kharkov "under control of the Soviet of Workers and Peasants Deputies, as well as territories in the far south of Russia, in the North Caucasus, where [various peoples] are passing over in whole groups to the Soviet power and arms in hand are freeing their lands from the hired bands of British Imperialism. . . . At the Centre of all these stupendous developments, is the standard bearer of world revolution, Soviet Russia, inspiring the workers and peasants of the oppressed peoples with faith in victory and supporting their liberation struggle for the benefit of world socialism," although, of course, "Soviet Russia has never looked upon the Western regions as its possessions." This statement, denying any imperialist plans by Soviet Russia for the Western parts of the Russian empire was made together with what amounted to implicit claims of legitimate title to formerly tsarist-dominated areas in the South and East. The difference in emphasis was meant to quiet the fears of Western Europe regarding a Red imperialism—the Baltic countries serving as illustrations—and to assure them of beneficent Soviet intentions. Regarding the West—i.e., the Baltic countries—Stalin wrote that Soviet Russia "had always considered . . . these regions [to be] the inalienable possession of the laboring masses of the nationalities inhabiting them." The deception lies in the code words "laboring masses," for the workers of any nation were expected to join Soviet Russia because of the "fraternal" bonds among the nationless working classes.

Referring to the Soviet advance in Latvia, Stalin had "information that the establishment of a Provisional Soviet Government is to be officially proclaimed in Latvia within the next few days." Stalin's "information" was, of course, correct. Two days later–December 17–the Provisional Soviet Government of Latvia "announced the transfer of state power to the Soviets," stating, "We know that . . . behind us stands the RSFSR with which we shall continue to be closely bound, *and not by external ties alone.*"[34] This hinted at the coming federal association of Soviet Latvia and RSFSR.

On December 22, Stalin underlined the immense importance of Latvia and the Latvian Rifles Regiments, or *strelki,* in breaking through the "partition wall," at the same time expressing indignation at the attempts of "a government that calls itself socialist" (he meant Germany) to intervene. As noted earlier, Germany, despite defeat, had not yet given up its *Ostpolitik.* "The revolution," wrote Stalin, "is mounting swiftly and irresistibly in Latvia. The glorious Red Riflemen have already captured Valka and are victoriously surrounding Riga. The recently formed Soviet Government of Latvia is leading the Latvian workers and landless peasants to victory with a sure hand. Exposing the equivocal policy of the Berlin Government and the German occupation forces, it declares unreservedly, 'We . . . reject all intervention on behalf of [the German barons and Ulmanis regime] even if such intervention is threatened by a [German] Government that calls itself socialist.' The Latvian Soviet Government relies only on the assistance of the revolutionary proletariat of all countries and of Russia first and foremost. It says: 'We call for aid and expect it from the genuinely revolutionary proletariat of the whole world and especially of the RSFSR.' Need it be said that the Soviet Government of Russia will render every possible assistance to Latvia, now in process of liberation, and to its heroic Riflemen?"[35]

Stučka's early December prediction, not surprisingly, was right on target. The proclamation of the Latvian Soviet Republic took place on January 13 and "foreign dignitaries" Sverdlov and Kamenev were present to mark the occasion. Kamenev recalled the heroic days of November 1917, when of all the world's people–the separate identity of Latvia being stressed for obvious reasons–only "our brothers," the Latvian Rifles aided in the seizure of power.[36] Somewhat later that month, Latvia's President Stučka, playing his role to the hilt, protested vigorously, when Germany, disputing the arrest of a German diplomat in Riga, addressed its complaint to the government of Russia rather than to that of "independent" Latvia.[37] In the meantime, however, the "rulers" of Soviet Latvia were proceeding rapidly to establish legal bases for union with Soviet Russia, with the "approval" of Sverdlov.[38] On January 17, the Latvian Congress of Soviets decided to base its internal functioning upon the Constitution of Soviet Russia and "to accept without change its basic statutes." The Congress further entrusted the Latvian Soviet of People's Commissars "to work out a new situation of cooperation between the RSFSR and Latvia . . . in their common (working class) struggle against the intervention of foreign imperialists. . . ." Except for minor differences rising out of peculiarly Latvian conditions, the Government of Soviet Latvia became a fairly accurate replica of the Soviet Russian government. "Because of economic conditions peculiar to our land," notes Stučka, "we decided not to emulate slavishly the construction of Soviet power of the RSFSR." Early in February, Russian currency was officially introduced into Latvia.[39]

These rituals were clearly intended as displays to the West of how "self determination" would work out in the course of the advancing world revolution. Through all this Lenin himself remained largely inconspicuous, perhaps to prove that all had transpired in a natural and unplanned manner.[40] Latvia, like the Ukraine and Belorussia, had passed through its phases of independence under a revolutionary government, and, as was to be expected, had opted for fraternal unity. In fact the process was so artificial that Stučka, in a labored polemic, tried to explain to his Latvian Bolshevik cohorts the "slippery" business of Latvian independence.[41] Stučka hardly made things clearer by acknowledging that the Latvian Communists in Petrograd–the party leaders, including himself–had known in November of the "impending advance" of the Red Army into Latvia. Therefore, he wrote, they had agreed to the Russian proposal to proclaim "the independence of Latvia," having correctly anticipated "that the freedom of Latvia would in actuality be won by the Latvian proletariat. Only malicious foes and ignorant war correspondents," he added, "can speak of the conquest of Latvia by the Russian Red Army." Late in November, Stučka had "explained" the paradox of "internationalistic nationalism" in words which might even today be used as an apologetic for Russian imperialism: "*Either a countless number of powerless and tiny states, all under the heel of imperialism, or the same number of Soviet republics within a single solid socialistic unity.* There is no other way."[42]

Showcase Soviet Latvia was especially concerned with demonstrating to the West that the advancing Soviet revolution held no mortal perils for the European bourgeoisie. In January, President Stučka appeared before a bourgeois group to assure it that there was no danger of a massacre, that the "irresistibly advancing" Red movement did not distinguish between nationalities. "We want equal rights for all people. We do not even want to kill capitalists," but only to "destroy their economic power . . . . As soon as they have become workers the (class) distinction will be removed."

In sum, Lenin, systematically, since the war's end had been constructing the scaffolding for the soon-to-be-erected Third International. In April 1919, the Riga Soviet announced that the wall between Russia and Germany was "crumbling," bluntly declaring that Latvia was "the gateway through which the Russian revolution must invade Western Europe." It was, the Riga Soviet proclaimed, the *strelki's* duty "to reach the Prussian frontier as quickly" as possible.[44] "Through the collapse of German imperialism and the outbreak of the revolution in Hungary the Red troops can now venture to push forward against Europe in the north and south (through the Ukraine) simultaneously; the divisions of the Red Army fighting in Latvia have to deliver the decisive blow." At the same time, as was done in Latvia by Stučka, Lenin, even while promising military aid for Hungary, also kept broadcasting that Bolshevism in the West would bear a humane face, different from that which it had been compelled to wear in Russia, that Hungary had provided a better example than had Russia of the peaceable way in which Soviet power should be introduced, and that where there was no resistance to historical inevitability there was also no reason for the bourgeoisie to fear violent measures against their persons.[45]

Of the fifty delegates, associated with thirty-nine countries, who convened in Moscow on March 2, 1919, all but a few happened at the time to be in Russia and did not have to smuggle their way through the anti-Soviet blockade. Many of them had for years been expatriates but were, nevertheless, accredited with representing their native lands.[46] Since the predominant majority of the "delegates," in fact, represented only themselves, one can imagine the excitement created when a delegate directly from Germany (one of two dispatched) unexpectedly appeared. Eberlein was a real representative of a Communist party which had risen beyond the confines of the former Russian empire: the KPD, which had just been founded by Liebknecht and Luxemburg. Most significantly, he came from the country referred to in the Communist Manifesto as the heartland of communism and the country whose proletariat Lenin, trying to undercut its native leaders, had been so ardently wooing.

But once again, as at the Women's and Youth conferences in Bern and at Zimmerwald, Lenin was doomed to frustration by the democratic and anti-centralist spirit of German Socialism. Luxemburg, on January 12,[47] had informed Eberlein that she preferred to see some time elapse before a Third International came into being. Although the KPD had agreed to send two delegates to Moscow, its Central Committee had adopted Luxemburg's position,[48] and that decision, antagonizing all the other "delegates," was fully elucidated by Eberlein, who echoed Luxemburg's prophetic fears that Lenin would organize a Jacobin-type body which would act in the name of the workers but without actually consulting them.[49]

Although a minority of one man opposed turning the informally arranged Moscow meeting into a founding conference, Lenin could not without some qualms brush aside the authentic voice of the German Communist Party and for a time that caused him to refrain from taking decisive action. Then, after making some futile attempts to persuade Eberlein to change his stance[50]—which Eberlein had no authority to do—Lenin went ahead anyway, in effect asserting that he and Russian Bolshevism, and not the sluggish Germans, represented the "will" of the international proletariat. Eberlein, in the debate on the question, referred to the still fragmentary nature of the European Communist movement and pleaded that the conference "carefully consider" the wisdom of constructing a Third International "on such flimsy foundations."[51] Zinoviev lashed back, speaking Lenin's mind.

"You want first to see the formal founding of communist parties in all countries? You have a victorious revolution [in Russia] which is worth more than a formal founding." Thus he disparaged the quality of German Social Democratic leadership as compared to the Bolsheviks. In an even more contemptuous comment, Zinoviev told the German, as though the latter was not versant with the situation in his own country and his own party, that the KPD would within months be establishing a German proletarian regime. "And now you ask us to delay?" Zinoviev's argument was grotesquely disproportionate as compared with Eberlein's polite and reasonable statement. Continuing in that spiteful vein he declared that "upon mature consideration" the Russian party "proposes the immediate founding of the Third International," to "show the whole world that we are both spiritually and organizationally armed."[52] On March 5, the conference unanimously, but for a single abstention (undoubtedly Eberlein), declared itself the First Congress of the Communist International. *Pravda,* next day, carried Lenin's boast that the "ice" had been broken and that "the Soviets (had) triumphed throughout the world." The Zimmerwald Left position had, so to speak, been elevated to the status of guidelines for the new international. The only change since Lenin had expressed his views in September 1915, was in the roles of Russia and Germany. Now it was the former which would carry the revolution's field marshal into Germany (and the West) instead of, as earlier, Lenin had hoped to be swept into Russia and Eastern Europe in the wake of an all-conquering German army in revolution.

CHAPTER VIII

THE FOCUS ON THE EAST
THE RISE OF STALIN

Lenin's great hopes for action in the West vanished during the summer of 1919. By October, Lenin did not believe that the Western proletariat could stage a revolution except in reaction to revolutions in the East.[1] Lenin, who had dreamed of leading a German revolution and had given so much of himself to achieve that goal, had to confront the fact that the working classes of the West did not perceive him as their liberator. Nor, for that matter, were they seeking liberation from the status quo post-bellum. Lenin had confidently expected the war's horrors to prompt the Western workers to rise. When that did not occur, Lenin blamed it on the leaders of Western socialism who had become the principal "social prop of the bourgeoisie." By 1919, ironically, Lenin had discovered that imperialism, the very phenomenon which, according to him, had made world wars and hence a Western revolution inevitable, was, in fact, the cause for the anti-revolutionary bent of the European workers.[2] The "superprofits," which thirty percent of the world's people derived from exploiting the remaining seventy percent,[3] Lenin said, had given the capitalists the means for buying off union and leftist leaders. Lenin probably would have been more accurate had he charged the Western proletariat as a whole, and not merely its leaders, with a desire to enjoy the plunder of the colonial world. But to put it that way would have insulted the workers *per se;* and Lenin was not about to alienate forces who could be rallied to fight capitalism, if only after the source of their wages (as well as industrial profits) had been destroyed.

Lenin's aim to lead the world revolution, as we have seen, required that he constantly restructure his theory of its inception in terms of his existing base of political operations. For geo-political reasons, Russia was ideally suited to Lenin's forecast of the world revolution growing out of the overthrow of imperialism in the colonies. Although perhaps not influencing the formulation of his latest "theory," it was in practice fitted like a glove to the fact that a crackling chain of fireworks, in the form of Asian revolutionary ferment, would above all disembowel the empire of Great Britain, the imperialist power which was also the mainspring of anti-Bolshevik intervention. Britain's most vital imperialist interests lay within easy target range of revolutionary propaganda from Russia, the more effective in that Russia, having become the world's revolutionary center, could declare herself cleansed of tsarist imperialistic policies.

This was the direction Lenin took beginning in the autumn of 1919 when the Red Army had re-established contact with Bolshevik-controlled Turkestan. The Communists in Turkestan, during their time of isolation from Moscow, had continued the role played by the pre-revolutionary Russian bureaucracy. In an October 1919 decree, instructing a commission to investigate conditions in Turkestan, Lenin specified that self determination of the peoples of Turkestan and the abolition of all national inequality and privilege of one nation at the expense of another "was the basis of the entire policy of the Soviet Government of Russia." A simultaneous letter to the Turkmen Communists directed them to cooperate with the commission because the establishment of "correct relations" with the peoples of Turkestan had "without exaggeration a gigantic and world historical significance." For all of Asia, Lenin wrote, and for all the colonies of the world, "for a thousand million people," the relations of the Soviet Workers Peasant Republic to the weak, hitherto oppressed peoples would have an "immediate and practical" significance. Lenin implored the Turkmen Communists to "display by deeds the sincerity" of Russia's desire to erase her evil past "for the supreme struggle with world imperialism headed by Britain."[4]

The Second All-Russian Congress of Communist Organizations of the Peoples of the East met in November 1919. Lenin's speech before that body was intended to agitate the peoples of Asia and the rest of the Europe-colonized world against imperialism.

> The most essential thing now is the relationship of the peoples of the East to imperialism, and the revolutionary movement among these peoples. It is self evident [here Lenin presents himself

> as the leader of the colonial world against the West] that this revolutionary movement of the peoples of the East can now develop successfully only in direct association with the revolutionary struggle of our Soviet Republic against international imperialism.

As he had done at the previous year's congress of Moslems, Lenin pointed to "*The backwardness of Russia* [my italics], her tremendous expanse, and the fact that she stands *between Europe and Asia,* between the West and the East" presaging that "*the entire course of development in the immediate future* [I stress these words to show that Lenin was by then completely committed to his Eastern orientation] would evince itself in an ever broadening struggle against international imperialism, which would *inevitably be tied to the struggle of the Soviet Republic against the forces of united imperialism–of Germany, France, Britain and the U.S.A.*" (my italics). Lenin was informing the colonial world that Russia was no longer linked with their European enslavers; indeed, that, armed with Lenin's Soviet system, Russia had accepted the task of leading the colonial peoples against imperialist Europe.[5]

Lest colonial nationalists lose heart at the thought of defeating the modern imperialist armies, Lenin declared that the Russian Civil War had proven "to us and to communists of all countries that, in the fires of civil war, the rise of revolutionary enthusiasm goes hand in hand with a powerful internal strengthening because peasants and workers stand together." This notion of peasant-worker unity was, of course, the special point Lenin was making to prove that Russia, unlike the other European powers, could relate to the backwardness of the colonial world. Lenin went on: "In Western Europe we see the dissolution of imperialism," noting that the new German empire, although socialist and republican, had remained imperialistic. Lenin also observed–contradicting himself–that Europe's imperialists had become more than ever rapacious, citing the Versailles Treaty as proof that they were even devouring European countries. (It did not make much sense for Lenin to label as "imperialistic" the chief victim of the merciless Versailles Treaty.) Seemingly carried away by the notion that imperialistic cannibals did not stop even at devouring one another, Lenin portrayed all of Western Europe as having become an object of exploitation by the United States. Imperialism in short, knew no law but that of pillage; it existed the world over and involved every country.

The main thrust of Lenin's speech exposed the revolutionary decadence of Europe; the putrefaction of its "socialism" as compared with that of morally strong Russia. Lenin still had a few vestigially kind words for the "civil war" which the German proletariat was soon bound to wage against "the German [social] imperialists."[6] But for all intents and purposes Lenin had shoved Europe, as a whole, excluding Russia into a backwater, to be brought back upon the scene at such time as the revolutionary forces of the East had taken from the Western proletariat everything but its chains, thereby restoring its once great potential for revolutionary action.

The concluding ideas of Lenin's speech became his final precepts for the course of world revolution. They may be summarized as follows:

> 1. Revolution in the West depends on revolutions in the East. The prime target of any Western country's workers, therefore, must be their own nation's imperialism, its exploitation of subject peoples.
> 2. The revolutions in the East (the colonial world in general) will be hastened by the rising nationalism among the world's subject nations and by increasing awareness of the majority of the world's people that they need no longer remain victims of exploitation.
> 3. The backward peoples of the world need not despair at the thought of fighting against advanced technology. The success of the Russian revolution, and especially the joint mutiny of workers and peasants against capitalism and feudalism, had shown them how it was to be done. Indeed, the workers of the East enjoyed an advantage in that they had not passed through the school of capitalist factories. (Unlike the Russian workers and peasants, therefore, the colonial peoples had never acquired property or trade union consciousness.)
> 4. Since the communist literature of the past had never before taken account of the revolutionary potential of colonial nations there was no theoretical guideline for them, and each colonial nation would have to chart its own way for achieving national

> liberation, all such actions being bound eventually to coalesce in the world revolution.[7]

The late 1919 articles in *Zhizn' Natsional'nostei* conveyed the above message, the conclusion being that all hopes placed on revolution in the West had been futile and that the stress of world revolutionary activity should be concentrated in the East.[8] The new Bolshevik line was quickly put into practice. A propaganda train, called "The Red East" (the first such left Moscow in January 1920),[9] carried literature, posters, films and agitators through Turkestan, enlightening its peoples about imperialist exploitation. A headquarters for communist missionaries, set up in Turkestan, sent agitators into Persia, Afghanistan and India to broadcast anti-British denunciations. Similar performances were given in Azerbaijan, which, in 1919, was still under British sway, and Bolshevik propaganda in shipyards, oilfields and factories of Baku was extremely effective. (When the Baku Congress of Eastern Peoples met in 1920 the British patrolled the northern Turkish coast trying to prevent Turkish delegates from crossing the Black Sea. Persians crossing the Caspian to get to Baku were bombed by British planes.) So frightened were the British of Moscow's propaganda barrage, that even in India the possession of a ruble note was made a crime. Bolshevik proclamations also proved effective in Mesopotamia, Afghanistan and Egypt.

In October 1919, writes E. A. Ross, Soviet Russia was "beleaguered by the armies of Kolchak, Denikin and Yudenich, all fed, armed and motivated from London. British imperialism seemed about to [destroy] the socialist experiment. . . . Eight months later the British had their hands full trying to put out the fires Moscow had lighted at the corner-posts of their Asiatic Empire." In May 1920, a British cabinet meeting was told that the Bolsheviks were "making difficulties" for the government "all over the East" and later in the year Curzon complained to Chicherin that Moscow had unleased "a real hurricane of propaganda, intrigue and conspiracy against British . . . power in Asia."[10]

The Second Congress of Comintern

Lenin's decision that world revolution had to start in the East and be led by Russia (i.e., by Lenin) best explains the utter breakdown of communications between Lenin's cohorts and the West European delegates who met in Moscow at the Second Congress of the Third International (July-August 1920).

Lenin, of course, did not expect the revolutions in the colonies to reach fruition for decades. In the meantime, therefore, he was above all concerned lest Western communists, in each country, bedevil their capitalist governments to the point at which the European bourgeoisie would unite to crush helpless Russia. Lenin wanted the Western Reds to do what they could for Soviet Russia but only within legal limits. (Such thinking gave rise to the later-called "peaceful coexistence"). His pamphlet *Left Wing Communism, A Disease of Immaturity,* was specifically written to instruct the delegates attending the Second Comintern Congress to act in moderation. Such counsel seemed strange to the zealots who had traveled to the Mecca of revolution, thinking not in the least of waiting for imperialism's overthrow in the colonies, but, as Lenin had done in Russia, of ousting their own European governments. The delegates were not all radical to the same degree. Some were not even communists but were left wing socialists (from Germany and France for example) who had been invited precisely because their gradualist mentality suited Lenin's overall strategy.

Lenin's pamphlet specifically cautioned the immature (often young) and hence reckless communists of the West against risking open conflict. Instead, as the Bolsheviks had done in Russia since 1906, they were to take part in parliamentary and trade unionist activities. This was essential, according to Lenin, because the working masses of the West, and the peasantry in particular, were more subject than their Russian brethren to deeply-rooted "bourgeois-democratic and parliamentary prejudices." For that reason tactics of compromise were even more suitable in the West than had been the case in Russia.[11] The radical Western delegates could not possibly have understood such advice coming from Lenin, for, if anything, it sounded exactly like reformism. Nor could they accept the fact that Lenin had relegated them to a secondary role in his scheme for world revolution, a role in which, under Lenin's discipline, they were to hold their fire until Lenin had decided that their moment of glory had arrived.

Small wonder, then, that the Comintern's Second Congress exploded in a series of bitter controversies. On the one side of each separate argument stood Lenin's henchmen, who dominated the proceedings numerically, and also by way of rigged committees.[12] On the other side of each particular quarrel stood one or another group of outraged delegates from one or another country of Western Europe or the United States, none of whom had had any premonition that their function in Moscow had been worked out in advance, and that they were there only to be manipulated in accordance with Lenin's purposes.

At the very outset Lenin was confronted by bitter English shop stewards, who, asked by Lenin to join their hated native Labour Party, inquired caustically whether they had come to Moscow only to learn from Russians how to cope with the situation in England. It made no sense to the British that a tightly managed internationally organized party should be directing the unionized English proletariat. The British shop steward position was, moreover, "left wing" and "childish" since it rejected collaboration with parliament.[13]

Thunder from the "left" erupted next from Dutch Tribunist Wjnkoop the Congress gadfly, who assailed the Centrist delegates whom Lenin was inviting to join the Comintern. Since Lenin wanted even the most militant-minded revolutionaries to act in moderation, he had every reason to allow reformist socialists to join the propaganda chorus designed to forestall anti-Soviet military aggression. (Here were shades of the subsequent united fronts of the twenties and thirties and of "collective security" against fascism.) But such rationale eluded the lefts. As they saw it, they were being ignominiously lumped together with the very persons and parties whom they had for years been castigating, using Lenin's own vocabulary. Lenin, Zinoviev and Co., in the very act of building an anti-Kautsky coalition seemed to be committing all the sins of Kautsky.[14]

Whatever the merits of that opinion, it was not the impression Lenin wanted the delegates to take home with them. Also, while the Congress met, the Red Army had taken the offensive, driving the Polish invaders of the Ukraine back into Poland. A march on Warsaw was in progress, its daily advances being marked by pins on a huge map that hung in the Congress hall. Around August 1, therefore, Lenin and Co., suddenly confronted by the possibility of a revolution in Germany, ceased parrying the savage anti-Centrist thrusts from the "immature lefts" and themselves turned their wrath against the Centrists. The result was that the conditions for entering the Comintern were made much more rigidly anti-reformist than Lenin had originally wanted them to be. This became a total loss from Lenin's point of view, because the Red Army, routed at Warsaw, was not able "to probe the German border with its bayonets," as Lenin later said he had expected would occur.[15]

To propagate his new Eastern line, Lenin himself took the floor—the only time he did so at the Congress—to preach the importance of colonial revolutions against imperialism. The few delegates from Asian countries were delighted, but the Western delegates, and the British, in particular, became even more confused. The latter were told not to incite a workers' rising against the English bourgeoisie but to stand up in Parliament and attack British imperialism in India and demand Irish independence.[16]

American communists, headed by John Reed, and the English shop stewards were instructed to join "bourgeois" trade unions and to bore from within. They were told, at the same time, to affiliate themselves with an International Federation of Trade Unions (Profintern) so that Moscow could maintain disciplinary control over the communists who were working within the traditional trade unions. It was not explained to the Americans and the British how they could at one and the same time operate in two mutually hostile trade unions, but the angry Anglo-American protests were quashed by the Congress "voting machine."[17]

In general, for reasons mentioned, Lenin wanted all activity by Western communist parties subject to centralized control. The communists and fellow traveling groups thus acquired the function of serving Soviet foreign policy and eventually Soviet foreign trade purposes as well. There can be no doubt but that this policy was instrumental in helping Soviet Russia to survive, to become a viable link between East and West and, thus, the generating force of world revolution.

To tie things up, the Russians, in the final congress sessions, proposed that the Executive Committee of Comintern meet in Moscow (it was admittedly impractical, indeed impossible, at the moment for it to convene elsewhere) and that its membership be dominated by Russian Bolsheviks. The device through which this was accomplished was in the establishment of legal and illegal sections of each country's party; the latter guaranteeing control of Lenin's group. Wjnkoop and German communist Levi quickly exposed the true purpose of the scheme. But, as in all matters, the Russians had the votes. Not only did they create an Executive Committee they could dominate but they even managed to exclude Holland from representation therein because the audacious Wjnkoop had never ceased sarcastically exposing what lay beneath the words of Lenin, et al.[18]

Because of the rigid conditions for admission to Comintern—which (we recall) Lenin had not wanted—the outcome of the Second Congress was the splitting off of communist from socialist parties and continuing friction between the parties of each country, occasionally papered over by popular frontism. However, because only communist parties entered the Comintern and accepted Russian-imposed discipline they became the handmaidens of Lenin's Eastern-oriented policy without really understanding what role they were playing. In practice the party's function, in each nation, became that of aiding Muscovite policy without even troubling to try to understand it. That, in turn, meant luring any dissident elements within a nation, whatever their mutual antagonisms, to support Lenin's Russia. At the same time, each "national" party took advantage of "bourgeois democracy" to organize itself as a legal party, although, in fact, ruled by secret Soviet agents.

Another facet of the same design was the disavowal of tsarist imperialist acts which had victimized China and Persia. This was the rationale for the treaty with Afghanistan, on February 28, 1921, which recognized the "freedom and independence of Khiva and Bukhara" and promised Afghanistan return of some frontier regions annexed by Russia "if the local population" so desired: in a word, "self determination." The Russo-Turkish Agreement of March 16, 1921 ended Russia's right to capitulations and released Turkey from all obligations incurred in dealings with the tsar.

Remaining to be settled in final form by 1922 was the matter of constructing a constitution that would officially unite six of the existing Soviet republics—RSFSR, Ukraine, Belorussia plus the three Transcaucasian "states," conquered by the Red Army in 1920 and 1921.

Meanwhile Soviet Russia had continued to sow the seeds of revolution against imperialism wherever they were likely to take root. Soon after the Second Comintern Congress, the "enslaved peoples of Persia, Armenia and Turkey" were asked to send representatives to a newly-formed League for Eastern Liberation which met September 1-8, 1920 in a Baku Conference. About 2,000 delegates showed up, among them Turks, Persians, Parsees, Armenians, Georgians, Kirghiz, Khivans, Kurds, etc., but only fourteen came from India and only seven from China. This was a staged event as is evident from the fact that almost half the delegates came from Azerbaijan or from the Soviet Caucasus. Zinoviev, President of the Executive Committee of the Comintern, was chosen honorary president of the

Baku Conference and most significantly described it as a "supplement, a second part, a second half," of the just concluded Moscow Comintern Congress. His opening address called upon the billion and a half peoples dependent on English capital to unite and to introduce the Soviet system. He asked for a holy war "against English and French robber capitalists."[19]

Soon thereafter came crude efforts to reproduce, for Eastern consumption, the type of display made a year and a half earlier in the West. The Kirghiz-Kazakh region was allowed a facade of independent statehood and the same was done with Turkestan. In October 1920, an Autonomous Kirghiz Republic was proclaimed and its government even contained Commissariats of the Interior, Justice, Agriculture and the like, although all of them were expected to act on directives of Moscow through Communist Party channels. In Latvia, the use of Western-style administrative organs to advertise a nation's independence could enjoy the appearance of normal developments. But in places like Kirghizia (area 76,100, population 1.5 million in 1950)[20] such devices were clearly designed to present the Central Asia republics as though they were passing through their bourgeois democratic phases. Such absurd demonstrations in nomadic regions were, of course, intended to lure the more advanced countries of the East into eventual union with the Soviet Union.

In Turkestan, in 1920, and early 1921, respectively, the officially "independent" People's Republic of Khiva and Bukhara were set up. Just what the term "independent" meant in reality may be judged from the "Treaty of Alliance Between the RSFSR and the Bukhara Soviet Republic," signed March 4, 1921 in Moscow. The treaty among other things contained the following stipulations:

> Taking into account the revolution in Bukhara, called forth by the will of the workers, the RSFSR recognizes its obligation to designate the former Khanate of Bukhara as the Bukhara Soviet Republic.
>
> Recognizing fully that between the working masses of two countries there can exist no differences of interests [and that both are fighting against imperialism, we realize] that only the closest alliance of the workers of East and West can secure victory and that all of the Soviet Republics must enter into a brotherly union. It is on this basis that the RSFSR and the Bukhara Soviet Republic have decided to conclude this agreement.

> At the same time as the present treaty is drawn up, a military-political agreement will be made. It should be noted that until this treaty is ratified there remains in effect the provisional military-political agreement concluded by the representatives of the RSFSR and Bukhara in November, 1920.
>
> The Bukhara Soviet Republic obliges itself not to turn over [any] enterprises to private uses or to exploit them through government enterprises of the Bukhara Soviet Republic.
>
> The RSFSR takes upon itself the obligation to help the workers of Bukhara by placing at the disposal of the government of the Bukhara Soviet Republic instructors, among these being military instructors, knowledgeable in the native languages, teachers, textbooks, materials for typesetting, etc.

In addition to retaining the right to exploit natural resources, the RSFSR retained the right, unencumbered by tariffs, and, as in 1919 Latvia, to use Russian money as native currency.[21]

The People's Republics of Central Asia and the People's Republic of the Far East were not yet deemed ready for this type of administrative integration.[22] For practical purposes the Ukraine, Belorussia and the Caucasian "republics," all possessing the showcase features of "independence," were already unified through treaties binding each with the RSFSR, by the subordination of each Republic's Communist party to the Moscow center, and by the universal authority of the Red Army.

Everything stood ready for the creation of a USSR, but in March 1921, Lenin hinted strongly to the communists of the Transcaucasian republics that he was particularly concerned with the mood of the recently conquered Georgians, and that he wanted the process of annexation (self determination) handled much more delicately than had been the case in constituting the RSFSR.[23] The explanation for this—to sum up this book's basic message—was that Lenin's policy for leading the world revolution depended on the army of the revolution establishing "dictatorships of the proletariat" wherever possible, whereupon, in every revolution–conquered country a brief period of "official" independence had to be instituted to "prove" that the eventual unification of that country with the workers of the world (Russia) was not the result of annexation.

This was the line of thought which, in December 1922, prompted Lenin to reproach Stalin and his underlings, for practicing tsarist-type oppression in Georgia, which had hurt, besides "ourselves. . . the entire International," and "the hundreds of millions of Asians who [will soon] appear upon the stage of history following directly in our footsteps."[24] Lenin's obsession with federation as a step toward "international" unity through apparently voluntary action,[25] of "self determination," explains why the seemingly trifling matter of using certain words to camouflage the annexation of Georgia blew up into Lenin's deathbed struggle with Stalin. That this, and nothing else, was at issue emerges clearly from a survey of the Lenin-Stalin relationship since 1917.

In the first Soviet government, Stalin became Commissar of Nationalities, a natural choice considering his 1913 paper on the national question and his role, in the course of 1917, as Lenin voice on the subject.[26] As chief of Narkomnats, Stalin faithfully executed Lenin's directives regarding self determination. In this work, so important to the "leader" of the world revolution, Stalin convinced Lenin that he had chosen the right man to carry out the subtly fraudulent assignment through which Lenin masked his personal aspirations.[27] Stalin, moreover, was willing to accept Lenin's dicta at face value, and if he disagreed,[28] he did so without making a public fuss,[29] in the way Bukharin, Piatakov and various others, over the years, had reacted to Lenin's views on the subject.

During the civil war Lenin became increasingly impressed with Stalin. His uncompromising ruthlessness in maintaining military discipline apparently seemed a trait of immense value to a Lenin whose hopes for world revolutionary leadership must have ballooned as Bolshevism overcame one seemingly insurmountable obstacle after another. It is hardly a coincidence if in the years of desparate struggle, beginning in 1917, Lenin allied himself closely with non-Russians, among them the Latvians, Stučka, Peters, Smilga, and Latsis, the Pole, Dzerzhinskii, the Finnish Rakhia and Jews, including Sverdlov and Trotsky. It seemed that Lenin was making use of the special venom which only national minority Bolsheviks could bring to tasks that would require the killing of many Russians. In this respect the Georgian, Stalin, displayed the greatest talent for violence in the name of Lenin's revolution. This characteristic of Stalin was far too important for Lenin to be offset by anything as trivial as a personal affront. Indeed, what Adam Ulam describes as Stalin's "strange power over Lenin," arising from his brutal and insolent manner toward the latter,[30] was in my opinion, nothing less than Lenin's admiration for Stalin's Nechaevism, that is, his unbrooked dedication to revolutionary fanaticism. Above all others, Stalin had emerged truly as the "man of steel" devoid of all traditional moral sensibility. Only Stalin could equal, if not surpass, Lenin in this trait; Lenin, notorious all his life for his unnecessarily vicious verbal onslaughts upon fellow revolutionists, Lenin, the man behind the initial wholesale post-November killing of innocents, including even *intelligenty,*[31] and, at least indirectly, the founder of the Gulag Archipelago.

When the civil war was over, Lenin more than ever needed Stalin's iron stomach. For then the dirtiest work yet lay ahead, as the party no longer unified by war, inevitably began to relax and to develop factions along various polemical lines. For the job of eliminating Bolshevik dissidents Lenin automatically turned to Stalin thereby launching the apprenticeship for a subsequently magnificent career as liquidator of communists. The ability to "exert pressure," Trotsky writes, was what Lenin "prized so highly in Stalin."[32]

Between 1920 and 1922 Lenin was directly responsible for placing the party-state machine under Stalin's control. As Trotsky bluntly implies, he relied on Stalin "for centralization with a firm hand," and only Stalin served in both the original Politburo and Orgburo, allowing him to staff the provincial party secretaries with his own candidates. Lenin, according to Trotsky "made no bones" about Stalin's heading Rabkrin, telling Preobrazhenskii that there was no better man than Stalin for the post that would "control all the units of our Soviet mechanism." Stalin's incessant packing of the entire party apparatus with his own stalwarts, many of whom were at odds with Lenin, did not deter the latter, at the March 1921 Tenth Party Congress, from instituting a Control Commission, headed by Stalin, with the power to purge dissenters. A year later, at the Eleventh Congress, it became the Central Control Commission with the power, through local control commissions, to punish party members of local and provincial party committees. The Congress, in addition forced each Soviet republic to establish its own Central Control Commission responsible to Moscow, i.e., to Stalin.

Control at the party center thus became a feature of self determination. In view of Lenin's concern for centralizing the nationalities, it is obvious why he wanted Stalin to hold the reins. At the time Preobrazhenskii expressed doubt that any one person could manage two vast bureaucratic empires along with many other responsibilities. However, declaring Stalin to be the only Bolshevik strong enough to run either Narkomnats or Rabkrin, Lenin said it was necessary to let him handle both jobs, so that disgrace and ruin resulting from "petty intrigues" should be avoided.[34] Worse yet, Stalin, days later was named party secretary, placing even greater power in his hands. Through the spring of 1922, Lenin clearly considered Stalin to be an absolutely irreplaceable person, an attitude probably reinforced as a consequence of Lenin's turn to the East. Stalin's Asian background, as Lenin saw it, enabled him to repeat the purpose he had served in 1913 but on a much larger scale. (A decade earlier Lenin had employed the "marvellous" Georgian to "author" a tract made up of Lenin's ideas designed to counteract the anti-centralist and pro-Menshevik trend among the national minority Marxists.)[35]

Judging from Lenin's undiluted faith in Stalin over so many difficult years, is it conceivable that a mere personality trait so troubled the dying Lenin; that it was Stalin's rudeness, or, rather the reflection of that rudeness in the behavior of Stalin's henchmen toward Georgian Bolsheviks that gave Lenin so much grief?[36] This question must be answered with a resounding "No!" As noted above, the entire struggle between Lenin and Stalin arose over a detail of policy formulation, but one of extreme importance to Lenin's rigid notion of how a world revolution, emanating from Russia and led by Lenin was to proceed. As death drew near, Lenin was fighting to preserve, in every last detail, the formula for success which he had invented and which was so intimately bound to his heroic ego image. In complaining of Stalin's rudeness, Lenin was trying to convey—what he could not directly admit—that the behavior of Stalin's clique in Georgia had done damage to the self portrait of Lenin as the leader of the world revolution. Considering his own monstrous acts of Great Russian chauvinism—as in the Baltic States—it was pure hypocrisy for Lenin to whine about brutalities of a similar nature perpetrated by Stalin or his associates.

What so rankled Lenin was not the incident involving fisticuffs in Georgia, but the fact that it was Georgia in which the unfortunate incident had occurred. But could Lenin explain his true feelings (the place rather than the incident) without appearing to be a vain glory seeker? Lenin's embarrassment is plainly seen in the awkward wording of his testament, where it concerned Stalin's removal as party secretary. In that post, Lenin suddenly wanted a person who differed from the "too rude" Stalin, not in ability, but only in being "more patient, more loyal, more polite and more attentive to comrades, less capricious, etc."[37] That is, Lenin wanted a man having all of Stalin's qualities but a different personality. But inasmuch as it had been precisely Stalin's personality which had made him Lenin's unquestioning choice to control the party apparatus, his statement, in effect, negated itself. Indeed, the reason he gave for requesting Stalin's removal from office–lack of consideration for party comrades–was so vague (Was the revolution less important than the bruised feelings of some comrade?) that Lenin himself had to admit that it seemed an insignificant trifle. This trifle, he added, might, in time, become important enough to cause a split in the party. But whom did he expect to convince with such a prognostication?

Because Trotsky's comments, made in 1928, throw much inadvertent light on the motives underlying the Lenin testament, they call for analysis at this point. Trotsky, in 1928, needless to say, was overly eager to portray the Stalin of 1922-1923 in as unflattering as possible a light and to show Lenin as guided in his actions by sharply delineated, purely political (rather than personal), attitudes concerning the damages which Stalin's bureaucratization of the party had wrought.

Quoting from the testament, Trotsky writes: "Stalin, having become General Secretary, has concentrated enormous power in his hands, and I am not sure he always knows how to use this power with sufficient caution." Going on to explain, Trotsky distorts the meaning of Lenin's words. "It is not the question of the political influence of Stalin, which at that period was insignificant, but of administrative power which he had concentrated in his hands, 'having become General Secretary.' This is a very exact and carefully weighed formula; we shall return to it later."

But Lenin had referred to "enormous power" in Stalin's hands and it was absurd for Trotsky to write that a man having "enormous" administrative power was "insignificant" politically. Moreover, Lenin had written, "I am not sure that he always knows how to use this power with sufficient caution," an ambivalent statement and by no means the "carefully weighed" formula which Trotsky claims to have perceived. If anything the opposite describes it better. Trotsky goes on to note that Lenin "only ten days later" sharpened his attack on Stalin by adding a "supplementary proposal which also gave to the whole document its final physiognomy." Trotsky then repeats the famous passage from the testament in which Lenin proposes "to the comrades" that they "find a way [Lenin himself did not have any immediate suggestions to offer] to remove Stalin from [the position of General Secretary] and appoint to it another man who in all other respects* [Trotsky's asterisk] differs from Stalin only in superiority–namely more patient, more loyal, more polite and more attentive to comrades, less capricious, etc." Trotsky's asterisk leads to a footnote explaining the awkwardness of Lenin's statement–which I have ascribed to Lenin's uncertainty about what to do–as follows: "We must not forget that the testament was dictated and not corrected, hence stylistic difficulties in places; but the thought is completely clear."

In fact the thought is far from clear as even Trotsky somewhat indirectly admits. "During the days when the testament was dictated, Lenin was still trying to give his critical appraisal of Stalin as restrained an expression as possible. In the coming weeks his tone would become sharper and sharper. . . . But even in the testament enough is said to motivate the demand for a change of General Secretary; along with rudeness and capriciousness, Stalin is accussed of *lack of loyalty.* At this point the characterization became a heavy indictment." In fact, Trotsky's evaluation is unsound, as is obvious by his need to make so much of of "rudeness," "capriciousness," and to twist Lenin's "more loyal" into "Stalin is accused of *lack of loyalty.*" (Italics are Trotsky's) Trotsky tries artificially to enhance the dimensions of Lenin's attack upon Stalin by misinterpretating a petulant comment by Lenin as if it had demonstrated a fierce hostility.

But at that point Lenin was far from sure that he wanted Stalin demolished, as Trotsky would have his readers believe. This is clearly revealed when the testament was brought to light in the Secretariat at a later date, and, as Trotsky writes, "in the circle" of Stalin's "closest associates," Stalin and his friends easily turned the whole thing into a joke precisely because of Lenin's wavering tone.

Trotsky writes: "In tendering his resignation as a matter of form, the General Secretary capriciously [note Trotsky's not too appropriate use of Lenin's word at this point] kept repeating, 'Well, I really am rude . . . . Ilyich suggested that you find another who would differ from me *only* in greater politeness. Well, try to find him.' 'Never mind," answered the voice of one of Stalin's then friends, "We are not afraid of rudeness. Our whole party is rude, proletarian'." Trotsky's rebuttal: "A drawing-room conception of politeness is here indirectly attributed to Lenin. As to the accusation of inadequate loyalty, neither Stalin nor his friends had a word to say."

But in actual fact, Lenin himself had made little out of the notion of disloyalty, probably because he had meant to use the word only with respect to Stalin's attitude toward Lenin's own person. And his charge of rudeness leveled against Stalin was also artificial because it derived entirely from the single episode of physical violence used in Georgia which Lenin so deeply deplored for reasons previously noted.[38] Physically helpless to prevent incidents which he thought might ruin his entire *Lebenswerk,* Lenin became desperate, in his final conscious months, to attempt–without knowing how–to remove from Stalin's grasp all the immense power he had for years been thrusting into it.

Lenin could not attack Stalin publicly, although by the end of 1922, he was willing to do so within the inner party councils. But if, in his testament, he could not be straightforward about why he wanted Stalin's removal as Secretary, his subsequent public comments did not even allow him to mention Stalin's name in proposing that he be removed from positions of power. Unable to do that he was forced to devise a tortuous plan. In his last two published articles (*Pravda,* January 23 and March 4, 1923), Lenin linked the success of Russia in leading the revolution in the East to a scheme for reorganizing and combining the Central Control Commission and Rabkrin and placing them both under the jurisdiction of the Central Committee, thereby greatly diminishing their influence. Only by so doing, Lenin said, in effect, could the USSR survive amid a hostile capitalist camp. Only that way could a tiny minority of industrial workers, backed by a peasant economy, make painful progress toward socialism, continue to develop technologically, thus providing the model needed by the struggling East.[39] In short, a reorganization of its bureaucracy, enabling it to survive, would allow the Soviet Union to lead the colonial world to its revolutionary triumph. Stated even more briefly this boils down to the following nonsense: A renovation of Soviet bureaucracy equals world revolution. A wider gap between cause and effect can scarcely be imagined. The reason for such irrationality was that Lenin could not permit himself to scream out to the world that Stalin was riding roughshod over the house that he, Lenin, had built. Lacking all choice, Lenin was reduced to making the pathetic proposal that the man who controlled it, Stalin, be removed from his immensely powerful bureaucratic apparatus, staffed from top to bottom with his hand-picked lackeys. Conceivably a healthy Lenin might have been able to do the job. But, as his testament reveals, Lenin knew that he lacked the strength and that without his personal leadership the task he proposed was beyond the means of the party. Moreover, who, at the time, could possibly have understood what exactly lay at the root of the dying man's seemingly bizarre requests or what it was that Stalin had done to require such drastic action to be taken against him. Nevertheless, the Central Committee did at least go through the motions of observing Lenin's wishes. Nothing that was done, however, made any impact upon Stalin's power.[40]

CHAPTER IX

SUMMARY AND REFLECTIONS

Before 1914, although well known as the leader of Russia's most radical Marxist faction, Lenin never enjoyed the status of a major figure in the Second International. However, the outbreak of World War One, along with changing Lenin's residence, from Poland to Switzerland, also changed his international, not to mention, his self image. For a person harboring Lenin's ambitions–it seems clear that since the turn of the century he had visions of himself as the leader of the world revolution–the situation could scarcely have been more propitious. In the face of the very "imperialist" war which, in 1909, Karl Kautsky had predicted would bring on a German revolution, the Marxist elite of all the warring powers, including Germany, had, to Lenin's (delighted?) surprise, surrendered like sheep to the spirit of chauvinism, allowing their proletarian followers to die by the millions in foul trenches.

Surely, Lenin thought, this condition could not endure for too long. Surely the German proletariat, so long regarded as the bellwether of European Marxism, was bound to rise, and, there being none other available to act as their leader, Lenin would be happy to oblige. In Germany, Kautsky and most other Social Democrats had remained silent, only Liebknecht daring to speak up against the war, as far as Lenin knew. In Switzerland, the home of most of the exiles during the war, as Alfred Senn's *The Russian Revolution in Switzerland, 1914-1917* so well depicts, Lenin had at his disposal various cells of Bolsheviks abroad. Although certain members of them often heatedly disagreed with Lenin, on one or another issue, they were, in general, prepared to do his bidding. To his Russian "corps" Lenin soon added a small company of young Swiss left socialists, all in all giving Lenin an apparatus that he could count upon. Aside from that he continued to publish the Bolshevik Central Organ, *Sotsial-Demokrat,* and since all important Russian Bolsheviks had been arrested or driven underground or abroad, Lenin, in effect, became the Central Committee of the Bolshevik Party, with the power to publish exactly what he wished and to maneuver as he saw fit.

Proceeding rapidly to shed the mantle of Russian leader for that of *the true* internationalist, Lenin considered his first priority the task of somehow making direct contact with the betrayed German workers. Since he had no direct channel, Lenin, in Bern, made every conceivable effort to project his views into Germany through international women's and youth conferences which met in Bern in the spring of 1915 and which were largely dominated by German delegates. However, in each case, his views calling for civil war in each country went against the conference majority. Frustrated, but undaunted, Lenin prepared most meticulously to use his tiny contingent to make a splash at a conference to be held at Zimmerwald in September 1915, and he succeeded brilliantly. Having virtually no following throughout Europe he was able to place himself on the map of socialist consciousness as the voice of the so-called Zimmerwald Left, the group irreconcileably opposed not only to those who supported a country's war effort but even opposing those who tolerated it in the name of defending the fatherland, or in the name of pacifism.

As already suggested, Lenin viewed Germany as the key to an all-European revolution. Better yet, as in the course of the war, Germany swallowed various nations or parts of nations in the Russian Empire, and, in the West, engulfed Belgium and a part of France, Lenin conceived the notion of a victorious Germany army rebelling, becoming converted into a Germany of the people's bayonets, ready to conquer the Russian empire and Western Europe for the proletarian cause. Around this motif, Lenin developed a whole series of ideas based on the rather far-fetched belief that he could convince the workers of Germany (in or out of uniform) that the war was not theirs but that of the bankers who were reaping profits from their blood.

In any case, Lenin found time enough in Switzerland—and on what else was he he spend his vast energies?—to prepare for assuming the leadership of the German revolution.

So from his pen flowed a succession of fascinating ideas, each in its own way a Lenin creation, yet having at least some basis in Marxist thought. As he gave up the role of Russian leader for the bigger one of Europe's, he also jettisoned the idea of a United States of Europe replacing it with the notion of socialism in a single country–Germany. (Ironically, as he never anticipated, Russia, in 1917, was to become that single country.) What was the revolutionary army of the single country (Germany) supposed to do? As Lenin foresaw, it would continue to overrun territories not for the imperialist purpose which had sparked the war, but in order to spread the revolution, thus unifying the European proletariat, who shared a common class interest. If for a time, the country of the revolution continued to dominate the conquered peoples, that would be done for the sake of advancing each subjected nation first to the status of bourgeois democratic republic (following the Marxist writ) and then helping it to go beyond that stage into a dictatorship of the proletariat.

It is in connection with that order of progression that Lenin's emphasis upon the right of nations to self determination and, indeed, independence (if only for a brief moment) was so important to him. This line of thinking by Lenin also explains the total frustration of Bukharin, Piatakov and other Bolsheviks. They considered Lenin's advocacy of defeat of his own (or any fatherland) to be absurd as long as he was simultaneously calling for the right of each nation to independence. What they did not understand was Lenin's motif connected with the idea of a revolutionary German army's conquest of a Europe headed by Lenin. Such a conquest could be justified only if it was supported, at least in theory, not in order to impose a new tyranny upon subject peoples but to liberate and to unite the proletarians among them. The latter, according to the *Communist Manifesto,* did not even have a fatherland. Eventually, of course, it could be anticipated that a proletarian-dominated Europe would proceed to unify the entire world on the same principles.

However, whichever way one looked at it, a German military conquest of many nations and the overthrow of their governments through revolutions masterminded by Lenin had to lead to a period of dictatorship. This anticipated dictatorship Lenin proceeded to depict as that which Marx had really meant when he had used the phrase "dictatorship of the proletariat," although there was no way at all of proving that Marx had foreseen what would happen in the period 1914-1917 and had expected the dictatorship to apply to conditions occurring long after his death.

This made it necessary for Lenin to undertake a voyage of "research" (actually highly selective reading) mainly in the writings of Marx and Engels since about 1850. From those writings he culled such bits and pieces as could be assembled to explain that dictatorship could be viewed as either slavery or freedom, depending on which "class" controlled it, whom it represented, and what its ultimate aim was. As Lenin read Marx and Engels, a dictatorship was the beginning of ultimate freedom if the proletariat, acting through its oligarchic representatives, controlled state power. In that case the laws would be made to benefit the working class, to destroy the former ruling class, and this would pave the way for an eventual dying off of the state, leading to the dawn of the freedom of communism. The word "democracy," as commonly used, said Lenin, really meant the rule of the bourgeoisie and was, in fact, a dictatorship suppressing the majority; so that democracy of the bourgeoisie was dictatorship, whereas a dictatorship of the proletariat was democracy; but, as Lenin emphasized, the very notion of democracy implied the use of some statist force or other and freedom could only arrive when there was no longer any need for democracy. However liberty-loving Lenin's words sounded, they were, after Lenin held power, greatly qualified, and he freely admitted that the dictatorship of the proletariat might take many hundreds of years to die off. The important thing, here, to keep in mind is that all of this elaborate formulation was simply theoretical preparation for the day when the German army converted itself into a revolutionary force—when exactly that would be Lenin had no idea—and Lenin would have ready for use a formula justifying the unification of conquered Europe under the domination of a single (temporary) state, ruled by a Bolshevik oligarchy, which he would command.

Lenin saw evidence of the impending German revolution in monopoly capitalism's creation of a state of perpetual world wars. Lenin's *Imperialism*, based almost entirely on German source data—in a sense proving the war guilt of Germany, later written into the Treaty of Versailles—demonstrated that the German bankers favored a war to redivide the world's colonial loot in favor of Germany, which had been cheated out of its rightful share. However, it was not particularly the German bankers whom Lenin intended to indict—Hobson had years earlier castigated British imperialism in similar terms but the bankers of all nations who made huge profits from imperialism as well as from war. *Imperialism*, perhaps Lenin's best known book, offered no ideas at all that had not been previously enunciated. But, joined to the themes of "socialism in a single country," "self determination of nations," "the state as the revolutionary dictatorship in the name of eventual freedom," it became part of a four-ply array of polemical weapons. These argued 1) for a revolutionary dictatorship in Germany; 2) for dictatorial (democratic) conquering Germany to establish temporary bourgeois republics in subject nations (simply to prove that such nations had gone through the proper historical process) 3) thus enabling them to progress toward proletarian dictatorship, and then (along with the power which had conquered its own and their bourgeoisie) 4) to move on toward universal statelessness or proletarian world brotherhood. Implicit in this scheme was the notion that the conquering dictatorship should retain control while shepherding the less powerful nations into the fold of internationalism.

Just as Lenin was ready to despair of the German revolution, the Russian revolution emerged like a *deus ex machina.* Without hesitation, Lenin embarked for Russia, taking along his faithful entourage and his ideological machinery, made in Switzerland. In Russia, however, it had to be readjusted to conditions in a peasant country, and so Lenin's April Theses became a blend of ideas, developed for a proletarian nation, but requiring an absurd blending with the idea of a revolution by the poorest peasants of Russia, the fieldhands. Lenin's April Theses won the day among the restive soldiers and workers, particularly in Petrograd. But while Lenin was still looking toward Germany for a revolution (and was therefore reluctant to tone down the militancy of that in Russia), the July Days' revolt, led by the Petrograd garrisons, caused him tremendous momentary confusion and even necessitated his going into hiding.

Had the April Theses proved to be his undoing? They might well have, except for a development in Latvia to which historians have paid virtually no attention. It happened that the Latvians were, by 1917, not only the best troops in the Russian army, but were also sold on Lenin's ideas as expressed in the April Theses which quite unintentionally coincided with the most cherished desires of the Latvian peasant-soldiery (the *strelki*). When Lenin considered the time for seizing power to be at hand in the fall of 1917–this because, in desperation, he saw no other way of achieving his goals–he had the good fortune to find on his side the 50,000 Latvian sharpshooters, who not only decided the issue of the seizure of power but who participated in the subsequent civil war to magnificent effect. It can be truly said that they saved Lenin's shaky regime in the year of its hardest trial, i.e., before his party was able to piece together an army and after a year-long Bolshevik anti-war campaign throughout the Imperial army.

Lenin, who, in March 1918, seemed to be giving away much of Russia at Brest-Litovsk, enjoyed another stroke of good fortune when Gemany soon thereafter was defeated and began to withdraw from Russia. This gave the Bolsheviks the chance to reoccupy the Ukraine and Belorussia and temporarily to invade Estonia, Latvia and Lithuania. Immediately Lenin, still expecting a German revolution, again called upon the Latvians to re-conquer Latvia, which they pretty well did, and then tried again to use the faithful Latvian Rifles as shock troops for the conquest of Germany. While this was transpiring, Lenin, using a handful of expatriates in Russia, allegedly representing almost every European country, announced that the Third International had arisen. Lenin, in every possible way, such as sovietizing the Ukraine and Belorussia (and, of course, allowing them self determination, i.e. a Bolshevik dictatorship), by trying the same technique in the Baltic countries, Latvia being the logical showpiece, and by encouraging the Hungarian Bolshevik regime under Bela Kun, etc., made every effort to accomplish from Russia (going West) what he had previously hoped would be achieved (going East) from Germany.

However, the revolution in the West fizzled and Lenin diagnosed that failure by asserting that imperialist controls of the colonial world by Western Europe, particularly English possessions in Asia, were propping up the rule of capitalist governments in the West. Since Great Britain was also the power directing the anti-Bolshevik intervention and was also most vulnerable to Lenin's propaganda in the Middle East, in Central Asia, and even in India, Lenin, aided by Stalin, Commissar of Nationalities, concentrated upon fomenting revolutions in Asia while calling for quiet among communist parties in the West. He feared that the bourgeois nations of the West might undertake a joint crusade against Bolshevism, even after intervention had ceased. But at the Second Comintern Congress, in July-August 1920, Lenin had a difficult task convincing the Western Communists that their job was simply to bide their time and await the revolutions in Asia. However, despite the bickering at the Congress, Lenin was able to impose Bolshevik discipline upon the Western Communist movement and to concentrate upon developments in the East.

If the rise of Stalin happened to coincide with the demise of Lenin, that was, as I have stressed, because of a combination of Stalin's brutality, which was especially required for the policy of "self determination" and the fact that Stalin, because of his Georgian background fitted so neatly into the Leninist design of producing bourgeois-democratic showcases in countries soon to be absorbed into the communist Russian empire. The dispute with Stalin which made the final months of Lenin's life so bitter came about because Lenin was obsessed with his world revolutionary scheme and wanted nothing like the brutal incident, produced in Georgia by Stalin's henchmen, to destroy it. In the long run, of course, it did not matter much. Lenin died, Stalin succeeded him and, through Stalin, Lenin's ideas lived on although it was not until the end of World War II that they were put into practice in Eastern Europe. Since then, however, as Russia has grown ever stronger militarily, the Lenin formula has advanced further into Europe, and has penetrated Latin America, the Middle East, Africa, and Central and Southeast Asia. Lenin's formula for expansion is the major problem of those who oppose the rapid Communist advance. The geopolitics of Lenin, i.e., his notion of self-determination, cannot be countered by Wilsonian self determination because the nations of the world are too poor and too backward to attempt to see much hope for themselves in democracy, American style.

NOTES

Notes to Introduction

1. R. Pipes, *Struve, Liberal on the Left, 1870-1905* (Cambridge: Harvard University Press, 1970), pp. 82-83.

2. A. K. Wildman, *The Making of a Workers Revolution, Russian Social Democracy, 1891-1903* (Chicago: University of Chicago Press, 1967), p. 1. "The rapid swing to Marxism occurred only after the famine, and the records of the period indicate that it was precisely the famine which provided the stimulus."

3. N. K. Krupskaya, *Reminiscences of Lenin* (New York: International Publishers, 1970), p. 11.

4. V. I. Lenin, *Polnoe Sobranie Sochinenii,* 5th Edition (Moscow, 1960), XLVI, pp. 1-2. (Hereafter, *P.S.S.*).

5. Ibid., I, p. 71.

6. Ibid., I, pp. 81-82. Lenin cites from *Kapital,* Bd. II, p. 436. A footnote in Lenin, *P.S.S.* I, p. 575 gives the date of publication of *Kapital* as 1955, a Soviet edition, and refers to page 439.

7. Krupskaya, *Reminiscences,* p. 11.

8. Ibid., p. 13.

9. Lenin, *P.S.S.,* I, pp. 310, 312.

10. Ibid., I, pp. 521, 527 and *passim.* According to Pipes, Lenin's aim "in reality was not to pillory Struve but to correct and amplify him. The tone he assumed was that of a teacher, not that of a prosecutor, and his strictures were friendly and constructive." (Pipes, *Struve,* p. 138). As I read it, Lenin's tone was condescending and although Lenin's hostility was not as specifically directed at Struve as it would later be, its presence is unmistakeable.

11. N. Harding, *Lenin's Political Thought* Vol. I, *Theory and Practice in the Democratic Revolution* (London: Macmillan, 1970), p. 89.

12. P. Struve, "My Contacts and Conflicts with Lenin," *The Slavonic Review,* XII, April 1934, pp. 573-595, and XIII, July 1934, pp. 66-84.

13. Lenin, *P.S.S.*, II, p. 452.

14. Ibid., VI, p. 150.

15. Ibid., VI, p. 21.

16. Ibid., VI, p. 39. Kautsky's emphasis on "bourgeois intellectuals" was specially noted by Lenin.

17. In the *Manifesto,* Marx and Engels asserted that the class war in its final stages would make for a process of dissolution within the ruling class, "a small part of the ruling class" breaking ranks to join with "the revolutionary class which holds the future in its hands." (This same notion is, of course, basic to the conception of the Communist vanguard of the proletariat as described in chapter two of the *Manifesto.*) The *Manifesto* continues: "Just as formerly a part of the nobility went over to the bourgeoisie, so at this point a portion of the bourgeoisie transfers itself to the proletariat; namely a sector of the bourgeois ideologists [men like Marx and Engels, for instance] who have educated themselves to a theoretical understanding of the entire motion of history." Thus did Marx and Engels indirectly account for their personal history-shaping function in writing the *Manifesto,* at the same time clearly distinguishing between leaders and followers. (For a more complete discussion of this see my letter to the *New Republic,* September 7, 1974, under the title "Stalin Legend" along with Sidney Hook's reply.)

18. O. Hammen, *The Red '48ers, Karl Marx and Friedrich Engels,* (New York: Scribners, 1969), pp. 272-73.

19. Ibid., pp. 355-56.

20. *Marx-Engels Gesamtausgabe,* ed., V. Adoratsky (Moscow, 1935) Part 3, III, p. 346.

21. Ibid., XXVI, p. 480.

22. R. Tucker, ed., *The Marx-Engels Reader* (New York: Norton, 1972), p. 599.

23. M. Hillquit, *From Marx to Lenin* (New York: The Manford Press, 1921), pp. 26-27.

24. K. Kautsky, *The Dictatorship of the Proletariat* (London: The National Labour Press, Ltd.), n.d.

25. N. Berdyaev, *The Origin of Russian Communism* (Ann Arbor: University of Michigan, 1960), p. 104.

26. Lenin, *P.S.S.,* VI, p. 28.

27. O. Hammen, "Marx and the Agrarian Question," *American Historical Review,* June 1972, p. 681.

28. Lenin, *P.S.S.*, VI, p. 26.

29. Ibid., VI, p. 27.

30. Ibid., pp. 132-33.

31. Tucker, *Marx-Engels Reader,* p. 352.

32. S. W. Page, "Lenin and Peasant 'Bolshevism' in Latvia, 1903-1915," *Journal of Baltic Studies,* III/2, Summer, 1972, pp. 95-112.

33. *Supra,* pp. 134-137.

34. In 1848 "the matter of going to the land, of using agrarian discontent, of organizing societies and holding meetings in the country was pressed by Marx and Engels and their faithful supporters." (Hammen, *The Red '48ers,* p. 267; see also Hammen's "Marx and the Agrarian Question," p. 680 in which he points out that Marx and Engels were prepared to "identify themselves with the grievances of diverse groups–worker, agrarian, national . . . even religious–that promised to advance the movement.

35. See Hammen, "Marx and the Agrarian Question," p. 681; also Frederick a de Lana's communication to *The American Historical Review,* February, 1973, pp. 194-96 for material on Marx's attitude toward peasants in 1871.

36. A term later used unjustly by Stalin and others to attack Trotsky.

37. G. Plekhanov, *Selected Philosophical Works,* 5 Vols. (Moscow, no date) I, pp. 395, 405, 410; see also F. Bystrykh, "Rasvitie Vzgladov Lenina Po Agrarnomu Voprosu," *Proletarskaia Revoliutsiia,* 1928, No. 1, 72, p. 1. The League for the Liberation of Labor, writes Bystrykh, was unable to include the peasant question in its program. The program states that "the urban revolutionary movement receives neither support nor sympathy from the peasants" and called "the political indifference and intellectual backwardness of the peasants the strongest bulwark of tsarism."

38. *Supra,* pp. 15-16.

39. Lenin, *P.S.S.*, p. 300.

40. In his preface Lenin wrote: "This book (received by me only after the greater part of this present volume was in typeset) constitutes the most significant contribution of the latest economic literature since the third volume of Capital." He added "It is extremely interesting to note to what degree the basic features of this general process in Western Europe coincide with those in Russia, despite the latter's peculiarities with regard both to economic and non-economic factors." (Lenin, *P.S.S.*, III, pp. 7-9.)

41. Lenin, *P.S.S.*, IV, pp. 88-94
42. Ibid., IV, pp. 99-156.
43. K. Kautsky, *Die Agrarfrage* (Stuttgart, 1899), p. 295. "The industrial proletariat cannot free itself unless it also liberates the agricultural population."
44. Some of Kautsky's chapter titles are: "The Proletarization of the Peasant." (Ibid., pp. 164-193); "The Increasing Difficulties of Commodity-Producing Agriculture." (pp. 194-231); "Does Social Democracy need an Agrarian Program–*Hinaus aufs Land!*" (pp. 303-308).
45. Lenin, *P.S.S.*, IV, pp. 434-436.
46. *RS-DRP Vtoroi ocherednoi S"ezd Ross. sots.-dem rabochei partii polnyi tekst protokolov* (Geneva, 1903), p. 207. (Hereafter, *Vtoroi S"ezd*) To this purist objection Akselrod replied that the call for return to the *otrezki* had agitational value. (Ibid., p. 210).
47. Lenin, *P.S.S.*, pp. 434-437.
48. Written February-March, 1902.
49. Lenin, *P.S.S.*, VI, p. 305.
50. Ibid., VI, pp. 305-306.
51. Ibid., VI, p. 306.
52. *Infra*, p. 1.
53. Lenin, *P.S.S.*, VII, pp. 155-56.
54. Ibid., VII, pp. 177-78.
55. Ibid., VII, pp. 181-87.
56. Ibid., VII, pp. 198-99.
57. *Vtoroi S"ezd*, p. 210.
58. Ibid., p. 206.
59. Lenin, *P.S.S.*, VIII, p. 217.
60. Ibid., VIII, pp. 217-18.
61. Ibid., VI, pp. 52-53.
62. *Tretyi Ocherednoi S"ezd Ross. Sots-Dem Rabochei Partii, Pol'nyi Tekst Protokolov* (Geneva, 1905), pp. xx-xxi.
63. Ibid., pp. 109-22.
64. Ibid., pp. 203-10.
65. See S.W. Page, "Lenin and Peasant 'Bolshevism,'" pp. 99-101.
66. Lenin, *P.S.S.*, XI, p. 88.
67. Ibid., XI, p. 89. In his "Lecture on the 1905 Revolution," (early 1917) Lenin described the peasant movement in 1905 as having reached "greater dimensions" than the workers' movement. "*Over one-third of the*

districts of the entire country were subject to the so-called 'peasant disorders.' . . . The peasants burned down about 2,000 estates and divided up the means of livelihood which the robber nobility had snatched from the people. Unfortunately their work was not carried out completely. Unfortunately the peasant destroyed only one-fifteenth of the nobles estates . . . . Unfortunately the peasants were too disorganized and not sufficiently aggressive. That was one of the basic reasons for the failure of the revolution." (Lenin, *P.S.S.,* XXX, p. 322.)

68. Lenin, *P.S.S.,* XI, p. 18.

69. L. Schapiro, *The Communist Party of the Soviet Union* (New York: Random House, 1959), p. 76.

70. Lenin, *P.S.S.,* XI, p. 18.

71. L. Trotsky, *The Permanent Revolution and Results and Prospects,* (New York: Pathfinder Press, 1970), pp. 75-115.

72. Lenin, *P.S.S.,* XI, p. 71.

73. Trotsky, *Permanent Revolution,* p. 115.

74. Lenin, *P.S.S.,* XVII, pp. 381-82.

75. L. Trotsky, *My Life* (New York: Grosset and Dunlap, 1960), p. 182.

76. Lenin, *P.S.S.,* X, p. 53.

77. Ibid., XII, pp. 150-53. See also S. Page, *Lenin and World Revolution* (New York: McGraw Hill, 1972), p. 6.

78. *Protokoly Ob"edinitel'nogo S"ezda RSDRP* (Moscow, 1926), pp. 26-27, 364.

79. Ibid., pp. 37-39.

80. Ibid., p. 41.

81. Ibid., p. 88.

82. Lenin, *P.S.S.,* XII, pp. 363-370.

83. "Who will dispose of the people's rights and property? The bureaucrats? The Trepovs? Do you want to give over the land to Trepov and the bureaucrats? No! Every peasant will oppose that . . . . Therefore we explain to the peasant that the people must elect all officials so that the land be given over entirely to the peasants. That is why my nationalization project, under conditions of a fully secure democratic republic, is the correct course for our agitators and propagandists, showing them that the peasant land demands must serve as the basis for their political and especially for their republican propaganda. The peasant Mishin, for instance, Duma deputy from Stavropol, took an instruction from his electors

verbatim out of the newspaper *The Russian State.* In this instruction a change of land bureaucrats is demanded, as well as the building of grain elevators and the giving of all land to the treasury. This demand is. . . a reactionary prejudice, for the present treasury and tomorrow's constitutional Russia, is the treasury of police-military despotism. But we must not simply throw this demand away as a prejudice, we must 'hook on' to it in order to persuade the Mishins how matters really stand; . . . that the demand for turning over the land to the treasury is a poorly expressed but an extremely important and useful idea for the peasants. The turning over of the land to the treasury can be very useful to the peasants only when the state shall have become a fully democratic republic, when there will be complete freedom in the election of bureaucrats, destruction of the standing army, etc. So for all these reasons, I think that if you reject nationalization you will inevitably make the same mistakes made by our *praktiki,* agitators and propagandists as we made with our *otrezki* program of 1903." (*Protokoly Ob"edinitel'nogo S"ezda,* pp. 92-93.)

84. Lenin, *P.S.S.,* XVI, pp. 380-81.

85. Ibid., XVI, p. 423.

86. Ibid., VII, pp. 235-36.

87. *Vtoroi S"ezd,* p. 421.

88. In J. P. Nettl's colorful words, the formative RSDWP feared for its status and felt threatened by the party's "two precursors, the Bund and the SDKPiL [the latter led by Rosa Luxemburg] two snorting steeds whose impatience had helped put the creaking Russian cart on the road in the first place. Should there be an all-embracing party, or should they be separate but equal; and if not equal, who should predominate?" (J. P. Nettl, *Rosa Luxemburg,* 2 vols. [London, 1966] I, p. 252.).

89. R. Pipes, *The Formation of the Soviet Union* (New York: Atheneum, 1968), p. 33.

90. S. Page, "Lenin and Self-Determination," *Slavonic Review,* April 1950, p. 345.

91. Lenin, *P.S.S.,* VII, p. 105.

92. Ibid., pp. 117-120.

93. Ibid., p. 122. The quarrel between *Iskra* and the Bund was partly a reflection of the conflict between assimilationist Jews and nationalist-Yiddishists. Should the Jews lose their identity; was there a need or was there not for a separate Jewish culture; was there or was there not a need

for separate Jewish workers' organizations? (See R. Abramovich, *Tsvei Revoluties,* citied in J. Nedava, *Trotsky and the Jews* (Philadelphia, 1972), pp. 90-91.

94. Lenin, *P.S.S.,* VII, p. 234.

95. Lenin, 4th Edition, VI, p. 470. Leonard Schapiro sums up the essential cause of the party's division by noting that "Lenin always attached much more importance to the question of organization than to doctrine. And so far as organization was concerned there was certainly unanimity that *Iskra* should dominate the party. As events were to show, where Lenin miscalculated was in assuming that there would be the same agreement on the necessity for Lenin to dominate *Iskra.*" (L. Schapiro, *The Communist Party* (New York: Random House, 1959), pp. 46-47.

96. *Vtoroi S"ezd,* pp. 170-72.

97. Ibid., pp. 139-41.

98. Nettl, I, p. 278. Mary-Alice Waters, ed., *Rosa Luxemburg Speaks* (New York: Pathfinder Press, 1970), pp. 113-14.

99. P. Frölich, *Rosa Luxemburg* (New York, 1972), p. 30.

100. Appeared in *Die Neue Zeit* and the then Menshevik-controlled *Iskra.*

101. Waters, *Luxemburg,* pp. 116-17.

102. Page, "Lenin and Self Determination," *Slavonic Review,* April 1950, pp. 343-47.

103. *Iskra,* No. 44, July 15, 1903.

104. Page, "Lenin and Self Determination," p. 347.

105. J. Stalin, *Marxism and the National Question* (New York: 1942), pp. 8-9; also V. Leder, "Natsional'ny vopros v polskoi i russkoi Sotsial-Demokratii," *Proletarskaia Revoliutsiia,* 1927, 2-3 (61-62), p. 190.

106. "The federalist inclinations of the various national groups" writes Leninist Leder, "were hurting the general party movement." (Leder, "Natsional'ny vopros," p. 190.)

107. The Unity Congress was a mockery of its designation. The revolution had left the Social-Democratic movement in tatters, and it was important at the time not to open old sores. No fundamental views were changed and both Russian factions, unlike their common hard line of 1903, were intent upon appeasing the national minority SDs. Indeed the first agenda item of the Congress was the establishment of a committee to take up the national question; its actual purpose being to bring the Poles,

the Bund and the Latvian SDs into the All-Russian party, making whatever concessions necessary. (See *Protokoly Ob"edinitel'nogo S"ezda,* pp. 26-27.)

108. For the sake of unity, the August Congress, among other things, adopted a resolution conceding that the Bund's demand for national cultural autonomy was not incompatible with the point in the party programme concerning the right of nations to self-determination. (B. Wolfe, *Three Who Made a Revolution* (Boston: Beacon, 1948), p. 581. Lenin furiously denounced this Menshevik surrender of the party's 1903 position, declaring that the August Conference of "liquidators" had by its "notorious resolution on 'national cultural' autonomy. . . adapted socialism to nationalism." (Lenin, *Collected Works,* 45 Vols. [Moscow: Progress Publishers, 1963-1970] XVIII, p. 412.)

109. Lenin's description of him at the time, in a letter to Gorky.

110. For persuasive evidence of this, see L. Trotsky, *Stalin* (London: Hollis and Carter, 1946), pp. 157-58.

111. After Stalin's arrest in 1913, Lenin tried to replace him with other Transcaucasians to serve as a vehicle for Lenin's propaganda on the national question. (B. Wolfe, *Three Who Made a Revolution,* pp. 583-87).

112. S. Page, "Lenin and Self-Determination," pp. 350-51.

113. Lenin, *P.S.S.,* XXV, p. 257.

114. Ibid., p. 364; Nettl, *Luxemburg,* II, pp. 591-95.

115. Nettl, II, 583-87.

116. Lenin, *P.S.S.,* XXV, p. 278.

Notes to Chapter One

1. Lenin, *P.S.S.,* XLVIII, p. 322.

2. Ibid., p. 332.

3. "Our connections with St. Petersburg (via Warsaw) have now become impossible. . . . To satisfy you as to my identity . . . , from 1907 to 1911 I represented RSDWP in the International Socialist Bureau. My party pseudonym is Lenin, my actual name is Ulianov . . . . Comrade Branting, leader of the Swedish party, knows me. You can telephone him." (Ibid., pp. 327-328.)

4. The success of "Pravdism" in St. Petersburg had been grudgingly admitted by Martov. (See O. H. Gankin and H. H. Fisher, *The Bolsheviks*

and the World War (Stanford: Stanford University Press, 1940), p. 102.

5. Lenin, *P.S.S.*, XXV, pp. 450-51.

6. Siromiatnikova, M. "Bernskaia Konferentsiia zagranichnikh organisatsii R.S.D.R.P. v. 1915 g. (s primechaniami G. L. Shklovskogo)," *Proletarskaia Revoliutsiia,* No. 5 (40), 1925, pp. 136-37.

7. The actual title of the article was "The Tasks of Revolutionary Social-Democracy in the European War." (Lenin, *P.S.S.,* XXVI, pp. 1-7.)

8. Alfred Rosmer notes that Lenin's was a Russian-based position and to prove his point indicates its similarity to that of the Russian liberals in the course of the Russo-Japanese war. "The latter were defeatists for the same reason as Lenin, which was that a Russian victory would strengthen tsarism, whereas a defeat would cause it to fall." (A. Rosmer, *Le Mouvement Ouvrier Pendant la Premié*re *Guerre Mondial, De Zimmerwald à la Révolution Russe,* 2 vols. (Paris, Mouton, 1959) II, p. 104.

9. In a letter of September 27, Karpinskii proposed a change in the wording of the sixth paragraph of the "Theses" lest it convey the erroneous idea that "the Russian Social-Democrats wish for victory of the Germans and defeat of the Russians. Note here the possible connection: the German Social Democrats struggle against . . . Tsarism and the Russian Social-Democrats greet the victory of German arms. This idea should be so formulated as to explain what would be the meaning of the victory of the Russian troops and what would be the meaning of their defeat (objectively)." (Gankin and Fisher, *The Bolsheviks,* p. 148.)

10. *Leninskii Sbornik,* (Moscow, 1930) XIV, p. 142.

11. Isaac Deutscher, *The Prophet Armed, Trotsky: 1879-1921,* Vol. I (New York: Vintage, 1965), p. 236.

12. Lenin, *P.S.S.,* XXVI, p. 166.

13. Gankin and Fisher, *The Bolsheviks,* pp. 219-21.

14. A. E. Senn, *The Russian Revolution in Switzerland, 1914-1917* (Madison: University of Wisconsin, 1971), p. 31; Gankin and Fisher, *The Bolsheviks,* p. 149. According to *Krasnyi Arkhiv,* 1939, No. 1, p. 52, Lenin's audiences included Okhrana agents.

15. Lenin, *P.S.S.*, XXVI, p. 108.

16. *Leninskii Sbornik,* XIV, pp. 135, 150-51. "I said these things," Kharitonov quoted Lenin, "to test the audience. If after such statements they do not hiss me, then things are going relatively well." (C.V. Tiutkin, "Leninskie referaty o voine (osen' 1914)," *Istoriia SSSR,* No. 2, Mart-Aprel, 1967, p. 38).

17. Lenin, *P.S.S.*, XXVI, pp. 15-23.

18. The following comment on Lenin's early November Zurich lecture strongly reflects a resentment toward Lenin's arrogance in trying to transplant his Russian-bred notions in the modernized West. "Here we are now in a region of heavy industry. Comrade Lenin represents a land of fools and slaves but acts like an authority on socialism before whom all tremble. Taking a vacation from Bolshevism, the careerist depicts himself as Ferdinand of Spain—'I shall save internationalism, I give you revolution; a new tactic.' There you have it! This is Bolshevism transposed to a place where European attitudes prevail." (*Leninskii Sbornik,* XIV, p. 141.)

19. *Leninskii Sbornik,* No. 2, p. 195; cited in Siromiatnikova, "Bernskaia Konferentsiia . . . 1915 g., *Proletarskaia Revoliutsiia,* No. 5 (40), 1925, p. 141.

20. Gankin and Fisher, *The Bolsheviks,* pp. 162-64; see also Ia. G. Temkin, *Lenin i Mezhdunarodnaia Sotsial-Demokratiia, 1914-1917* (Moscow, 1968), p. 113.

21. Temkin, *Lenin,* pp. 117-18.

22. Gankin and Fisher, *The Bolsheviks,* pp. 162-64.

23. Senn seems quite correct in noting that "the conference's image was obviously Lenin's greatest concern," telling a friend, a year after the event, that a large number of delegates was not essential for an effective conference, the important thing being the quality of the delegates as "true representatives of the masses, true revolutionaries, Bolsheviks . . . . " (Senn, *The Russian Revolution in Switzerland,* p. 39). See also Senn's "The Bolshevik Conference in Bern, 1915," *Slavic Review,* XXV, December, 1966, p. 676. Since the activity of the Bolshevik Central Committee and the Committee for Organizations Abroad had become defunct in the first months of the war, the revival in Switzerland of *Sotsial-Demokrat* by Lenin and Zinoviev made them the party's effective Central Committee. But, as Senn observes, "a more formal structure" seemed called for, and hence the conference of representatives abroad, "a more general party conference" being impossible to arrange. The Conference, Senn succinctly observes, served Lenin 1) by electing a new Committee of Organizations Abroad "that group was now formally transferred from Paris to Bern," and 2) by rallying "the various Bolshevik groups to Lenin's position," despite sniping, mainly by Bukharin, at Lenin's slogan of "civil war" and his call for "defeat of one's own government."

24. Lenin, *P.S.S.*, XXVI, pp. 161-67.

25. In the sense that his view of self-determination meant a confluence of nations through "proletarian" fraternization.

26. *Sotsial-Demokrat,* December 12, 1914. (Lenin, *P.S.S.*, XXVI, pp. 90-105.)

27. "The war," Balabanova writes, "had closed the various countries behind impenetrable curtains, and passions, intrigues, fears, conspiracies of silence, agencies for the diffusion of false news, spies and *agents provocateurs* had succeeded in distorting facts, situations and attitudes of individuals to such an extent that one finished by living in a world far from reality." (Angelica Balabanova, *Impressions of Lenin* [Ann Arbor: University of Michigan, 1964] pp. 38-39.)

28. Siromiatnikova, "Bernskaia Konferentsiia . . . ", *Proletarskaia Revoliutsiia,* No. 5 pp. 186-88; See also, S. W. Page, *Lenin and World Revolution* (New York: McGraw-Hill, 1972), pp. 13-15.

29. Lenin, *P.S.S.*, XXVI, p. 354.

30. Stanley Washburn writes: "the world's history records nothing that has even approximated to this German drive which fell on one Russian Army, the bulk of which remained at its post and perished. . . . If the statement that the Germans fired 700,000 shells in three hours is true, and it is accepted in the Russian army, one can readily realize what must have been the condition of the army occupying that line of works." (C. F. Horne and W. F. Austin, eds., *Source Records of The Great War,* 7 vols. III, pp. 183-84.)

31. R. H. Bruce Lockhart, *British Agent* (New York: Putnams, 1933) p. 104.

32. Lenin, *P.S.S.*, XXVI, pp. 273-76. To the reactionary war aims of men like Purishkevich, Lenin linked Potresov, Akselrod, Plekhanov, Chkheidze, the Bund and others of Menshevik stripe.

33. Temkin, *Lenin,* pp. 122-29.

34. N. Krupskaya, *Reminiscences of Lenin* (New York: International Publishers, 1960), pp. 302-303. Lenin's wife recalls her husband's impatience in putting up "with the role of a sort of shadow-leader in the momentous events that were taking place around him and in which he longed with all his being to take a direct part."

35. According to Balabanova, a Menshevik delegate to the Women's Conference, it was "ludicrious" for Lenin to be sitting "days on end in . . . a

coffeehouse" receiving information from the female Bolshevik delegates at the convention and giving them instructions." These were meticulously followed, for "at each ballot" if there was even "the slightest modification of a resolution, the meeting was interrupted to allow the Bolshevik delegates" to confer with Lenin. (Balabanova, *Impressions of Lenin,* p. 40). Lenin's attempt to control every last move of the convention is borne out also by a Krupskaia anecdote. Lenin tried vainly on one occasion to have Inessa Armand "go immediately" to convince Zetkin "of the correctness of our position," to argue her out of sliding "toward pacifism at the present moment," and to "sharpen all issues." Lenin never ceased pressing fresh ideas upon Armand which were, in his words, certain to "persuade Zetkin." And although Inessa assured Lenin that such missions would be useless, Lenin "insisted ardently that she do as he wished." See *Vospominaniia O Vladimire Il'ich Lenine,* 5 vols. (Moscow, 1969) I, pp. 408-409. Through his female messengers, Lenin was trying to induce the Women's Conference to come out for the formation of a new international. However, the attendant "mothers, wives and widows" did not consider themselves authorized to take so drastic an action. According to Balabanova, the delegates begged Lenin's "deputies" to yield so that the final resolution could be a unanimous one. But the difficult negotiations with the obdurate Lenin could produce only a compromise. The Bolshevik minority signed the resolution with an addendum stating that the Women's Congress had not "achieved its purpose. It could have laid the foundation for the construction of a new international. But it has not done so." (Balabanova, p. 41.)

36. At the Youth Convention, Lenin similarly caused "confusion and despair" because the delegates did not regard a vote on the formation of a new international to be within their realm of competency. Balabanova writes:

> In my memory still echoes the desperate outcry of the young German delegate: 'Being liable to conscription, I have faced great dangers in crossing the border and overcome many obstacles to get here and bring you the German Socialist youth's proof of their antiwar sentiments and their belief in the brotherhood of peoples. I have come here to take back to Germany the assurance that the war has not severed the class bonds, that we proletarians

> are brothers fighting for the same cause. Think what relief and encouragement this news might bring to the front and the back areas. And you, comrades, want to destroy all this, you want me to return with the news that unanimity has not been reached, exactly what our adversaries affirm!'
>
> These words of warning, uttered in a voice unsteady with emotion, could not induce the Bolshevik delegates to give in. After consulting Lenin—who this time guided the discussions from his home by phone—they became even more intransigent and used, for the first time, that retaliation to which they were to resort later even in diplomatic relations with governments. They left the assembly hall.
>
> After various attempts to come to some sort of agreement the convention was adjourned. As in the previous case, a delegation went to Lenin. The outcome was the same: Lenin authorized the youth of his group to vote in favor of the resolution proposed by the majority of the delegates, provided the statement of the Bolshevik minority be included in the minutes of the meeting.

(Balabanova, *Impressions of Lenin,* pp. 42-43.)

37. Angelica Balabanova, *My Life as a Rebel* (Bloomington: Indiana University, 1973), pp. 132-33. Balabanova's account of Lenin's intransigence at the Bern Youth Conference is fully supported by Willi Münzenberg. (See Gankin and Fisher, *The Bolsheviks,* pp. 302-307).

38. Senn, *Russian Revolution,* p. 42.

39. Z. A. B. Zeman and W. B. Scharlau, *The Merchant of Revolution, The Life of Alexander Israel Helphand (Parvus) 1867-1924* (London: Oxford University, 1965) pp. 131-151, 158; G. Katkov, *Russia, 1917, The February Revolution* (New York: Harper, 1967), pp. 80-81.

40. A. E. Senn, "Solzhenytsin and the Historical Lenin," *Canadian Slavonic Papers,* XIX, No. 2, June, 1977, p. 156. See also B. Souvarine, "Solzhenytsin and Lenin," *Dissent,* Summer, 1977. Souvarine has scathing criticism for the falsifications in the books cited in footnote 39, especially with regard to matters concerning the Lenin-Helphand relationship, Lenin's return to Russia and Lenin and "German gold." I have drawn upon the above mentioned questionable sources only for materials about which there can be no controversy. On the same subject, see also Souvarine's

long and extremely persuasive letter in response to criticism of his Summer, 1977 article in *Dissent,* Winter, 1978.

41. Lenin, *P.S.S.,* XLIX, p. 81.

42. N. K. Krupskaya, *Reminiscences of Lenin* (New York: International Publishers, 1960), p. 309.

43. Gankin and Fisher, *The Bolsheviks,* p. 311.

44. Krupskaya, *Reminiscences,* p. 309. For extensive data on this activity by Lenin see, *P.S.S.,* XLIX, pp. 77-138.

45. Lenin, *P.S.S.,* XLIX, pp. 116-117.

46. Ibid., XXVI, p. 283.

47. Ibid., pp. 323, 454.

48. Ibid., pp. 323, 333.

49. Ibid., pp. 337-338.

50. Ibid., p. 342.

51. Ibid., p. 342.

52. K. Kautsky, *Sozialisten und Krieg* (Prague, 1937), pp. 542, 547.

53. Gankin and Fisher, *The Bolsheviks,* pp. 338-339.

54. The Zimmerwald Left was made up of Lenin, Zinoviev, Berzins, Radek, Borchardt, Platten, Höglund and Norman.

55. D. Shub, *Politicheskie Deiateli Rossii (1850ykh-1920ykh gg. Sbornik Statei* (New York: Waldon Press, 1969) pp. 166-167. Hoffman, a member of Lebedour's group, charged the Bolsheviks with being such daring revolutionaries because they were not residing in their own country. (Temkin, *Lenin,* p. 231.)

56. *Die Zimmerwalder Bewegung,* 2 vols. (The Hague: Mouton, 1967) I, *Protokolle,* pp. 129-30.

57. Lenin, *P.S.S.,* XXVII, p. 43. In his brief post-Zimmerwald comments on the conference, Lenin again compared his Zimmerwald actions pertaining to Germany with attitudes of Marx and Engels in 1847, when "*from abroad*—they had viewed the German Philistines with horror, and that they wanted to call for revolution from abroad, as they did in their famous 'Manifesto of the Communist Party', which directly and openly spoke of the need for violence." (Ibid., p. 44.)

58. Lenin, *P.S.S.,* LIV, p. 462.

59. According to the Conference minutes Lenin spoke only five times at Zimmerwald and then briefly. He preferred to let Radek and Zinoviev press the Bolshevik proposals while he remained in the background.

According to W. Gautschi, Lenin "in no way dominated the proceedings." See W. Gautschi, *Lenin als Emigrant in der Schweiz,* (Zurich: Bensiger, 1973), pp. 147-149. But even if Lenin spoke little, there can be no doubt that the Conference majority, whose views he contemptuously opposed, knew who was pulling the strings.

Notes to Chapter Two

1. Lenin, *P.S.S.,* XXVII, pp. 26-30.
2. Ibid., pp. 49-50.
3. Ibid., p. 114.
4. Ibid., p. 249.
5. Gankin and Fisher, *The Bolsheviks,* p. 379.
6. Gankin and Fisher, *The Bolsheviks,* p. 460. See also p. 458 for further sarcastic comment by Grumbach. "I praise Lenin [Radek shouts.] How can [he] think that I should have the presumption to praise Lenin—the only ruler of the Russian Bolsheviks! Lenin is being neither praised nor censured! Facts about Lenin are merely established in the same manner as a well intentioned citizen treats the actions of his Emperor or as a scientist treats the phenomena of nature." For comment on the strength of the revolutionary movement in Germany, see *Die Zimmerwald Bewegung,* I, pp. 226, 230. Laukant and Thalheimer suggest little in the way of mutinous sentiment.
7. Krupskaya, *Reminiscences,* p. 333.
8. Gankin and Fisher, *The Bolsheviks,* pp. 440-441.
9. Ibid., p. 421.
10. Lenin, *P.S.S.,* XXX, pp. 131-143.
11. Ibid., p. 142.
12. Ibid., p. 161. "*We* help to unite the revolutionary proletariat of France, Germany, and Italy. . . . This is the political objective of the Swiss revolutionary Social Democrats." (My italics. The "we" was, of course, Lenin.)
13. Ibid., pp. 218-219.
14. W. Lerner, *Karl Radek, The Last Internationalist* (Stanford, 1970), pp. 49-52. Lenin, writes Lerner, "had always been intrigued by Radek's potential as a contact with the German Left." To Armand on November 4, Lenin wrote: "Radek arrived and we made peace. Bitterness had almost reached the breaking point." Lenin, *P.S.S.,* XLIX, p. 318.

15. Lenin, *P.S.S.*, pp. 362-365.

16. Lerner, *Radek*, pp. 49-52.

17. Lenin, *P.S.S.*, pp. 336-337.

18. Ibid., XLIX, pp. 351-386.

19. "It is not true," Lenin wrote to Armand on February 14, 1917, "that revolutionary mass action in Switzerland is 'impossible.' Was there not a general strike in Zurich in 1912? And what happened in Geneva and in La Chaux-de-Fonds? Precisely now, during the war, mass action and even revolution in Switzerland is even more possible. (This would have significance for France and Germany.) There is a basis in the Swiss party for creating a left movement. This is fact. It would not be an easy job, but it would be worth doing." (Lenin, *P.S.S.*, XLIX, pp. 385-386. For extensive comment on Lenin's attempts to instigate a revolutionary climate in Switzerland, see A. E. Senn, *The Russian Revolution in Switzerland,* Chapter 16 "Splitting the Swiss.") Lenin's failure to draw attention to his ideas brought him to such a pathetic level of depression that he even proposed to Armand what was to be done to make the best revolutionary use of a situation in which Switzerland was drawn into the war. That being the case, Lenin ruminated "the French would occupy Geneva. To be in Geneva then is to be in France; and from there to be in contact with Russia. [Better than nothing] I am therefore thinking of turning over the *party* funds to you (for you to keep *on your person* sewed up in a special little bag) for the bank won't let you withdraw money during the war." (Lenin, *P.S.S.*, XLIX, p. 367.) But Lenin was apparently too depressed even to dwell extensively upon a hope dictated by despair, one in which he did not really believe. He concluded his brief note by writing: "these are merely plans [daydreams]. So far let us keep them to ourselves. I think that we shall remain in Zurich and that war is improbable." (Ibid.)

Notes to Chapter Three

1. See H. W. Kettenbach, *Lenin's Theorie des Imperialismus, Teil 1: Grundlagen und Voraussetzungen* (Cologne: Mindt, 1965). See also J. A. Hobson's *Imperialism,* (London: Allen and Unwin, 1938, first published in 1902) which, in language, even more caustic than Lenin's makes all of the latter's points. Hobson could not, of course have anticipated Kautsky's attempt, as Lenin viewed it, to interpret imperialism as a movement toward

internationalism. Kautsky's "ultra-imperialism," whether or not an apologetic for imperialism—particularly that of Germany—could be considered a normal derivative of Marxist reasoning. But of course, it ran directly opposite to Lenin's designs of the moment.

2. Kautsky defined "ultra-imperialism" as a form of capitalist internationalism.

3. N. Bukharin, *Imperialism and World Economy, with an introduction by V. I. Lenin* (London, n.d.), p. 139. An interpretation of the differences between Bukharin's and Lenin's theoretical expositions on the subject of imperialism is expounded in S. F. Cohen, *Bukharin and the Bolshevik Revolution* (New York: Knopf, 1973), pp. 35-37.

4. Lenin objected to Kautsky's failure to consider the war to be a product entirely of finance capital, as opposed to industrial capital, the economic force which had led to an earlier phase of imperialist expansion and conflict. Lenin wanted to pinpoint finance capital as the dynamic that impelled capitalist powers to try to annex not "*only* agrarian regions," but also, because the world was already parceled out, to grasp at "*any* territory whatsoever," making for inevitable and interminable wars. Kautsky, according to Lenin, had compromised with the bankers by suggesting that it was possible to fight against imperialism, "the politics of trusts and banks," without attacking "the economic foundation of trusts and banks," and for suggesting, as well, that the imperialists might conceivably unite through their international cartels, thus introducing a "phase of ultra-imperialism" during which the world might be exploited in peace by "an internationally united finance capital." (Lenin, *P.S.S.*, XXVII, pp. 388-391; see also Lenin's comments on the same subject in "Proletarian Revolution and Renegade Kautsky," Lenin, *P.S.S.*, XXXVII, pp. 238-239.)

5. Fritz Fischer, *Griff Nach Der Weltmacht* (Düsseldorf: Droste, 1961), pp. 15-35, provides a lengthy explanation of German imperialism in terms of such drives. For Bethmann-Hohlweg's war aims' program and its links to German finance capital, see Fischer, *Weltmacht,* pp. 107-117.

6. According to a recent observation, "Although historians remain unclear about the precise connection between German imperialism in 1911, 1914 and 1939, there is an increasing willingness to recognize the validity of the problem when stated this way." See G. D. Feldman, *German Imperialism, 1914-1918* (New York: Wiley, 1972), p. 6.

7. Lenin, *P.S.S.,* XXVII, p. 387.

8. Anyone consulting Lenin's notebooks for *Imperialism* (Lenin, *P.S.S.,* XXVIII, pp. 805-822) can see, by merely glancing at the index of source titles, that Lenin drew predominantly from German materials. The sources actually cited in the completed work are largely by German authors, an observation which struck me forcibly and helped lead to this book's basic thesis. Lenin's book gave the Pan-Germans free rein to "prove" Lenin's own critique of imperialism, as some random excerpts reveal: "So writes the German Professor Schulze-Gaevernitz, an apologist of German imperialism . . . ." (Lenin, *P.S.S.,* XXVII, p. 335), or "We notice that the representatives of bourgeois German–but not only German–scholarship, such as Riesser, Schulze-Gaevernitz, Liefmann and others, are all solid apologists for imperialism and financial capital." (Ibid., p. 344) or "Kautsky debates with Cunow, the German apologist for imperialism and annexations, who . . . cynically argues that imperialism is contemporary capitalism, that the development of capitalism is inevitable and progressive, which means one must bow down before imperialism and glorify it!" (Ibid., p. 390). Similar passages abound throughout the work. See Ibid., pp. 345-346, 352, 355-356, 358, 362-363, 371-373, 384 and *passim.*

9. Lenin, *P.S.S.,* XXX, pp. 5-6.

10. Gyorgy Lukacs brilliantly captured this essence of Leninism in his book of 1924. Lukacs writes:

> For the real revolution is the dialectical transformation of the bourgeois revolution into the proletarian revolution . . . . The bourgeoisie's recourse to counter-revolution indicates not only its hostility towards the proletariat, but at the same time the renunciation of its own revolutionary traditions. *It abandons the inheritance of its revolutionary past to the proletariat.* [My emphasis] From now on the proletariat is the only class capable of taking the bourgeois revolution to its logical conclusion. In other words, the remaining relevant demands of the bourgeois revolution can only be realized within the framework of the proletarian revolution, and the consistent realization of these demands necessarily leads to a proletarian revolution. Thus, the proletarian revolution now means, at one and the same time, the realization and suppression of the bourgeois revolution. The

> correct application of this situation opens up an immense perspective for the chances and possibilities of the proletarian revolution. At the same time, however, it makes heavy demands on the revolutionary proletariat and its leading party. For to achieve this dialectical transition the proletariat must not only have [correct] insight into, but must in practice overcome all its own petty-bourgeois tendencies and habits of thought (for instance, national prejudice) which have hitherto prevented such insight. Overcoming its own limitations, the proletariat must rise to the leadership of all the oppressed.

Lukacs, like Lenin, really did not expect the "proletariat," without educated and intellectual revolutionary guidance, to achieve "its own" standards of excellence. But like Lenin, he attributed mystical qualities to the "proletariat" and he related the question of self determination to the factor of proletarian self-discipline. Such a hoped-for suppression of the national instinct by proletarians was, of course, Utopian. Despite numerous Leninist-guided revolutions in the fifty-odd years since Lukacs' book was published, nationalist sentiment has nowhere become extinct. "The oppressed nations' struggle for national independence," Lukacs writes,

> is an undertaking of the greatest revolutionary self-education, both for the proletariat of the oppressing nations, *which overcomes its own nationalism by fighting for the full national independence of another people, and for the proletariat of the oppressed nation, which in its turn transcends its own nationalism by raising the corresponding slogan of federalism–of international proletarian solidarity.* [My emphasis]. For as Lenin says, 'The proletariat struggles for socialism and against its own weaknesses'.

G. Lukacs, *Lenin, A Study of the Unity of His Thought* (Cambridge: M.I.T., 1971), pp. 40-50. Coming from an intellectual, such a comment can only be viewed as a form of fanaticism.

11. Lenin, *P.S.S.,* XXX, pp. 17-58.

12. S. Page, "Lenin and Self Determination," *The Slavonic and East European Review,* April, 1950.

13. Ibid., The Jewish Bund, the Georgian and Latvian Social-Democrats, in general, opposed self determination as a device Lenin was using to undercut their separate national identities within RSDWP in order to eliminate their claims to autonomous status within the all-Russian party. Rosa Luxemburg had a more complex position to defend, because in Poland she was struggling against the nationalistically oriented P.P.S. (*Infra,* pp. 39-40.)

14. Richard Pipes, *The Formation of the Soviet Union,* (New York: Atheneum, 1968), pp. 48-49.

15. Lenin, *P.S.S.,* XXX, p. 117. See also *supra,* Chapter VIII.

16. Gankin and Fisher, *The Bolsheviks,* p. 220.

17. Ibid., p. 228. Lenin's *Sotsial-Demokrat* and the Bukharin-Piatakov group (publishers of *Kommunist*) were in constant contact, having plans to issue a jount collection of articles, presenting both points of view.

18. Ibid., p. 236.

19. Ibid.

20. Deutscher remarks that Bukharin's ideas, even though criticized by Lenin as being scholastic and doctrinaire, nevertheless exercised a strong influence on Lenin, "who adopted them and gave the a more realistic and supple expression." (See I. Deutscher, *The Prophet Unarmed, Trotsky: 1921-1929,* Vol. II, [New York: Vintage, 1959], p. 82.) Lenin's Testament, in effect, admitted this, when it described Bukharin as the party's foremost theoretician. Bukharin, for his part, soon after Lenin's death, admitted a certain debt to Lenin with regard to the latter's practical sense on the subject of the revolutionary state. See N. Bukharin, *Lenin as a Marxist* (London, 1925), pp. 28-33.

21. But does the state "die off?" See *Supra,* pp. 99-101.

22. Gankin and Fisher, *The Bolsheviks,* p. 237.

23. Ibid.

24. Lenin, *P.S.S.,* XXX, p. 79.

25. Ibid., p. 122. Lenin's article was entitled "A Caricature of Marxism and Imperialist Economism."

Notes to Chapter Four

1. N. K. Krupskaya, *Reminiscences,* p. 328.
Krupskaya continues:

> As far back as October, 1915 [right after Zimmerwald] Ilyich had written a reply to an article by Radek. . . in *Berner Tagewacht.* 'According to [Radek] it works out that *for the sake* of the socialist revolution he spurns a consistently revolutionary programme in the field of democracy. That is wrong. The proletariat can win only through democracy, i.e., through putting into effect full democracy and linking up every stop of its progress with democratic demands in their most emphatic wording. It is absurd to offset the socialist revolution and the revolutionary struggle against capitalism by *one* of the questions of democracy, in this case the national question. We must *combine* the revolutionary struggle against capitalism with a revolutionary programme and tactics in respect of *all* democratic demands, including a republic, a militia, election of government officials by the people, equal rights for women, self determination of nations, etc. So long as capitalism exists all these demands are capable of realization only as an exception, and in incomplete, distorted form. (Ibid., pp. 328-329).

2. *Leninskii Sbornik,* XIV, p. 204. (Hereafter *Sbornik*).
3. Krupskaya, *Reminiscences,* p. 331.
4. *Sbornik,* p. 214.
5. Ibid., p. 218.
6. Ibid., p. 223, 386.
7. Ibid., pp. 220-223.
8. Ibid., pp. 224-236.
9. Ibid., p. 248.
10. Ibid., pp. 224-228.
11. Ibid., pp. 368-379.

11a. At the time, ironically, Plekhanov had clearly perceived the state of affairs. See "Perepiska G. V. Plekhanova i K. Kautskogo," in Deutsch L., ed., *Gruppa Osvobozhdenie Truda,* 6 vols. (Moscow, 1924-28), V. p. 225. "Do you really agree with Bernstein?" Plekhanov asked Kautsky in a letter.

12. K. Kautsky, *Das Erfurter Program* (Stuttgart, 1892), pp. 147-149. As late as March, 1952, the notion that Kautsky supported a truly revolutionary doctrine at Erfurt was presented in a *Journal of Modern*

History article. See also W. H. Maehl, *German Militarism and Socialism* (Nebraska Wesleyan Press, 1968), pp. 64-65.

13. K. Kautsky, *The Social Revolution* (Chicago, 1902), p. 3.
14. Ibid., pp. 85-88.
15. Ibid., pp. 96-98.
16. Lenin, *P.S.S.,* XXXIII, pp. 109-110.
17. Ibid., p. 110.
18. Ibid.
19. Ibid., p. 111.
20. Lenin, having read Kautsky's *Social Revolution,* writes in his notes, "Even in 1890 Kautsky was against the introduction into the program of some measures anticipating the transfer period from capitalism to socialism." (*Sbornik,* p. 357).
21. Lenin, *P.S.S.,* XXXIII, p. 4.
22. Ibid., p. 5.
23. Ibid., pp. 7-8.
24. *Supra,* p. 80.
25. Lenin, *P.S.S.,* XXXIII, p. 34.
26. Ibid. Mocking the emphasis Lenin laid upon the once-used phrase "dictatorship of the proletariat," Kautsky referred to the term in German as "the little word,"–*das Wörtchen.*
27. *Supra,* p. 88.
28. C. E. Schorske, *The German Social Democracy, 1905-1917* (Cambridge: Harvard, 1955), pp. 248-49.
29. Lenin, *P.S.S.,* XXX, p. 15.
30. Luxemburg, p. 159.
31. Ibid., p. 179.
32. Ibid., p. 180.
33. Ibid., p. 181.
34. Ibid., p. 182.
35. Lenin, *P.S.S.,* XXXVII, pp. 290-291.
36. That oligarchy was Lenin's conception of the form which the dictatorship of the proletariat had to assume is clear from his shrill defense of the existing Soviet oligarchy against Kautsky's attack upon it in *Diktatur des Proletariates.* In his counterattacking *Renegade Kautsky* (1918) Lenin derides Kautsky for his ignorance in assuming that a dictatorship has to be exercised by a single person when it can be done "by a handful

of people, or by an oligarchy. . . ." (See Lenin, *P.S.S.*, XXXVII, p. 244.)

37. *Sbornik,* p. 255.

38. Ibid., pp. 266-267.

39. Ibid.

40. Ibid., p. 267.

41. Ibid., p. 271.

42. At the present time, of course, the ideas of *State and Revolution* have become enshrined in Soviet doctrine. See *Fundamentals of Marxism-Leninism,* 2nd Revised Edition (Moscow, 1963), pp. 509-538 and *passim.*

43. Lenin, *P.S.S.,* XXXVII, pp. 262-264.

44. Ibid., p. 302.

45. Ibid., pp. 302-303. This is an example of how Lenin used his geographically broadened perceptions (*Supra,* p. 77) of the national question as a global phenomenon for the purpose of aiding his tactical revolutionary program.

46. *Supra,* p. 81.

47. V. I. Lenin, *Collected Works,* 45 vols. (Moscow: Progress Publishers, 1963-1970), XXIII, p. 69.

48. Ibid., pp. 67-68.

49. Ibid.

50. Ibid., pp. 69-70.

51. Ibid., p. 70.

52. *Sbornik,* XIV, p. 228. In *State and Revolution,* Lenin observes that Engels, at this point, particularly stresses the basic theme "running like a red thread through all of Marx's work; namely, that the democratic republic is the nearest approach to the dictatorship of the proletariat." (Lenin, *P.S.S.,* XXXIII, pp. 70-71.)

53. *Sbornik,* p. 234. For Lenin's use of these ideas in *State and Revolution,* see Lenin, *P.S.S.,* XXXIII, pp. 73-74.

54. *Sbornik,* pp. 237-239.

55. Ibid., p. 239.

56. Ibid.

57. Ibid., pp. 250-253.

58. Ibid., p. 255.

59. In 1908 Lenin depicted the Soviets as having in effect converted the Russian revolutionary movement into the spiritual descendant of the Paris Commune. (See Page, *Lenin and World Revolution,* p. 6.)

60. Lenin, *P.S.S.*, XLVIIII, pp. 341-342.

61. S. Bloch, *Erinnerungen an Lenin* (Zurich, 1924), p. 5.

62. Lenin, *P.S.S.*, XXX, pp. 306-310.

63. Prior to Bloody Sunday, Lenin said, there had been in Russia mere sects of revolutionary organizers, "a few thousand members of local organizations, a half dozen revolutionary leaflets, appearing no more than once a month." (Ibid., p. 310.)

64. Lenin, *P.S.S.*, XXX, pp. 310-311.

65. Ibid., pp. 315-316.

66. Ibid., XII, pp. 24-25, 33, 57, 68 and *passim.*

67. Ibid., XXX, pp. 317-318.

68. Ibid., pp. 318-322.

69. Commenting in his notebook on Marxism and the State, Lenin notes that Marx's *Civil War in France* makes much of the active role the workers themselves played in taking over governmental functions. Lenin points out as *"very important"* that "the Russian revolution was approaching the same outcome, perhaps more timidly, on the one hand, than the Paris Commune, yet evincing, on the other hand, a broader base in the 'Soviets of Workers' Deputies' of 'Railway Workers' Deputies' of 'Soldier, Sailor Deputies' and of 'Peasant Deputies.' This should be particularly noted!" (*Sbornik,* p. 313).

70. Lenin, *P.S.S.*, XXX, p. 322.

71. Ibid., pp. 323-327.

72. Krupskaya, *Reminiscences,* pp. 333-335.

Notes to Chapter Five

1. Lenin, *P.S.S.*, XXXI, p. 87.
2. Ibid., p. 93.
3. Ibid., p. 16.
4. Ibid., p. 22.
5. Ibid., pp. 24-30.
6. Ibid., pp. 42-44.
7. Ibid., p. 44.
8. Ibid., p. 46.
9. Ibid., pp. 46-47.
10. Ibid., pp. 93, 56.

11. Ibid.

12. Ibid.

13. Soon after Lenin arrived in Russia he was subjected to harassment for being a spy and a traitor, he was threatened with violence and arrest by large contingents of soldiers and was forbidden, for a time, to appear before the soldiers' section of the Soviet. However, Menshevik and S.R. leaders feared that patriotic attacks upon Lenin might ramify to endanger their own uncertain status. Skobelev and Tsereteli appeared before demonstrators to quiet the cries against "provocateur" Lenin. Subsequently, the Soviet organ *Izvestiia* ran an article charging "dark forces" were trying to discredit Lenin, who had given his whole life to the working class. *Izvestiia* attacked Miliukov for adhering to Russia's imperialistic agreements and this diverted attention from Lenin. (For a good review of this episode, see A. Sergeev, "Na Voloske," *Novoe Russkoe Slovo,* June 23, 1978.) After the July Days' rising, the Mensheviks themselves used the "spy" weapon to discredit Lenin. (See *supra,* p. 125.)

14. F. Platten, *Lenin iz Emigratsii v Rossii, Mart 1917* (Moscow, 1925), p. 47.

15. Lenin, *Sochineniia,* 3rd Ed. (Moscow, 1926-1932), XX, p. 81.

16. N. N. Sukhanov, *The Russian Revolution of 1917,* ed. J. Carmichael, 2 vols. (New York: Harper, 1962), I, pp. 281-288.

17. *Pervyi legal'nyi Peterburgskii Komitet Bol'shevikov v 1917 g.* (Moscow, 1927), p.

18. *Petrogradskaia Obshchegorodskaia Vserossiiskaia Konferentsiia R.S.-D.R.P. (Bol'shevikov v Aprele 1917 g.* (Moscow, 1925), pp. 14-15.

19. See A. Rabinowitch, *Prelude to Revolution, The Petrograd Bolsheviks and the July 1917 Uprising* (Bloomington: Indiana University, 1968), pp. 42-47; and R. V. Daniels, *Red October, The Bolshevik Revolution of 1917* (New York: Scribners, 1967), p. 32.

20. For the best treatment of this subject see R. A. Wade, *The Russian Search for Peace, February-October, 1917* (Stanford, 1969), Chapters IV and V.

21. Daniels, *Red October,* p. 34.

22. Page, *Lenin and World Revolution,* pp. 40-41.

23. *Pravda,* May 6, 1917; citied in I. G. Tsereteli, *Vospominaniia o Fevral'skoi Revoliutsii,* 2 vols. (Paris: Mouton, 1963), I, p. 93.

24. Lenin, *P.S.S.,* XXXII, pp. 263-291; Page, *Lenin and World Revolution,* p. 47.

25. N E. Saul, *Sailors in Revolt. The Russian Baltic Fleet in 1917* (Lawrence: University of Kansas, 1978), p. 111.

26. Page, *Lenin and World Revolution,* pp. 43-44.

27. B. Elov, "Posle Iul'skikh Sobytii," *Krasnaiia Letopis,* No. 7, 1923, p. 96.

28. V. D. Bonch-Bruevich, *V. I. Lenin v Rossii* (Moscow, 1935), p. 86.

29. Lenin, *Sochineniia,* 2nd ed. 30 vols. (Moscow, 1926-32), XXI, p. 41.

30. Ibid., *P.S.S.,* XXXIII, p. 4.

31. Ibid., pp. 37-40.

32. Leon Trotsky, *History of the Russian Revolution,* 3 vols. (New York: Simon and Schuster, 1937), II, 54-55, 116, 252-253.

33. Page, *Lenin and World Revolution,* pp. 61-63.

Notes to Chapter Six

1. Page, "Lenin and Peasant 'Bolshevism' in Latvia," pp. 95-112.

2. U. Germanis, *Oberst Vacietis und die Lettischen Schützen im Weltkrieg und in der Oktober Revolution* (Stockholm: Almquist and Wiksell, 1974), p. 101.

3. Ibid., pp. 102-103.

4. S. W. Page, The Formation of the Baltic States (New York: Fertig, 1970), p. 84 n.

5. S. W. Page, "Lenin's April Theses and the Latvian Peasant Soldiery," in R. C. Elwood (ed.) *Reconsiderations On the Russian Revolution* (Cambridge: Slavica, 1976), pp. 154-155 (Hereafter, Page "Theses.")

6. *Infra,* p. 133.

7. A. K. Wildman, "The Bolsheviks of the Twelvth Army and Latvian Social Democracy," in R. C. Elwood, *Reconsiderations,* pp. 173-74.

8. Page, "Theses," pp. 155-156.

9. Ibid., p. 157. More specifically the conference went on record as saying that "the workers view the national question, in the sense of the language and culture, simply as a question of democracy in general, which can best of all be resolved not by way of insulation and national separatism, but through the formation of a broad union and democratic centralism . . . . In the first place [we are] for a democratically governed Latvia in a democratic Russia, or more broadly, in a Western European or worldwide

democratic republic." (Ibid., pp. 168-169.) This was really a roundabout way of saying that only an international organization, recognizing a tiny nation's existence, could give that nation at least a semblance of national identity.

10. Lenin, *P.S.S.*, XXXI, pp. 113-114.

11. According to M. L. Schlesinger, *Russland im XX Jahrhundert* (Berlin, 1908), pp. 142-145, the Latvians placed red flags in the hands of their kindergartners and taught them to sing revolutionary songs.

12. A. Ezergailis, "A German Leaflet on Fraternization, April, 1916," *The Slavonic and East European Review,* XLVIII, No. 113 (October, 1970), pp. 598-599.

13. A. A. Drizulis, A. Y. Kabikis, A. K. Kirshbaum, eds., *Oktiabr'-skoi revoliutsiia v Latvii, dokumenty i materialy* (Riga, 1957), pp. 127-128. (Hereafter *ORL*).

14. W. S. Woytinsky, *Stormy Passage* (New York: Vanguard, 1961), p. 319.

15. Lenin, *P.S.S.*, XXXI, p. 14.

16. Page, "Theses," n. 7. There is, of course, the possibility that Lenin deliberately seized upon the use of Courland by *Rech* because Courland was German-occupied and that he was still thinking in terms of a Germany army in revolution as the instrument he could use to further the "self determination" of nations under a Lenin-dominated all-European proletarian dictatorship.

17. Lenin, *P.S.S.*, XXXI, p. 435. "If Finland, if Poland or the Urkaine separate themselves from Russia, there is nothing bad about that. . . . He who says so, is a chauvinist."

18. For vivid descriptions of the emotional experiences of the Latvians, see A. Ezergailis, "1917 in Latvia: The Bolshevik Year," *Canadian Slavic Studies,* II No. 4 (Winter 1969), pp. 646-647; Lockhart, *British Agent* (New York: Putman's, 1933), p. 330; B. M. Weissman, *Herbert Hoover and Famine Relief to Soviet Russia: 1921-1923* (Stanford: Hoover, 1974) pp. 118-119. For additional information on refugees from Courland and from Latvia in general, see also *Presseabteilung Ober Ost* (Berlin, 1917), p. 431 and M. Markov, *Sovetskaia Latviia* (Moscow, 1940), p. 13. Markov reports that almost a million people (more than one-third of the population) abandoned Latvia in the course of the war.

19. Lenin, *P.S.S.*, p. 106 (Emphasis in the original.)

20. According to a Bolshevik comment, "The Soviets of the Landless capitulated to the bourgeoisie." V. Mishke, "Podgotovka Oktiabra v Latvii," *Proletarskaia Revoliutsiia,* No. 72 (1928), p. 58.

21. Lenin, *P.S.S.*, XXXI, p. 107.

22. *ORL,* pp. 29-30. The organ of the *strelki* reports that Krastkalns was then forcibly removed to Petrograd and handed over to the Provisional Government under condition that he not be allowed to "return to Riga while the war lasted." (Mishke, "Podgotovka," p. 56.)

23. *ORL,* pp. 29-30.

24. Lenin, *P.S.S.*, XXXI, p. 109. (Emphasis in the original.)

25. Sukhanov, *The Russian Revolution I,* pp. 282-283. (Emphasis in the original.)

26. Page, "Lenin and Peasant 'Bolshevism', etc.," pp. 101-012.

27. *Supra,* p. 28.

28. Lenin, *P.S.S.,* XXXI, pp. 166-167. (Emphasis in the original.)

29. Trotsky, *History of the Russian Revolution III,* p. 75.

30. Back in Riga, again, *Cina* replaced *Zinotajs,* the newspaper published by the Riga Soviet.

31. *ORL,* pp. 70-72. The figures cited differ only slightly from those in Germanis, *Oberst Vacietis.* Germanis points out that the new executive committee of the *strelki* was Bolshevik-controlled. See pp. 96-97.

32. *ORL,* pp. 70-72. Stučka wrote his *Pravda* article at Lenin's request. The conservative circles of the German Balts jeered at the Latvian bourgeoisie and other non-Bolshevik Latvians, whose "spoiled and beloved child" has crossed into the enemy camp. "So even the best troops of our front,"a Baron Lieven wrote, mocking the Russian Command's description of the Latvian Battalions, "are no longer available for further adventurist schemes." (Germanis, *Vacietis,* p. 198.) Reacting to storms of protest, a certain number of *strelki* delegates reneged on the May 17 resolution which they had originally supported. (Ibid., p. 199.)

33. A. Ezergailis, "1917 in Latvia," p. 646, *Cina,* No. 39, May 9, 1918.

34. According to Vacietis the Latvians had to support that Russian party which promised them freedom and independence. He stressed the importance to the *strelki* at the time of a slogan calling for a "Free Latvia." (Germanis, *Vacietis,* p. 277).

35. S. W. Page and A. Ezergailis, "The Lenin-Latvian Axis in the

November Seizure of Power," *Canadian Slavonic Papers,* XIX, No. 1, March 1977, pp. 34-35.

36. Lenin, *P.S.S.,* XXXIV, pp. 10-20; *Shestoi S'ezd RSDRP (b), Avgust 1917 g.* (Moscow, 1934), pp. 238-241. Point 7 of the resolution "on the Political Situation" gave token approval to Lenin's new line, but point 8 deflated it by cautioning the party that it must avoid taking premature chances and "prepare itself for the moment when all the necessary forces would be ready."

37. Page and Ezergailis, "The Lenin-Latvian Axis," pp. 36-41.

38. Ibid., pp. 42-44.

39. Ibid., pp. 44-45.

40. Ibid., pp. 45-46.

41. Ibid., pp. 46-49. John Reed's unpublished first hand impressions of his late September 1917 travels in Latvia quite clearly establish that the Latvian troops were the major power within the XIIth Army and that their mood coincided with Lenin's desires.

42. M. Latsis, "Vozniknovene narodnogo Kommissariata vnutrennikh del," *Proletarskaia Revoliutsiia,* 1925 (no. 2) pp. 138-140. Lenin's closeness to the Latvian leaders is well illustrated by the fact that he entrusted to Jacob Peters, subsequently second in command of the Cheka, the translation into English of the November 8 Decree of Peace. See B. Beatty, *The Red Heart of Russia* (New York: The Century Company, 1918), pp. 222-224. For more on Peters' closeness to Lenin see A. R. Williams, *Journey into Revolution* (Chicago, 1969), pp. 147, 152-154 and passim.

43. P. Malkov, *Reminiscences of a Kremlin Commandant* (Moscow: Progress Publishers, no date) pp. 69-70. From December 1917 to March 1918, the Smolnyi contingent varied in numbers between 300 and 1,000 men. In March there were about 500 Latvians on "praetorian" guard duty. (Malkov, *Reminiscences,* pp. 69-70; Germanis, *Vacietis,* pp. 272-273.) All important Cheka posts were held by Latvians and Poles as late as 1922. See L. Bryant, *Mirrors of Moscow* (New York: Seltzer, 1923), pp. 52-53.

44. Y. Vaceetis, *History of the Latvian Sharpshooters,* pp. 8-9. (Manuscript in my possession.)

45. Ibid., p. 7. I. Peters, "Vospominaniia O Rabote v V CH K v Pervykh God Revoliutsii," *Proletarskaia Revoliutsiia,* 1924 (No. 10), p. 8, tells of tens of thousands of soldiers streaming into Petrograd and immediately turning to banditry.

46. Vaceetis, *Latvian Sharpshooters,* p. 7.

47. Ibid., p. 27.

48. G. Stewart, *The White Armies of Russia* (New York: MacMillan, 1933), p. 57; U. Germanis, "Some Observations on the Yaroslav Revolt in July 1918," *Journal of Baltic Studies,* (Fall, 1973), pp. 238-240; Page, *Russia in Revolution* (New York: Van Nostrand, 1965), pp. 146-148.

49. L. Trotski, *Die Geburt der Roten Armee* (Vienna: 1924), pp. 7-16.

50. Vaceetis, *Latvian Sharpshooters,* p. 26.

51. J. F. N. Bradley, *Civil War in Russia* (New York: St. Martin's Press, 1975), p. 60.

52. Ibid., p. 65.

53. Vaceetis, *Latvian Sharpshooters,* pp. 43-46.

54. Iu. Srechinskii, *Novoe Russkoe Slovo,* June 14, 1972; Vaceetis, *Latvian Sharpshooters,* p. 54.

Notes to Chapter Seven

1. Page, *Lenin and World Revolution,* pp. 95-97.

2. Ibid., pp. 94-100.

3. Lenin, *P.S.S.,* XXXV, p. 372.

4. Page, *Lenin and World Revolution,* pp. 100-101.

5. L. Fischer, *The Soviets in World Affairs* (New York: Knopf, 1930), 2 Vols., I, pp. 75-76.

6. Lenin, *P.S.S.,* XXXVII, p. 97.

7. J. Stalin, *Works,* 13 vols. (Moscow: Foreign Language Publishers, 1953-1955), IV, pp. 158-170.

8. Stalin, "Marxism and the National Question," *Works,* II, pp. 300-381.

9. Stalin, *Works,* IV, pp. 171-173.

10. K. Kautsky, *Die Diktatur des Proletariates* (Vienna, 1918).

11. Ibid., p. 20.

12. Lenin, *P.S.S.,* XXXVII, p. 304.

13. See L. Trotsky, *Lenin* (New York: Minton, Balch, 1925), pp. 150-151. "In particularly critical moments, when it was a question of a very responsible or risky tactical change of position, Lenin put aside everything else less important that permitted postponement . . . . He put aside,

not only all that was at variance, directly or indirectly with the central problem, but also that which might distract and weaken his assertion."

14. Ibid., pp. 151-152.

15. As it was subsequently labeled.

16. Cohen's *Bukharin,* pp. 69-87, has an excellent treatment of this subject.

17. Lenin, *P.S.S.,* XXXVI, pp. 277-278.

18. Ibid., XXXVII, p. 13.

19. Ibid., p. 589.

20. Ibid., p. 305.

21. Kautsky, *Diktatur,* p. 55. "A state-run economy is not yet socialism. Whether it is or not depends on the character of the nation. But Russia is a *peasant* country."

22. Lenin, *P.S.S.,* XXXVII, pp. 310-323. ("And Kautsky calls himself a 'Marxist'!," p. 323.)

23. Ibid., p. 331.

24. *Bor'ba Bol'shevikov za Sozdanie Kommunisticheskogo Internatsionala* (Moscow: 1934), pp. 105-106.

25. E. H. Carr, *The Bolshevik Revolution, 1917-1923,* vol. 1 (Baltimore: Penguin, 1966), p. 118.

26. *Bor'ba Bol'shevikov za Sozdanie,* pp. 105-106.

27. Lenin, *P.S.S.,* XXXVII, pp. 147-148.

28. Ibid., XXIV, p. 240. "Only quick action [taking power]," Lenin wrote in late September, 1917, "can and must prevent a separate [antirevolutionary peace] between the English and the German imperialists." (See also Ibid., pp. 393, 404.)

29. *The Times* (London), November 12, 1918; See also Mermeix, *Les Négociations Secrètes et les Quatre Armistices Avec Pièces Justicatives* (Paris, 1919), pp. 257-259.

30. F. Weiss, *Die Baltische Frage* (Berne, 1917), pp. 8-10; see also K. von Westarp, *Konservative Politik, im letzten Jahrzehnt des Kaiserreiches,* 2 vols. (Berlin, 1935), II, p. 600; A. Volck, *Völkisches Erleben* (Lübeck, 1924), pp. 218-220.

31. A. Winnig, *Am Ausgang der deutschen Ostpolitik* (Berlin, 1921), pp. 36-40.

32. Page, *Lenin and World Revolution,* p. 121.

33. P. Stučka, *Piat Mesiatsev Sotsialisticheskoi Sovetskoi Latvii*

(Moscow, 1919), Part I, pp. 8-12. "Sverdlov," writes Stučka, "was somewhat shocked by my assurance. With a smile he asked me, 'Are you not a bit premature. . . inviting me to a congress before you have even set one foot on Latvian soil? However, I shall be at your Congress.'" (Ibid., p. 8.)

34. Stalin, *Works,* IV, p. 436.

35. Ibid., pp. 187-189.

36. Stučka, *Piat' Mesiatsev,* pp. 12-13. Said Kamenev: "We have not forgotten. . . that when the proletariat of Russia, first in the world to take decisive action, finding no support in other countries, above all found it in you–your organized Rifles–our brothers."

37. Ibid., Part II, pp. 18-19; *Izvestiia,* February 1, 1919.

38. S. Page, *The Formation of the Baltic States,* p. 139, n. 61.

39. Stučka, *Piat' Mesiatsev,* Part II, pp. 11, 14, 38; *Izvestiia,* January 21, February 4, February 7, 1919.

40. Still, Lenin knew what was going on every stop of the way, and this probably contributed to the optimism in his comment to Vtsik on January 17, expressing the view that despite all the hardships of the year past and difficulties anticipated in the next six months, "we can look forward to the victory not only of the Russian but also of the world revolution." (Lenin, *P.S.S.,* XXXVII, p. 420.)

41. Page, *Formation,* pp. 137-138.

42. Stučka, *Piat' Mesiatsev,* Part I, pp. 21-22; Stučka, *Za Sovetskaia Vlast' v Latvii 1918-1920; Sbornik Statei* (Riga, 1964), p. 48. (Hereafter, Stučka, *Sbornik.*)

43. G. Popov, *The City of the Red Plague* (New York, 1932), pp. 70, 205, 257.

44. Ibid., p. 240; Stučka, *Sbornik,* p. 49; see also *Die Rote Fahne* (Riga), April 9, 1919, which carried a manifesto asking the "German workers in soldiers' uniforms who are fighting here against your Latvian brothers" to throw down their weapons "and come over to us. Those of you who wish to be 'honest counter-revolutionaries' go back home and fight in the open against your brothers in Bavaria who have founded the same kind of Soviet Republic as we. Or go to Württemberg. . . or to Essen . . . or to Berlin where workers' soviets are openly declaring themselves on the side of the Soviet Republics of Russia, Hungary and Bavaria. The revolution of the working classes is advancing victoriously; nothing can stop it from becoming a world revolution. . . . Who is not with us is against us."

45. Page, *Lenin and World Revolution,* pp. 138-139.

46. The flimsy requirements needed to qualify as a delegate may be judged from comments made on March 3 by Chicherin, speaking for the committee validating the mandates of delegates. He declared that a country's revolutionary party, no matter how small in numbers (even one or two people might suit this definition), would be considered representative of a given country for purposes of the current congress. Although lacking a mandate, "Comrade Rutgers" represented Holland with a "consultative vote," and he could speak for the Dutch Communist Party. "At the same time he has a consultative vote for the American League of Socialist Propaganda. But since he was in Japan only in the process of passing through, he can, where Japan is concerned, not be regarded as an outstanding member of a movement or as a mandate bearer with consultative voice." It was therefore necessary, Chicherin added, "to cross the Japanese group from our list." Had Comrade Rutgers spent a week in Tokyo, he would, by the standards of the Third International's founding congress, apparently have been eligible to represent three continents. (*Bibliothek der Kommunistischen Internationale, VII, Der I Kongress der Kommunistischen Internationale, Protokoll der Verhandlungen in Moskau vom 2 bis zum 6 März, 1919* [Hamburg, 1921], p. 56.)

47. She was murdered, along with Liebknecht, a few days later.

48. H. Eberlein, "The Foundation of the Comintern and the Spartakusbund," *The Communist International,* Nos. 9-10 (1929), p. 437.

49. R. Luxemburg, *The Russian Revolution* (New York: 1940), pp. 44-48.

50. Lenin, *Sochineniia,* 2nd ed., XXIV, p. 725.

51. E. Korotkii, B. Kun, D. Piatnitskii, eds., *Protokoli Kongressov Kommunisticheskogo Internatsionala, Pervyi Kongress Kominterna, Mart, 1919 g.* (Moscow, 1933), p. 134.

52. Ibid., pp. 135-136.

Notes to Chapter Eight

1. S. W. Page, "Lenin, Prophet of World Revolution from the East," *The Russian Review,* April, 1952, pp. 67-75.

2. Ibid.

3. Ibid.; also *Vtoroi Kongress Kominterna, Iul'-Avgust 1920 g* (Moscow, 1934), p. 29.

4. Lenin, *Sochineniia* (2nd Ed.) XXIV, p. 531.

5. Ibid., XXXIX, p. 318.

6. Ibid., p. 321.

7. Ibid.

8. See Pipes, *Formation,* p. 169.

9. *Zhizn' Natsional'nostei,* February 1, 1920.

10. E. A. Ross, *Russian Soviet Republic* (no. pub., n.d.) pp. 286-290; S. White, "Communism and the East: The Baku Congress, 1920," *Slavic Review,* September 1974, pp. 501-503.

11. Lenin, *P.S.S.,* XLIX, p. 49.

12. Page, *Lenin and World Revolution,* p. 155.

13. *Vtoroi Kongress,* pp. 59-61.

14. Page, *Lenin and World Revolution,* pp. 158-161.

15. Ibid., pp. 169-174.

16. *Vtoroi Kongress,* pp. 646-650, 113-114.

17. Page, *Lenin and World Revolution,* pp. 179-182.

18. *Vtoroi Kongress,* pp. 397-409. Radek told the bitterly challenging Wjnkoop, "It has been necessary for me to exchange very unflattering expressions with the Dutch colleagues." (Ibid., p. 453.)

19. Ross, *Russian Soviet Republic,* pp. 290-302. Zinoviev delivered a splendidly rabblerousing keynote address, noting among other things that "each English capitalist forces about 100 English workers and several hundred workers in the colonies to drudge for him . . . China, India, Turkey, Persia, Armenia can and must [fight hard to establish] the Soviet system . . . . Soviets must be created even when there are no town workers; in these cases we can create Soviet states of working peasants . . . . It is against English capitalism that . . . the most fatal blow must be dealt . . . . But at the same time we must educate the laboring masses of the East to hatred (against) the whole of the rich classes . . . whether they be Russians, Jews, Germans or Frenchmen . . . . We are not begging the English imperialist to take his feet off the table for the purpose of permitting the wealthy Turk to place his feet on it all the more comfortably." See also S. White, "Communism in the East," pp. 493, 507.

20. Theodore Shabad, *Geography of the USSR, A Regional Survey* (New York: Columbia, 1951), p. 371.

21. *Istoriia Sovetskoi Konstitutsii (v dokumentakh)* 1917-1956 (Moscow, 1957), pp. 271-274; Pipes, *Formation,* p. 255; Alexander Park, *Bolshevism in Turkestan* (New York: Columbia, 1957), pp. 63-87.

22. The economic bonds placed upon the Central Asian "autonomous" republics have been mentioned. *Supra,* p. 174.

23. Pipes, *Formation,* p. 241.

24. Lenin, *P.S.S.,* XLV, pp. 211-212.

25. Pipes calls this "pseudofederalism."

26. Stalin, *Works,* III, pp. 51-60; see also Carr, *The Bolshevik Revolution,* I, p. 267, who astutely remarks that the April 1917 party conference "was noteworthy for Stalin's first appearance as rapporteur on the national question."

27. The manner in which Lenin masked his personal aspirations is dealt with extensively in my *Lenin and World Revolution.*

28. Pipes rightly notes that Stalin was never "much impressed" by Lenin's concern for "diplomatic niceties" in connection with "the independence of republics." (Pipes, *Formation,* p. 270.)

29. See Leon Trotsky, *Stalin, An Appraisal of the Man and His Influence* (London: Hollis and Carter, 1947), pp. 266, 358; also R. C. Tucker, *Stalin as Revolutionary, 1879-1929* (New York: Norton, 1973), pp. 245-247, and Pipes, *Formation,* p. 270.

30. A. B. Ulam, *Stalin: The Man and his Era* (New York: Viking, 1973), pp. 183-184.

31. See B. D. Wolfe, *The Bridge and the Abyss, the Troubled Friendship of Maxim Gorky and V. I. Lenin* (New York: Praeger, 1967), Chapters VI to VIII.

32. Trotsky, *Stalin,* p. 270. Although making this point within the context of Stalin's behavior as military commissar during the civil war, Trotsky's characterization of Stalin is obviously intended to apply to all other situations as well.

33. Ibid., pp. 346-350.

34. B. Souvarine, *Stalin, A Critical Survey of Bolshevism* (New York: Longmans, Green 1939), p. 293.

35. S. W. Page, "Lenin and Self-Determination," *The Slavonic and East European Review,* April, 1950, pp. 342-358. At the time (*supra,* p. 44) the Georgian Social-Democrats, headed by Jordania, were shifting away from their earlier pro-Bolshevik orientation.

36. This position is maintained by H. J. Ellison, "Stalin and His Biographers: the Lenin-Stalin Relationship." See R. C. Elwood, *Reconsiderations on the Russian Revolution,* p. 264. Writes Ellison: "It was the rude

application of a policy, not the underlying policy itself, that Lenin was attacking."

37. *Vladimir Il'ich Lenin, Biografiia,* 2nd ed. (Moscow, Institute Marksisma-Leninisma, 1963), p. 642.

38. L. Trotsky, *On the Suppressed Testament of Lenin* (New York: Pathfinder, 1970, 1970), pp. 16-18.

39. Lenin, *P.S.S.*, XLV, pp. 383-406.

40. Ibid., pp. 599-600.

BIBLIOGRAPHY

Adoratskii, V., ed., *Marx-Engels Gesamtausgabe, Part 3, III,* (Moscow) 1935.

Balabanova, A., *Impressions of Lenin* (Ann Arbor: University of Michigan) 1964.

Balabanova, A., *My Life as a Rebel* (Bloomington: Indiana University) 1973.

Beatty, B., *The Red Heart of Russia* (New York: The Century Company) 1918.

Berdyaev, N. *The Origin of Russian Communism* (Ann Arbor: University of Michigan) 1960.

Bibliothek der Kommunistischen Internationale, VII, Der I Kongress der Kommunistischen Internationale, Protokoll der Vorhandlungen in Moskau von 2 bis zum 6 März, 1919 (Hamburg) 1921.

Bloch, S., *Erinnerungen an Lenin* (Zurich) 1924.

Bonch-Bruevich, V. D., *V. I. Lenin v Rossii* (Moscow) 1935.

Bor'ba Bol'shevikov za Sozdanie Kommunisticheskogo Internatsionala (Moscow) 1934.

Bradley, J. F. N., *Civil War in Russia* (New York: St. Martin's Press) 1975.

Bryant, L., *Mirrors of Moscow* (New York: Seltzer) 1923.

Bukharin, N., *Imperialism and World Economy, with an introduction by V. I. Lenin* (London) n.d.

Bukharin, N., *Lenin as a Marxist* (London) 1925.

Bystrykh, F., "Rasvitie Vzgladov Lenina Po Agrarnomu Voprosu," *Proletarskaia Revoliutsiia,* 1928, No. 1, 72.

Carr, E. H., *The Bolshevik Revolution, 1917-1923,* 3 vols. (Baltimore: Penguin) 1966.

Cohen, S. F., *Bukharin and the Bolshevik Revolution* (New York: Knopf) 1973.

Daniels, R. V., *Red October, The Bolshevik Revolution of 1917* (New York: Scribners) 1967.

Deutsch, L., *Gruppe Osvobozhdenie Truda*, 6 vols. (Moscow) 1924-28.

Deutscher, I., *The Prophet Armed, Trotsky: 1879-1921*. Vol. I, (New York: Vintage) 1965.

Deutscher, I., *The Prophet Unarmed, Trotsky, 1921-1929*. Vol. II (New York: Vintage) n.d.

Die Rote Fahne (Riga) April 9, 1919.

Die Zimmerwalder Bewegung, 2 vols. (The Hague: Mouton) 1967.

Drizulis, A. A., Kabikis, A. Y., Kirshbaum, A. K., eds. *Oktiabr'skoi revoliutsiia v Latvii, dokumenty i materialy* (Riga) 1957.

Eberlein, H., "The Foundation of the Comintern and the Spartakus Bund," *The Communist International*, Nos. 9-10 (1925).

Elov, B., "Posle Iul'skikh Sobytii," *Krasnaia Letopis*, No. 7, 1923.

Elwood, R. C., "Lenin and the Brussels 'Unity' Conference of July 1914," *The Russian Review*, vol. 39, No. 1, January, 1980.

Elwood, R. C., "Lenin and Pravda, 1912-1914," *Slavic Review*, June, 1972.

Elwood, R. C., ed., *Reconsiderations on the Russian Revolution* (Cambridge, Mass.: Slavica Publishers) 1976.

Engels, F., *Herr Eugen Dühring's Revolution in Science [Anti-Dühring]* (Chicago: Charles H. Kerr and Co.) 1935.

Ezergailis, A., "A German Leaflet on Fraternization, April, 1916," *The Slavonic and East European Review*, XLVIII, No. 113, October, 1970.

Ezergailis, A., "1917 in Latvia: The Bolshevik Year," *Canadian Slavic Studies*, II, No. 4 (Winter, 1969).

Ezergailis, A., *The 1917 Revolution in Latvia* (Boulder, Colorado: East European Quarterly, dist. by Columbia University Press) 1974.

Feldman, G. D., *German Imperialism, 1914-1918* (New York: Wiley) 1972.

Fischer, F., *Griff Nach Der Weltmacht* (Düsseldorf: Droste) 1961.

Fischer, L., *The Soviets in World Affairs*, 2 vols. (New York: Knopf) 1930.

Frölich, P., *Rosa Luxemburg*, (New York) 1972.

Fundamentals of Marxism-Leninism, 2nd Revised Edition (Moscow) 1963.

Gankin, O. H. and Fisher, H. H., *The Bolsheviks and the World War* (Stanford: Stanford University Press) 1940.

Gautschi, W., *Lenin als Emigrant in der Schweiz* (Zurich: Benziger) 1973.

Germanis, U., *Oberst Vacietis und die Lettischen Schützen im Weltkrieg und der Oktober Revolution* (Stockholm: Almquist and Wiksell) 1974.

Germanis, U., "Some Observations on the Yaroslav Revolt in July, 1918," *Journal of Baltic Studies,* Fall, 1973.

Hammen, O., "Marx and the Agrarian Question," *American Historical Review,* June, 1972.

Hammen, O., *The Red '48ers, Karl Marx and Friedrich Engels* (New York: Scribners) 1969.

Harding, N., *Lenin's Political Thought, Vol. I Theory and Practice in the Democratic Revolution* (London: Macmillan) 1970.

Hillquit, M., *From Marx to Lenin* (New York: The Hartford Press) 1921.

Hobson, J. A., *Imperialism* (London: Allen and Unwin) 1938.

Horne, C. F. and Austin, W. F., eds., *Source Records of the Great War,* 7 vols., 1923.

Istoriia Sovetskoi Konstitutsii (v dodumentakh) 1917-1956 (Moscow) 1957.

Izvestiia, February 1, 1919.

Katkov, G., *Russia, 1917, The February Revolution* (New York: Harper) 1967.

Kautsky, K., *Das Erfurter Program* (Stuttgart) 1892.

Kautsky, K., *Die Agrarfrage* (Stuttgart) 1899.

Kautsky, K., *Die Diktatur des Proletariates* (Vienna) 1918.

Kautsky, K., *Sozialisten und Krieg* (Prague) 1937.

Kautsky, K., *The Dictatorship of the Proletariat* (London: The National Labour Press, Ltd.) n.d.

Kautsky, K., *The Social Revolution* (Chicago) 1902.

Kettenbach, W. K., *Lenin's Theorie des Imperialismus, Teil I: Grundlagen und Voraussetzungen* (Köln: Verlag Wissenschaft und Politik) 1965.

Korotkii, E., Kun, B., Piatnitskii, D., eds., *Protokoli Kongressov Kommunisticheskogo Internatsionala, Pervyi Kongress Kominterna, Mart, 1919 g.* (Moscow) 1933.

Krasnyi Arkhiv, 1939, No. 1.

Krupskaya, N. K., *Reminiscences of Lenin* (New York: International Publishers) 1970.

Lana, F. a de, "Communication to *The American Historical Review,*" February, 1973.

Latsis, M., "Vozniknovene narodnogo Kommissariata vnutrennih del," *Proletarskaia Revoliutsiia,* 1925 (no. 2).

Leder, V., "Natsional'ny vopros v polskoi i russkoi Sotsial-Demokratii," *Proletarskaia Revoliutsiia,* 1927, 2-3 (61-62).

Lenin, V. I., *Collected Works,* 45 vols. (Moscow: Progress Publishers) 1963-1970.

Lenin, V. I., *Leninskii Sbornik,* 36 vols. (Moscow) 1952-1957.

Lenin, V. I., *Polnoe Sobranie Sochinenii,* 5th Ed.; 55 vols. (Moscow) 1958-1965.

Lenin, V. I., *Sochinenii,* 3rd Ed. (Moscow) 1926-1932.

Lerner, W., *Karl Radek, The Last Internationalist* (Stanford) 1970.

Lockhart, B. R. H., *British Agent* (New York: Putnam's Sons) 1933.

Lukacs, G., *Lenin, A Study on the Unity of His Thought* (Cambridge: M.I.T.) 1971.

Luxemburg, R., *The Mass Strike, The Political Party and The Trade Unions, and The Junius Pamphlet* (New York: Harper) 1971.

Luxemburg, R., *The Russian Revolution* (New York) 1940.

Maehl, W. H., *German Militarism and Socialism* (Nebraska: Wesleyan Press) 1968.

Malkov, P., *Reminiscences of a Kremlin Commandant* (Moscow) n.d.

Markov, M., *Sovietskaia Latviia* (Moscow) 1940.

Marx, K., *Capital* (New York: Modern Library) n.d.

Mermeix, *Les Négociations Secrètes et les Quatre Armistices Avec Pièces Justicatives* (Paris) 1919.

Mishke, V., *Podgotovka Oktiabra v Latvii,"* Proletarskaia Revoliutsiia, No. 72 (1928).

Nedava, J., *Trotsky and the Jews* (Philadelphia) 1972.

Nettle, J. P., *Rosa Luxemburg,* 2 vols. (London) 1966.

Park, A., *Bolshevism in Turkestan* (New York: Columbia) 1957.

Page, S. W., "Lenin and Self-Determination," *The Slavonic and East European Review,* April, 1950.

Page, S. W., "Lenin's April Theses and the Latvian Peasant Soldiery," in R. C. Elwood, ed., *Reconsiderations on the Russian Revolution* (Cambridge: Slavica Publishers) 1976.

Page, S. W., "Lenin and Peasant 'Bolshevism' in Latvia, 1903-1915," *Journal of Baltic Studies,* III/2, Summer, 1972.

Page, S. W., *Lenin and World Revolution* (New York: McGraw-Hill) 1972.

Page, S. W., "Lenin, Prophet of World Revolution from the East," *The Russian Review,* April, 1952.

Page, S. W., "Stalin Legend," *The New Republic,* September 7, 1974.

Page, S. W., *The Formation of the Baltic States* (New York: Fertig) 1970.

Page, S. W. and Ezergailis, A., "The Lenin-Latvian Axis in the November Seizure of Power," *Canadian Slavonic Papers,* XIX, No. 1, March, 1977.

Pervyi legal'nyi Peterburgskii Komitet Bol'shevikov v 1917 g. (Moscow) 1927.

Peters, I., "Vospominaniia o Rabote v V CH K v Pervykh God Revoliutsii," *Proletarskaia Revoliutsiia, 1924 (No. 10).*

Petrogradskaia Obshchegorodskaia Vserossiskaia Konferentsiia R.S.D.R.P. (Bol'shevikov v Aprele 1917 g.) (Moscow) 1925.

Pipes, R., *Struve, Liberal on the Left, 1870-1905* (Cambridge: Harvard University Press) 1970.

Pipes, R., *The Formation of the Soviet Union, Communism and Nationalism, 1917-1923.* (New York: Atheneum) 1968.

Platten, F., *Lenin iz Emigratsii v Rossii, Mart 1917* (Moscow) 1925.

Plekhanov, G., *Selected Philosophical Works,* 5 vols. (Moscow) n.d.

Presseabteilung Ober Ost (Berlin) 1917.

Protokoly Ob"edinitel'nogo S"ezda RSDRP (Moscow) 1926.

Rabinowitch, A., *The Bolsheviks Come to Power, The Revolution of 1917 in Petrograd* (New York: Norton) 1976.

Rabinowitch, A., *Prelude to Revolution, The Petrograd Bolsheviks and the July 1917 Uprising* (Bloomington: Indiana University) 1968.

Ross, E. A., *Russian Soviet Republic* (no publ.) n.d.

Rosmer, A., *Le Mouvement Ouvrier Pendant la Première Guerre Mondial, De Zimmerwald a la Révolution Russe,* 2 vols. (Paris: Mouton) 1959.

Saul, N. E., *Sailors in Revolt, The Russian Baltic Fleet in 1917* (Lawrence: University of Kansas) 1978.

Schapiro, L., *The Communist Party of the Soviet Union* (New York: Random House) 1959.

Schorske, C. E., *German Social Democracy, 1905-1917* (Cambridge: Harvard University Press) 1955.

Schlesinger, M. L., *Russland im XX Jahrhundert* (Berlin) 1908.

Senn, A. E., "Solzhenytsin and the Historical Lenin," *Canadian Slavonic Papers,* XIX, No. 2, June, 1977.

Senn, A. E., "The Bolshevik Conference in Bern, 1915," *Slavic Review,* XXV, December, 1966.

Senn, A. E., *The Russian Revolution in Switzerland, 1914-1917* (Madison: University of Wisconsin) 1971.

Sergeev, A., "Na Voloske," *Novoe Russkoe Slovo,* June 23, 1978.

Shabad, T., *Geography of the USSR, A Regional Survey* (New York: Columbia) 1951.

Shub, D., *Politicheskie Deiateli Rossii (1850ykh-1920ykh gg.) Sbornik Statei* (New York: Waldon Press) 1969.

Siromiatnikova, M., "Bernskaia Konferentsiia zagranichnikh organisatsii R.S.D.R.P. v 1915 g. (s primechaniami G. L. Shklovskogo) *Proletarskaia Revoliutsiia,* No. 5 (40) 1925.

Souvarine, B., "Solzehnytsin and Lenin," *Dissent,* Summer, 1977.

Srechinskii, Iu., *Novoye Russkoye Slovo,* June 14, 1972.

Stalin, J., *Marxism and the National Question* (New York) 1942.

Stalin, J., *Works,* 13 vols. (Moscow) 1953-55.

Stewart, G., *The White Armies of Russia* (New York: Macmillan) 1933.

Stučka, P., *Piat Mesiatsev Sotsialisticheskoi Sovetskoi Latvii* (Moscow) 1919.

Stučka, P., *Za Sovetskaia Vlast' v Latvii 1918-1920; Sbornik Statei* (Riga) 1964.

Struve, P., "My Contacts and Conflicts with Lenin," *The Slavonic and East European Review,* XII, April, 1934 and XIII, July, 1934.

Sukhanov, N. N., *The Russian Revolution of 1917,* ed., J. Carmichael, 2 vols. (New York: Harper) 1962.

Temkin, Ia. G., *Lenin i Mezhdunarodnaia Sotsial-Demokratiia* (Moscow) 1968.

The Times (London) November 12, 1918.

Tiutkin, C. V., "Leninskie referaty o voine (osen' 1914)" *Istoriia SSSR,* No. 2, Mart-Aprel, 1967.

Tretii Ocherednoi S"ezd Ross. Sots.-Dem Rabochei Partii, Poln'yj Tekst Protokolov (Geneva) 1905.

Trotski, L., *Die Geburt der Roten Armee* (Vienna) 1924.

Trotsky, L., *History of the Russian Revolution,* 3 vols. (New York: Simon and Schuster) 1937.

Trotsky, L., *My Life* (New York: Grosset and Dunlap) 1960.

Trotsky, L., *On the Suppressed Testament of Lenin* (New York: Pathfinder) 1970.

Trotsky, L., *Stalin* (London: Hollis and Carter) 1946.

Trotsky, L., *The Permanent Revolution and Results and Prospects* (New York: Pathfinder Press) 1970.

Tsereteli, I. G., *Vospominaniia o Fevral'skoi Revoliutsii,* 2 vols. (Paris: Mouton) 1963.

Tucker, R., *Stalin as Revolutionary, 1879-1929* (New York: Norton) 1973.

Tucker, R., ed., *The Marx-Engels Reader* (New York: Norton) 1972.

Vaceetis, Y., *History of the Latvian Sharpshooters.* (Typed mss. in my possession).

Vladimir Il'ich Lenin, Biografiia, 2nd ed., (Moscow) 1963.

Volck, A., *Völkisches Erleben* (Lübeck) 1924.

Vospominaniia o Vladimire Il'ich Lenine, 5 vols. (Moscow) 1969.

Vtoroi Kongress Kominterna Iul'-Avgust 1920 (Moscow) 1934.

Wade, R. A., *The Russian Search for Peace, February-October, 1917* (Stanford) 1969.

Waters, Mary-Alice, ed., *Rosa Luxemburg Speaks* (New York: Pathfinder Press) 1970.

Weiss, F., *Die Baltische Frage* (Bern) 1917.

Weissman, B. M., *Herbert Hoover and Famine Relief to Soviet Russia* (Stanford: Hoover Institution) 1974.

Westarp, K. von, *Konservative Politik im letzten Jahrzehnt des Kaisserreiches,* 2 vols. (Berlin) 1935.

White, S., "Communism and the East: the Baku Congress, 1920," *Slavic Review,* September, 1974.

Wildman, A. K., "The Bolsheviks of the Twelvth Army and Latvian Social Democracy," in Elwood, R. C., ed. *Reconsiderations on the Russian Revolution* (Cambridge: Slavica) 1976.

Wildman, A. K., *The Making of a Workers Revolution, Russian Social Democracy, 1891-1903* (Chicago: University of Chicago Press) 1967.

William, A. R., *Journey Into Revolution: Petrograd, 1917-1918* (Chicago: Quadrangle) 1969.

Winnig, A., *Am Ausgang der deutschen Ostpolitik* (Berlin) 1921.

Wolfe, B. D., *The Bridge and the Abyss, the Troubled Friendship of Maxim Gorky and V. I. Lenin* (New York: Praeger) 1967.

Wolfe, B. D., *Three Who Made a Revolution* (Boston: Beacon Press) 1948.

Woytinsky, V. S., *Stormy Passage* (New York: Vanguard) 1961.

Ulam, A., *The Bolsheviks* (New York: Macmillan) 1965.

Ulam, A., *Stalin, the Man and his Era* (New York: Viking) 1973.

Zeman, A. B. and Scharlau, W. B., *The Merchant of Revolution. The Life of Alexander Israel Helphand (Parvus) 1867-1924* (London: Oxford University Press) 1965.

Zhizn' Natsional'nostei.

INDEX

EAST EUROPEAN MONOGRAPHS

The *East European Monographs* comprise scholarly books on the history and civilization of Eastern Europe. They are published by the *East European Quarterly* in the belief that these studies contribute substantially to the knowledge of the area and serve to stimulate scholarship and research.

Political Ideas and the Enlightenment in the Romanian Principalities, 1750-1831. By Vlad Georgescu. 1971.
America, Italy and the Birth of Yugoslavia, 1917-1919. By Dragan R. Zivjinovic. 1972.
Jewish Nobles and Geniuses in Modern Hungary. By William O. McCagg,Jr. 1972.
Mixail Soloxov in Yugoslavia: Reception and Literary Impact. By Robert F. Price. 1973.
The Historical and National Thought of Nicolae Iorga. By William O. Oldson. 1973.
Guide to Polish Libraries and Archives. By Richard C. Lewanski. 1974.
Vienna Broadcasts to Slovakia, 1938-1939: A Case Study in Subversion. By Henry Delfiner. 1974.
The 1917 Revolution in Latvia. By Andrew Ezergailis. 1974.
The Ukraine in the United Nations Organization: A Study in Soviet Foreign Policy. 1944-1950. By Konstantin Sawczuk. 1975.
The Bosnian Church: A New Interpretation. By John V. A. Fine, Jr., 1975.
Intellectual and Social Developments in the Habsburg Empire from Maria Theresa to World War I. Edited by Stanley B. Winters and Joseph Held. 1975.
Ljudevit Gaj and the Illyrian Movement. By Elinor Murray Despalatovic. 1975.
Tolerance and Movements of Religious Dissent in Eastern Europe. Edited by Bela K. Kiraly. 1975.
The Parish Republic: Hlinka's Slovak People's Party, 1939-1945. By Yeshayahu Jelinek. 1976.
The Russian Annexation of Bessarabia, 1774-1828. By George F. Jewsbury. 1976.
Modern Hungarian Historiography. By Steven Bela Vardy. 1976.
Values and Community in Multi-National Yugoslavia. By Gary K. Bertsch. 1976.
The Greek Socialist Movement and the First World War: The Road to Unity. By George B. Leon. 1976.
The Radical Left in the Hungarian Revolution of 1848. By Laszlo Deme. 1976.
Hungary between Wilson and Lenin: The Hungarian Revolution of 1918-1919 and the Big Three. By Peter Pastor. 1976.
The Crises of France's East-Central European Diplomacy, 1933-1938. By Anthony J. Komjathy. 1976.
Polish Politics and National Reform, 1775-1788. By Daniel Stone. 1976.
The Habsburg Empire in World War I. Robert A. Kann, Bela K. Kiraly, and Paula S. Fichtner, eds. 1977.
The Slovenes and Yugoslavism, 1890-1914. By Carole Rogel. 1977.
German-Hungarian Relations and the Swabian Problem. By Thomas Spira. 1977.
The Metamorphosis of a Social Class in Hungary During the Reign of Young Franz Joseph. By Peter I. Hidas. 1977.
Tax Reform in Eighteenth Century Lombardy. By Daniel M. Klang. 1977.
Tradition versus Revolution: Russia and the Balkans in 1917. By Robert H. Johnston. 1977.
Winter into Spring: The Czechoslovak Press and the Reform Movement 1963-1968. By Frank L. Kaplan. 1977.
The Catholic Church and the Soviet Government, 1939-1949. By Dennis J. Dunn. 1977.
*The Hungarian Labor Service System, 1939-1945.*By Randolph L Braham. 1977.
Consciousness and History: Nationalist Critics of Greek Society 1897-1914. By Gerasimos Augustinos. 1977.

Emigration in Polish Social and Political Thought, 1870-1914. By Benjamin P. Murdzek. 1977.

Serbian Poetry and Milutin Bojic. By Mihailo Dordevic. 1977.

The Baranya Dispute: Diplomacy in the Vortex of Ideologies, 1918-1921. By Leslie C. Tihany. 1978.

The United States in Prague, 1945-1948. By Walter Ullmann. 1978.

Rush to the Alps: The Evolution of Vacationing in Switzerland. By Paul P. Bernard. 1978.

Transportation in Eastern Europe: Empirical Findings. By Bogdan Mieczkowski. 1978.

The Polish Underground State: A Guide to the Underground, 1939-1945. By Stefan Korbonski. 1978.

The Hungarian Revolution of 1956 in Retrospect. Edited by Bela K. Kiraly and Paul Jonas. 1978.

Boleslaw Limanowski (1835-1935): A Study in Socialism and Nationalism. By Kazimiera Janina Cottam. 1978.

The Lingering Shadow of Nazism: The Austrian Independent Party Movement Since 1945. By Max E. Riedlsperger. 1978.

The Catholic Church, Dissent and Nationality in Soviet Lithuania. By V. Stanley Vardys. 1978.

The Development of Parliamentary Government in Serbia. By Alex N. Dragnich. 1978.

Divide and Conquer: German Efforts to Conclude a Separate Peace, 1914-1918. By L. L. Farrar, Jr. 1978.

The Prague Slav Congress of 1848. By Lawrence D. Orton. 1978.

The Nobility and the Making of the Hussite Revolution. By John M. Klassen. 1978.

The Cultural Limits of Revolutionary Politics: Change and Continuity in Socialist Czechoslovakia. By David W. Paul. 1979.

On the Border of War and Peace: Polish Intelligence and Diplomacy in 1937-1939 and the Origins of the Ultra Secret. By Richard A. Woytak. 1979.

Bear and Foxes: The International Relations of the East European States 1965-1969. By Ronald Haly Linden. 1979.

Czechoslovakia: The Heritage of Ages Past. Edited by Ivan Volgyes and Hans Brisch. 1979.

Prima Minister Gyula Andrassy's Influence on Habsburg Foreign Policy. By Janos Decsy. 1979.

Citizens for the Fatherland: Education, Educators, and Pedagogical Ideals in Eighteenth Century Russia. By J. L. Black. 1979.

A History of the "Proletariat": The Emergence of Marxism in the Kingdom of Poland, 1870-1887. By Norman M. Naimark. 1979.

The Slovak Autonomy Movement, 1935-1939: A Study in Unrelenting Nationalism. By Dorothea H. El Mallakh. 1979.

Diplomat in Exile: Francis Pulszky's Political Activities in England, 1849-1860. By Thomas Kabdebo. 1979.

The German Struggle Against the Yugoslav Guerrillas in World War II: German Counter-Insurgency in Yugoslavia, 1941-1943. By Paul N. Hehn. 1979.

The Emergence of the Romanian National State. By Gerald J. Bobango. 1979.

Stewards of the Land: The American Farm School and Modern Greece. By Brenda L. Marder. 1979.

Roman Dmowski: Party, Tactics, Ideology, 1895-1907. By Alvin M. Fountain, II. 1980.

International and Domestic Politics in Greece During the Crimean War. By Jon V. Kofas. 1980.